Global Issues

Series Editors

Paolo D. Farah
West Virginia University
John D. Rockefeller IV School of Policy and Politics West
Virginia University
Morgantown, USA

Jim Whitman
Wakefield, UK

The rapid pace of globalizing dynamics has brought in its wake a proliferation of crises, governance challenges and large-scale stresses, unprecedented in their range, seriousness and urgency. These emerging conditions and relations are variously global is their range, inclusiveness and impacts; and many of them are outpacing our legal, political and ethical systems of deliberation and control. Climate change, the ravages of contagious diseases and financial turmoil are all cases in point. Similarly, the transformative implications of new scientific and technological developments, from Big Data to gene editing, are already upon us. This book series is dedicated to providing insights into the complex interaction of human and natural systems; modes of cooperation and conflict; and the ways and degrees to which human values can be reconciled and more effectively enacted. The concentration throughout is on an integration of existing disciplines toward the clarification of political possibility as well as impending crises.

The series is published in cooperation with gLAWcal - Global Law Initiatives for Sustainable Development.

Halil Göksan

Global Law of Sustainable Development

palgrave
macmillan

Halil Göksan
North Bergen, NJ, USA

ISSN 2947-8863 ISSN 2947-8871 (electronic)
Global Issues
ISBN 978-3-031-74546-1 ISBN 978-3-031-74547-8 (eBook)
https://doi.org/10.1007/978-3-031-74547-8

This Palgrave Macmillan imprint is published by the registered company Springer Nature Switzerland AG.
The registered company address is: Gewerbestrasse 11, 6330 Cham, Switzerland

Acknowledgments

This book is the result of many hours spent for the accomplishment of my doctoral thesis while working full-time and going through significant life events, becoming a husband and, later, a father. I therefore firstly dedicate this book to my lovely daughter, Eva Ipek, and her loving mother, Ferin Merve. My parents sacrificed their lives for me and my brothers. I also dedicate this book to my selfless parents. My infinite appreciation also goes to my former colleague and my beloved friend Laurie McNabb for reviewing and proofreading this book.

Disclaimer

Contents

Abbreviations

CSD	Commission of Sustainable Development
CSOs	Civil society organizations
DAC	Development Assistance Committee
DSD	Decade of sustainable development
ECOSOC	United Nations Economic and Social Council
EU	European Union
GA	General Assembly
GAL	Global administrative law
GCM	Global Compact for Migration
GLSD	Global law of sustainable development
HLPF	High-level Political Forum
IACSD	Inter-Agency Committee on Sustainable Development
ICJ	International Court of Justice
IDGs	International development goals
IFI	International financial institutions
IGOs	Intergovernmental organizations
IIPC	Intergovernmental Inter-Sessional Preparatory Committee
IMF	International Monetary Fund
INP	Intergovernmental Negotiations Process
IOs	International organizations
IUCN	International Union for Conservation of Nature and Natural Resources
MDGs	Millennium Development Goals
MNCs	Multinational corporations
MS	Member states
NGOs	Nongovernmental organizations
OECD	Organisation for Economic Co-operation and Development

OEWG	Open-Ended Working Group
OWG	Open Working Group
PrepCom	Preparatory Committee
SDGs	Sustainable development goals
SDSN	Sustainable Development Solutions Network
SG	Secretary-general
UN	United Nations
UNCED	United Nations Conference on Environment and Development
UNCHE	United Nations Conference on the Human Environment
UNCSD	United Nations Conference on Sustainable Development
UNEP	United Nations Environmental Programme
UNESCO	United Nations Educational, Scientific and Cultural Organization
UNFCCC	United Nations Framework Convention on Climate Change
UNGA	United Nations General Assembly
UNGC	United Nations Global Compact
UNSTT	UN System Task Team
UN DESA	United Nations Department for Economic and Social Affairs
WCED	World Commission on Environment and Development
WSSD	World Summit of Sustainable Development
WWF	World Wildlife Fund

Introduction

How would it be possible to describe the legal nature of the Sustainable Development Goals (SDGs)? Are they global policy objectives, or might they have a legal nature? Would it be, for example, possible to determine whether the SDGs are rules of "law"? This book aims to provide an answer to the question of whether the SDGs are rules of law at the global level.

The SDGs were adopted by the United Nations General Assembly (UNGA) on 25 September 2015[1] and constitute one of the greatest achievements of "the peoples of the United Nations" as a landmark framework for a sustainable future. Seventeen goals and 169 targets of the SDGs were formulated through a unique process involving all the Members States (MS) of the United Nations (UN) and numerous international organizations (IOs), as well as non-governmental organizations (NGOs). In terms of their origins, I present that the SDGs go back as far as to an UNGA resolution adopted in 1983.[2] It was in this Resolution 38/161 of 1983 that the UNGA decided to establish the renowned World Commission on Environment and Development (WCED). Four years

[1] "Transforming Our World: The 2030 Agenda for Sustainable Development, UNGA Resolution, UN Doc. A/RES/70/1," September 25, 2015, 1.

[2] "Process of Preparation of the Environmental Perspective to the Year 2000 and Beyond, UNGA Resolution, UN Doc. A/RES/38/161," December 19, 1983.

later, the WCED issued its report entitled "Our Common Future" (Brundtland Report),[3] which was later endorsed by the UNGA.[4]

The Brundtland Report defined that "sustainable development is development that meets the needs of the present without compromising the ability of future generations to meet their own needs."[5] Given this definition, in terms of its scope, the notion of sustainable development extends beyond national boundaries. Moreover, it is "genuinely international[/global] in nature, meaning that its origins cannot be tracked down to any national programme or political discourse".[6] Since 1983, the concept of sustainable development has constantly advanced and unfolded into specific rules as part of global action plans throughout many international conferences and negotiations.[7] Moreover, the SDGs, with 17 goals, 169 targets and 232 indicators, are currently the most enriched articulation of this global concept.[8]

Nevertheless, from the standpoint of international law, this enrichment and crystallisation of the substance and scope of the principle of sustainable development is often considered as a progress outside the "jurisdiction" of international law because such norm-making exercises produce only "outcome documents" or "action plans" that are adopted through soft and non-binding instruments in terms of international law. The global support given to these norms even led the International Court of Justice (ICJ) to hold that these norms and standards must be "taken into consideration" and must be "given proper weight."[9] These norms and standards

[3] In recognition of Ms Gro Harlem Brundtland's role as the Chair of the WCED. Ms Brundtland is a former Prime Minister of Norway (1981, 1986–1989, 1990–1996) and former Director-General of the World Health Organization 1998–2003.

[4] "Report of the World Commission on Environment and Development, UNGA Resolution, UN Doc. A/RES/42/187," December 11, 1987.

[5] "Report of the World Commission on Environment and Development, UN Doc. A/42/427," August 4, 1987, 54.

[6] Helge Jörgens, "Governance by Diffusion: Implementing Global Norms through Cross-National Imitation and Learning," 2004, page 247.

[7] In addition to being a global concept, Helge Jörgens adds that sustainable development "is a strongly normative concept 'used to prescribe and evaluate changes in living conditions.'" See in ibid.

[8] It is also important to note that, since 2002, sustainable development is considered to be "a key element of the overarching framework for United Nations activities." See, "World Summit on Sustainable Development, UNGA Resolution, UN Doc. A/RES/57/253," December 20, 2002, para. 3.

[9] Gabčíkovo-Nagymaros Project (Hungary v. Slovakia), 7 paragraph 140. See also, W. Michael Reisman, "Soft Law and Law Jobs," *Journal of International Dispute Settlement* 2, no. 1 (February 1, 2011): 28.

to which the ICJ referred were mostly articulated in the outcome documents of the Rio Conference of 1992 on Environment and Development (UNCED),[10] as well as in the United Nations Framework Convention for Climate Change (UNFCCC) that was opened for signatures at the UNCED.[11]

In other words, there is a strong normative concept for sustainable development, which incorporates norms and standards that must be taken into consideration and must be given proper weight. Furthermore, not only has the concept of sustainable development "received wide support in a vast array of non-binding international legal documents," but it can also "be found in 112 multilateral treaties, roughly 30 of which are aimed at universal participation [which] points to a certain level of consensus among the international community concerning the relevance of sustainable development for international law."[12] However, the legal nature of the concept of sustainable development in international law is not clear, and there exist ample discussions around this question in the literature since the beginning of the 1990s.[13]

However fascinating this question might be, sustainable development is not any more a simple concept. Today, it consists, at least, of 17 goals, 169 targets and 232 indicators adopted as a result of a unique process at the global level.[14] I therefore think that it is timely and worthwhile to examine whether sustainable development has its own legal field at the global level, namely the field of *Global Law of Sustainable Development* (GLSD).

This brings me back to the question whether the SDGs are rules of law at the global level. This recalls the notorious question of jurisprudence

[10] Namely, Rio Declaration and Agenda 21.

[11] For example, despite this rather strong statement of the ICJ, a commentary on the Rio Declaration saw daylight only in 2015. See Jorge E. Viñuales, ed., *The Rio Declaration on Environment and Development: A Commentary* (Oxford University Press, 2015).

[12] Virginie Barral, "Sustainable Development in International Law: Nature and Operation of an Evolutive Legal Norm," *European Journal of International Law* 23, no. 2 (May 1, 2012): 383–84.

[13] In this regard, refer to the bibliography at the end of Barral's article with respect to different approaches to the legal nature of sustainable development in international law, in Barral, "Sustainable Development in International Law." See also, Riccardo Pavoni and Dario Piselli, "The Sustainable Development Goals and International Environmental Law: Normative Value and Challenges for Implementation," *Veredas Do Direito* 13 (2016): 13–60.

[14] Evidently, sustainable development is not only about the SDGs. There are many international treaties, such as the UNFCCC, dealing with significant aspects of sustainable development.

"What is law?" and, specifically, how would it be possible to identify what law is at the global level? In legal theory, this question is a matryoshka-doll-type question with a myriad of enchaining questions.[15] The smallest matryoshka doll, namely the question of "What is law?", is the key question of general jurisprudence to which legal theorists and legal philosophers have been providing answers for centuries. Therefore, many concepts and approaches are available in contemporary legal theory with respect to the identification of law at the global level.[16] In this book about the emergence of GLSD, I will follow the footprints of H.L.A. Hart and his rule of recognition-based theory from an exclusive legal positivist approach.[17] In addition, I will attempt to surpass some shortcomings of Hart's theory with Brian Z. Tamanaha's socio-legal and legal pluralist inputs.

Briefly, in line with Hart's theory of law, law is understood in this book from a legal positivist approach, and the underlying concept of law in GLSD is based on the two following theses of Hart: the union of primary and secondary rules thesis and the social rule thesis. According to Hart, primary rules constituting a social practice would be qualified as law if they are supported by secondary rules. Therefore, in order to be able to qualify the SDGs as the laws of GLSD, the existence of secondary rules would be

[15] Jules L. Coleman and Ori Simchen, "'Law,'" *Legal Theory* 9, no. 1 (March 2003): 5.

[16] Nicolas Levrat, "Legal Studies and Global Governance," in *Globalisation, Multilateralism, Europe: Towards a Better Global Governance?*, ed. Mario Telò, 2013, 159–72.

[17] Following Ronald Dworkin's criticism, Hart's legal positivism is divided into two opposing approaches: inclusive legal positivism and exclusive legal positivism. The relationship between law and morality is at the core of the debate between Hart and Dworkin. Dworkin asserts that morality is what makes law "law." Hart essentially rejects this idea; however, he left the door open in a way to suggest that he might not be rejecting it at all. This has seriously influenced the course of their debate, and, as a result, legal positivists were divided into two aforementioned camps. While exclusive legal positivists maintain that moral principles can never be a validity condition of "law," inclusive legal positivists claim that morality may be included among the criteria that make law "law" under certain conditions. See, *inter alia*, Scott J. Shapiro, "The Hart-Dworkin Debate: A Short Guide for the Perplexed," SSRN Scholarly Paper (Rochester, NY: Social Science Research Network, March 5, 2007); Keith Culver, "Leaving the Hart-Dworkin Debate," *The University of Toronto Law Journal* 51, no. 4 (2001): 367–98; Jules L. Coleman, "Negative and Positive Positivism," *Journal of Legal Studies* 11 (1982): 139–64; Jules L. Coleman, "Beyond Inclusive Legal Positivism," *Ratio Juris* 22, no. 3 (September 1, 2009): 359–94; Ronald Dworkin, *Law's Empire* (Harvard University Press, 1986); Brian Leiter, "Beyond the Hart/Dworkin Debate: The Methodology Problem in Jurisprudence Symposium: Has Law Moral Foundations," *American Journal of Jurisprudence* 48 (2003): 17–52; Wilfrid J. Waluchow, *Inclusive Legal Positivism* (Clarendon Press, 1994).

required. In Hart's theory, secondary rules are rules for recognising (rule of recognition), changing (rule of change), and adjudicating (rule of adjudication) primary rules. Even though all three of these types of secondary rules are necessary for a complete legal system, Hart argues that the existence of the rule of recognition is sufficient in order to qualify primary rules as law. Accordingly, this book is essentially an examination of whether a rule of recognition exists with respect to the identification and recognition of the SDGs as laws of GLSD.

However, Hart's theory of law is not a perfect fit to be applicable in contexts other than state law, as it is an account of state law.[18] As such, as a basis for a concept of law at the global level, it needs to be complemented and reinforced with Tamanaha's non-essentialist legal pluralist perspective. For Tamanaha, "law is a human construction" and as such, "every concept of law has social origins that link it to a particular conceptual background."[19] Therefore, as law is a human construction, there is remarkable diversity in the world. Given such diversity, the search for a unified legal concept that would reveal the necessary and essential features of law is unsound.[20] Accordingly, Tamanaha asserts that law has no essence, and it is impossible to capture the essence of law. In other words, for Tamanaha, the identification criteria of law in different contexts might be completely different. Accordingly, Tamanaha even provides a non-exhaustive list of general categories of the types of law; such as, state law, customary law, religious law, international law, transnational law,

[18] Keith Culver and Michael Giudice, *Legality's Borders: An Essay in General Jurisprudence* (Oxford University Press, 2010), 24.

[19] Brian Z. Tamanaha, "What Is 'General' Jurisprudence? A Critique of Universalistic Claims by Philosophical Concepts of Law," *Transnational Legal Theory* 2, no. 3 (September 15, 2011): 291.

[20] An essentialist vision of law contends that there are necessary and universal truths about law that makes law "law." A prominent proponent of this essentialist vision of law, Joseph Raz explains this vision as follows: "[F]or only necessary truths about the law reveal the nature of the law. We talk of 'the nature of law', or the nature of anything else, to refer to those of the law's characteristics which are of the essence of law, which make law into what it is. That is those properties without which the law would not be law." see in Joseph Raz, *Between Authority and Interpretation: On the Theory of Law and Practical Reason* (Oxford: Oxford University Press, 2009), 24–25. See also Tamanaha's criticism of such a vision in Brian Z. Tamanaha, "Necessary and Universal Truths about Law?," *Ratio Juris* 30, no. 1 (March 1, 2017): 3–24.

indigenous law, etc.[21] In line with these arguments, I argue that there is tailor-made recognition and identification criteria of law at the global level in the field of sustainable development. In other words, I contend that GLSD rests on a rule of recognition of its own.

In addition to these contributions of Tamanaha's non-essentialist legal pluralist perspective to the underlying concept of law in GLSD, a reinforced version of Hart's rule of recognition will be brought into play in accordance with Tamanaha's views. In fact, Tamanaha explains and demonstrates that "Hart's ultimate rule of recognition requires a co-ultimate social convention regarding whose actions have the status of law."[22] Accordingly, in this book, Hart's ultimate rule of recognition is re-entitled as "primary social convention" and Tamanaha's co-ultimate social convention as "secondary social convention" in the context of GLSD.

Based on this theoretical background, the question whether the SDGs might be considered as the laws of GLSD necessitates examining and verifying whether there exist: first, a secondary social convention regarding which global actors' common acts would have the status of law within the framework of GLSD; second, a primary social convention among the said global actors with respect to the identification and recognition of rules as the laws of GLSD; and third, within the primary social convention, conclusive criteria[23] for the identification and recognition of rules as the laws of GLSD, or in other words, conclusive criteria for distinguishing law from non-law within the context of GLSD.

In this respect, my initial hypotheses are as follows: firstly, I argue that States, IOs and NGOs, or civil society organisations (CSOs)—including multinational corporations (MNCs), financial institutions, scientific institutions/academia, etc.[24]—are parties to the secondary social convention of GLSD. Secondly, I contend that a primary social convention has emerged among States, IOs and NGOs with respect to the identification and recognition of rules as the laws of GLSD. Thirdly, I sustain that the

[21] Brian Z. Tamanaha, *A General Jurisprudence of Law and Society* (Oxford University Press, 2001), 224–30.

[22] Brian Z. Tamanaha, "Socio-Legal Positivism and a General Jurisprudence," *Oxford Journal of Legal Studies* 21, no. 1 (January 1, 2001): 9. This will be further developed and explained in Chap. 2.

[23] H. L. A. Hart, *The Concept of Law*, 3rd ed, Clarendon Law Series (Oxford: Oxford University Press, 2012), 94–95.

[24] Throughout this book, NGOs, CSOs, "major groups" are used interchangeably and includes, MNCs, financial institutions, scientific institutions/academia.

primary social convention of GLSD includes the following conclusive criteria: (1) States-led, (2) inclusiveness, (3) consensus, (4) universality, and (5) pluralism.

In this sense, this book will test these hypotheses through a chronological examination starting with the UN Conference on the Human Environment of 1972 in Stockholm (UNCHE) and ending with the adoption of the SDGs at the UNGA in September 2015. With this chronological perspective in mind, each ten-year period starting from 1972 will be called as a decade of sustainable development (DSD) and a chapter will be dedicated to each of these decades.

Accordingly, after having provided the details of the theoretical foundations of the underlying concept of law of GLSD, as well as my hypotheses with respect to the primary and secondary social conventions of GLSD, the first chapter will offer a close overview of the literature on global law and how the underlying concept of law of GLSD is embedded in the existing literature.

The second chapter—first DSD, 1972–1982—starts with the UNCHE and ends with the creation of the WCED. By observing the process leading to the UNCHE and its aftermath, including progress preceding the WCED, the chapter concludes that, during the first DSD, (i) the concept of sustainable development had acquired a concrete shape; (ii) a common understanding among global actors was reached in order to move beyond international cooperation and towards a global and systemic approach to effectively address the challenges of sustainable development; and (iii) States started to recognise the role and place of IOs and NGOs by paving the way for their further inclusion in efforts addressing the challenges of sustainable development.

The third chapter—second DSD, 1982–1992—scrutinises the process leading to the UNCED and its aftermath. With respect to the existence of the secondary social convention of GLSD, it is determined that States, as the prime potential global actor, recognised as a matter of fact—on various occasions and throughout the second DSD—the significant role of the IOs and NGOs and their place in the efforts to address the challenges of sustainable development. Accordingly, the chapter concludes that, at the end of the second DSD, there was significant evidence for the emergence of the secondary social convention regarding the status of States, Ios, and NGOs, as global actors whose common acts would constitute the laws of GLSD. Concerning the primary social convention of GLSD, I conclude that, despite some significant indicators with respect to the conclusive criteria for the identification and recognition of rules as the laws of GLSD, it had not yet been possible to talk about the emergence of the primary social convention of GLSD during the second DSD.

In Chap. 4—the third DSD, 1992–2002—the 19th Special Session of the UNGA – 1997 (Rio+5), the World Summit of Sustainable Development of 2002 (WSSD), the Millennium Summit, the creation of the Millennium Development Goals (MDGs), the work of the Commission of Sustainable Development (CSD), and the outcomes of the UN conferences of the 1990s are examined. Based on this examination, I conclude that the secondary social convention of GLSD was operational at the time of the new millennium. In terms of the primary social convention of GLSD, I demonstrate that, despite the full compliance with the conclusive criteria throughout the CSD and the WSSD, as well as the UN conferences, the fragmented picture of these efforts prevented the emergence of the primary social convention of GLSD during the third DSD.

Regarding the MDGs, the fourth chapter illustrates that there were many obstacles for even considering the creation of the MDGs as an exemplary norm-making exercise. In terms of the content of the SDGs, this chapter clarifies the nexus between the SDGs and other norm-making efforts of the 1990s in the field of sustainable development and concludes that the origins of the SDGs are to be found, in terms of *substance and content*, in the outcome documents of the UNCED, Rio+5 and the WSSD, as well as in the UN conferences of 1990s, and, in terms of *style and format*, in the MDGs.

The fifth chapter—fourth DSD, 2002–2012—addresses the UN Conference on Sustainable Development (UNCSD) of 2012. By analysing the process leading to the UNCSD and its aftermath, and by tracking down in its outcome document the references to the conclusive criteria of the primary social convention of GLSD, I conclude that, at the end of the fourth DSD, a primary social convention with precise conclusive criteria had taken shape regarding the identification and recognition of common acts of global actors as the laws of GLSD.

The sixth chapter provides an overview of the initiatives taken within the context of Post-2015 Development Agenda with respect to the materialisation of the goals and targets of the SDGs. I conclude in this chapter that, during the three-year long negotiation process, all five criteria were thoroughly observed, and, at the end of this unprecedented process, the very first rules of GLSD were finally adopted, namely the SDGs.

The final chapter offers concluding remarks and demonstrates that, the SDGs are far beyond being an ordinary UNGA resolution. The chapter adds that although the progress on most of the SDGs is not promising, the SDGs are not only about the content of the Global Goals. Rather, as the book illustrates, one of the most tangible achievements of the SDGs is the global actors' recognition of the SDGs as global rules of sustainable development.

CHAPTER 1

Theoretical Foundations of GLSD

1 Hart's Theory of Law

H.L.A. Hart is one of the key scholars of legal positivism, together with John Austin, Hans Kelsen and Joseph Raz. For Austin, the ultimate basis of a legal system is a sovereign and its commands backed by threat and force.[1] According to Kelsen, a rule of law exists in a legal system if it can be traced back through a chain of validity to the *grundnorm*, whose existence is presupposed and is believed to exist in "judicial consciousness".[2] For Kelsen, a legal system of this kind exists only if it reaches a certain level of efficacy. Even though it is possible to identify certain similarities between Austin's and Kelsen's approaches, Hart's arguments and constructions are quite different. Hart discards Austin's and Kelsen's ideas, and for him, "the ultimate basis of law is neither a justification nor a presupposition but a social construction from people thinking and doing certain things."[3] This is Hart's social thesis.

For Hart, rules are created through practice.[4] This practice that Hart theorised is evidently different than the habit of going to cinema once a week. For Hart, even though there are certain similarities between habits

[1] John Austin and Wilfrid E. Rumble, *The Province of Jurisprudence Determined*, Cambridge Texts in the History of Political Thought (Cambridge: Cambridge Univ. Press, 1995).

[2] Hans Kelsen, *Pure Theory of Law* (University of California Press, 1967).

[3] Hart, *The Concept of Law*, xix.

[4] Ibid., xxi.

H. Göksan, *Global Law of Sustainable Development*, Global Issues,
https://doi.org/10.1007/978-3-031-74547-8_1

and social rules, there are "three salient differences."[5] The first difference is about criticism. In the case of a habit, deviations from converging behaviours "need not be a matter for any form of criticism[,] [...] [while in the case of a rule, deviations] [...] are generally regarded as lapses or faults open to criticism, and [...] pressure for conformity[.]"[6] Secondly, in the case of a rule, "except by a minority of hardened offenders [...] criticism and demands are generally regarded as legitimate, or made with good reason, both by those who make them and those to whom they are made."[7] Hart terms the third distinction as the *internal aspect* of a social rule: "if a social rule is to exist some at least must look upon the behaviour in question as a general standard to be followed by the group as a whole."[8]

In addition, the idea of the union of primary and secondary rules is at the very centre of Hart's theory of social construction. This union provides necessary conditions for the existence of a legal system.[9] Furthermore, for Hart, the existence of secondary rules is what qualifies the primary rules to their status of being law. Thus, the existence of secondary rules in Hart's theory of law is the key for the identification and recognition of norms/rules as law.

The shortcoming in the Hart's theory of law is that he considers that the ideal concept of law is that of municipal/state law.[10] He even argued that international law is not a legal system, but is only a set of rules, because international law lacks secondary rules.[11] However, before reaching such a

[5] Ibid., 55.

[6] Ibid.

[7] Ibid., 56.

[8] Ibid., 56. As much as the idea of social construction seems fancy, it also comes together with some difficulties. As mostly criticised by Ronald Dworkin, some rules are not social practices, and some social practices are not rules. See in Ronald Dworkin, *Taking Rights Seriously* (Harvard University Press, 1978), 48–58. In his postscripts to *The Concept of Law*, Hart replies mainly to the critics of Ronald Dworkin and says that some considerable modifications are necessary, and he argues that only conventional rules form the basis of law. In this respect, he noted: "Rules are conventional social practices if the general conformity of a group to them is part of the reasons which its individual members have for acceptance." See in Hart, *The Concept of Law*, 255. He also added that conventional social rules include ordinary social customs and the rule of recognition.

[9] Hart, *The Concept of Law*, 213.

[10] Hart compares international law with municipal law because of the great analogy between these two. He argued that "no other social rules are so close to municipal law as those of international law." See in; ibid., 237.

[11] Ibid., 234. Undoubtedly, international law greatly evolved since Hart published *The Concept of Law* in 1960. Today, there is an overarching and predominant consensus about

conclusion, Hart did not inquire whether international law might have a different concept of law than the concept of municipal/state law.[12] Nonetheless, today, there is no reason to consider either municipal/state law nor international law as the absolute benchmark in distinguishing law from non-law at the global level. Such an essentialist vision of concept of law would render it impossible to discuss the emergence of a new concept of law at the global level. It is therefore necessary to surpass this shortcoming of Hart's theory of law with Tamanaha's socio-legal and legal pluralist inputs.

2 Tamanaha's Non-essentialist Version of Legal Pluralism

In terms of legal pluralism, Tamanaha mentions that legal pluralism is irresistible despite the fact that it has strong conceptual problems and challenges.[13] In the beginning of the 1990s, the popularity of legal pluralism spread more generally among international lawyers.[14] Influenced by this growing literature, international lawyers proposed pluralist solutions to the increasing legal problems of the twenty-first century's international legal system.[15] Among international lawyers, one can easily notice

genuine lawfulness of rules of international law other than few exceptions, see, for example, Dworkin's *A New Philosophy for International Law*.

[12] For a detailed account of the existence of rule of recognition in the context of international law, namely international rule of recognition, see Samantha Besson, "Theorizing the Sources of International Law," in *The Philosophy of International Law*, ed. Samantha Besson and John Tasioulas, 2010, 163–85. See also, John Tasioulas, "The Legitimacy of International Law," in *The Philosophy of International Law*, ed. Samantha Besson and John Tasioulas (OUP Oxford, 2010).

[13] Brian Z. Tamanaha, "Understanding Legal Pluralism: Past to Present, Local to Global," *Sydney Law Review* 30 (2008): 396.

[14] Among many others, see; Boaventura de Sousa Santos, "Law: A Map of Misreading. Toward a Postmodern Conception of Law," *Journal of Law and Society* 14, no. 3 (1987): 279–302; John Griffiths, "What Is Legal Pluralism," *Journal of Legal Pluralism and Unofficial Law* 24 (1986): 1–56; Sally Engle Merry, "Legal Pluralism," *Law & Society Review* 22, no. 5 (1988): 869–96; Gunther Teubner, "Global Bukowina: Legal Pluralism in the World-Society," SSRN Scholarly Paper (Rochester, NY: Social Science Research Network, 1996).

[15] Sally Engle Merry, "International Law and Sociolegal Scholarship: Toward a Spatial Global Legal Pluralism," in *Special Issue Law and Society Reconsidered*, vol. 41, 0 vols., Studies in Law, Politics and Society 41 (Emerald Group Publishing Limited, 2007), 149–68; Tamanaha, "Understanding Legal Pluralism"; Paul Schiff Berman, "The New Legal

numerous concepts and types of legal pluralism, such as transnational legal pluralism,[16] global legal pluralism,[17] constitutional legal pluralism,[18] internal and external legal pluralism[19] and normative pluralism.[20]

Among legal pluralists, for Tamanaha, "law is a human construction" and as such, "every concept of law has social origins that link it to a particular conceptual background."[21] As law is a human construction and as there is remarkable diversity in the world, the search for a unified legal concept that would reveal the necessary and essential features of law is unsound.[22] Tamanaha and others thus describe why the essence of law can never be found and why it is wrong to search for such an essence.[23]

Pluralism," *Annual Review of Law and Social Science* 5, no. 1 (2009): 225–42; William Twining, "Normative and Legal Pluralism: A Global Perspective Annual Herbert L. Bernstein Lecture in International and Comparative Law," *Duke Journal of Comparative & International Law* 20 (2010 2009): 473–518; Nico Krisch, *Beyond Constitutionalism: The Pluralist Structure of Postnational Law* (OUP Oxford, 2010); Nico Krisch, "Pluralism in International Law and Beyond," SSRN Scholarly Paper (Rochester, NY: Social Science Research Network, June 3, 2015); Roger Cotterrell, "A Concept of Law for Global Legal Pluralism?," in *Concepts of Law: Comparative, Jurisprudential, and Social Science Perspectives* (Routledge, 2016), 193–208.

16 Peer Zumbansen, "Transnational Legal Pluralism," *Transnational Legal Theory* 1, no. 2 (July 1, 2010): 141–89.

17 Paul Schiff Berman, *Global Legal Pluralism: A Jurisprudence of Law Beyond Borders* (Cambridge University Press, 2012).

18 Neil Walker, "The Idea of Constitutional Pluralism," *The Modern Law Review* 65, no. 3 (May 1, 2002): 317–59.

19 Nollkaemper, A. et al., "Inside or out: Two Types of International Legal Pluralism," in *ASIL Studies in International Legal Theory* (Cambridge University Press, 2013).

20 Jan Klabbers and Touko Piiparinen, *Normative Pluralism and International Law: Exploring Global Governance* (Cambridge University Press, 2013).

21 Tamanaha, "What Is 'General' Jurisprudence?," 291.

22 An essentialist vision of law contends that there are necessary and universal truths about law that makes law "law." A prominent proponent of this essentialist vision of law, Joseph Raz explains this vision as follows: "[F]or only necessary truths about the law reveal the nature of the law. We talk of 'the nature of law', or the nature of anything else, to refer to those of the law's characteristics which are of the essence of law, which make law into what it is. That is those properties without which the law would not be law." see in Raz, *Between Authority and Interpretation*, 24–25. See also Tamanaha's criticism of such a vision in Tamanaha, "Necessary and Universal Truths about Law?"

23 Brian Z. Tamanaha, "A Non-Essentialist Version of Legal Pluralism," *Journal of Law and Society* 27 (2000): 313. Refer to this article for a detailed account about how this non-essentialist vision allows legal scholars to surpass two main conceptual difficulties in legal pluralism; namely the questions related to the definition of law and, especially, how to distinguish law from social rules/norms. See also, William Twining, *General Jurisprudence:*

Once such a non-essentialist concept of law is adopted, what would be the next steps for discussing the emergence of a concept of law at the global level? Giudice draws a road map in this regard—through what he calls a "constructive conceptual explanation."[24] Accordingly, two critical questions appear with respect to the qualification of rules as the laws of GLSD:[25] First, how rules at the global level would be qualified as the laws of GLSD and second, who would be entitled to qualify these rules as law? To answer these questions, I need to refer back to Hart's theory.

In Hart's theory, secondary rules are rules for recognizing (rule of recognition), changing (rule of change), and adjudicating (rule of adjudication) primary rules. Even though all three of these types of secondary rules are necessary for a full-fledged legal system, the existence of the rule of recognition is sufficient to qualify primary rules as law. Therefore, the existence of a rule of recognition is the key in order to qualify social rules as law. Nevertheless, in Hart's theory of law, it is not clear how to determine the existence of a rule of recognition. Much of Hart's argument in this respect is intensively discussed among legal theorists.[26] For this reason, the way Hart initially explained the existence of a rule of recognition needs to be adapted and contextualised, especially with regard to the

Understanding Law from a Global Perspective, Law in Context (Cambridge: Cambridge University Press, 2009), 66.; Paul Schiff Berman, "Global Legal Pluralism," *Southern California Law Review* 80 (2007 2006): 1178.; Teubner,"The Two Faces of Janus," 1451.

[24] Michael Giudice, *Understanding the Nature of Law: A Case for Constructive Conceptual Explanation* (Edward Elgar Publishing, 2015), 66.

[25] Tamanaha notes in this regard as follows: "The first problem involves resolving the question of *who* must identify a phenomenon as law through their social practices for it to qualify as such." See in Tamanaha, "A Non-Essentialist Version of Legal Pluralism," 319.

[26] According to Hart, a rule of recognition is a social convention among legal officials accepting the same rule of recognition for the identification and recognition of primary rules and displaying a critical reflective attitude towards the accepted rule of recognition. This explanation raises a lot of questions. What is an official? What is a legal official? How to decide who is an official? Who decide(s) who is official? How to identify the acceptance of a rule of recognition by these officials? What does it mean to accept a rule of recognition? Is it enough if the majority of the officials accept a rule of recognition? Or is there another specific threshold? What does it mean to display a critical reflective attitude? Is it enough if a small number of legal officials display a critical reflective attitude? Or is this expected from all legal officials? For a brilliant account providing thorough answers to these and similar questions about Hart's rule of recognition, please refer to Tamanaha, "Socio-Legal Positivism and a General Jurisprudence." Accordingly, I am not going to duplicate Tamanaha's efforts in responding to these questions.

question concerning who would be entitled to qualify rules as law within the framework of GLSD.

According to Hart, a rule of recognition is a social convention among legal officials who accept the same rule of recognition for the identification of primary rules. Accordingly, the existence of a social convention among legal officials is crucial for the qualification of primary rules as law and for the conversion of "the regime of primary rules into [...] a legal system."[27] Consequently, in Hart's theory of law, another key element in the emergence of law out of rules is the notion of "legal officials."

Hart did not sufficiently explain the significance of the notion of legal officials in his theory of law.[28] In order to better apply his theory to the case of GLSD, it is necessary to utilise a new terminology instead of referring to the notion of legal officials. In this regard, Tamanaha refers repeatedly to "social actors" in his theory of "a non-essentialist legal pluralism." He notes that "[N]ew forms of 'law' can be said to exist whenever recognized as such by social actors."[29] Accordingly, the rule of recognition can be defined as a social convention among social actors—in the case of GLSD, as global actors—accepting the same rule of recognition for the identification and recognition of primary rules and displaying a critical reflective attitude towards the accepted rule of recognition.

However, while questing for such a rule of recognition at the global level,[30] the task is significantly more difficult than doing the same exercise in the case of municipal/state law or international law. This is because

[27] Hart, *The Concept of Law*, 94.

[28] There are abundant scholarly discussions around Hart's "legal officials, but this book is not the place to review these discussions. For scholarly discussions on this issue, see among others; Culver and Giudice, *Legality's Borders*, 1–33.; Jules L. Coleman, *The Practice of Principle: In Defence of a Pragmatist Approach to Legal Theory* (Oxford University Press, 2003); Kent Greenawalt, "The Rule of Recognition and the Constitution," *Michigan Law Review* 85, no. 4 (1987): 621–71; Andrei Marmor, *Positive Law and Objective Values* (Clarendon Press, 2001), 16–17; Tamanaha, *A General Jurisprudence of Law and Society*, 133–70; Jeremy Waldron, "Who Needs Rules of Recognition?," SSRN Scholarly Paper (Rochester, NY: Social Science Research Network, March 12, 2009).

[29] Tamanaha, "Socio-Legal Positivism and a General Jurisprudence," 28.

[30] I contend that GLSD rests on a rule of recognition of its own. In terms of comparison, for example, concerning GAL, Kingsbury asserts as follows: "[A]t present, any claims within GAL to be law do not rest on a rule of recognition, shared among relevant participants, which identifies and delimits a unified legal system of GAL. There may well exist, however, different rules of recognition within different social-institutional-sectoral groupings in specific practice areas of GAL. There certainly exist recognition practices in such areas, so that recognition is important to law, even if a single shared rule of recognition is difficult to dis-

norms of GLSD are still emerging. Nevertheless, d'Aspremont points a way out for this type of law-ascertainment situation—through an example about international legal rules—in emerging contexts.[31] If, d'Aspremont's views are transplanted into the emerging context of GLSD, what matters first is to find out who might be the authorities at the global level, sharing sufficient social consciousness and making use of similar law-ascertainment language, that are actually recognising some norms as constituting rules of GLSD. What secondly matters is to uncover the characteristics of the law-ascertainment language used by these authorities.[32]

D'Aspremont's views are entirely in line with the two questions I identified above and with Hart's arguments around the rule of recognition. What is missing in Hart's rule of recognition and d'Aspremont's arguments is related to who decides who will be the authorities making use of similar law-ascertainment language (or legal officials) accepting the same rule of recognition for the identification of primary rules. It is with respect to this question that Tamanaha provides a simple solution. In the literature, this is the famous chicken-and-egg problem[33] and Tamanaha maintains that "the recognition of legal officials, and the emergence of secondary rules, are contemporaneous events, both grounded in social

til." See in Benedict Kingsbury, "The Concept of 'Law' in Global Administrative Law," *European Journal of International Law* 20, no. 1 (February 1, 2009): 30.

[31] Jean d'Aspremont, "Herbert Hart in Post-Modern International Legal Scholarship," SSRN Scholarly Paper (Rochester, NY: Social Science Research Network, October 2, 2012), 18.

[32] This exercise obviously needs to be conducted with an inductive method. Moreover, d'Aspremont underlines that an interdisciplinary perspective, especially further sociological analyses, will be needed when such a theory becomes functional and applicable. He claims that "[e]ven if the social thesis, by bypassing the question of the validity [...] and grounding law-ascertainment in facts, were to lead legal science to encapsulate sociological analysis, such an enlargement of scope of the science of law [...] would then be the necessary condition for a lasting and solid theory of ascertainment of international legal rules." See, ibid., 19.

[33] This description about Hart's legal officials is quite common. Without getting into details, let me refer to Shapiro's brief explanation of this problem: "On the one hand, it seems that legal rules can only be generated by authoritative legal sources. Not anyone may make a legal rule—only those vested with legal authority may—yet it also appears that the authority of a legal source can only be generated by legal rules. Congress, the Supreme Court, the President, and Parliament are all themselves products of law. Hence, we find ourselves in a situation where we need law in order to make law. This leads to a classic 'chicken-egg' problem: If legal authority can only be created by rules, who makes the rules that creates the authority?" see in Scott J. Shapiro, "On Hart's Way Out," *Legal Theory* 4, no. 4 (December 1998): 471.

practices."[34] Tamanaha further contends that "Hart's ultimate rule of recognition requires a co-ultimate social convention regarding whose actions have the status of law."[35] In other words, for the identification and recognition of rules as the laws of GLSD, it is indispensable to identify global actors whose common acts would constitute the laws of GLSD. Accordingly, in this book, Hart's ultimate rule of recognition will be referred to as "primary social convention" and Tamanaha's co-ultimate social convention as "secondary social convention" in the context of GLSD.

3 Primary and Secondary Social Conventions of GLSD

Based on the aforementioned theoretical background, the question whether the SDGs might be considered as the laws of GLSD necessitates examining and verifying whether there exist: first, a secondary social convention regarding which global actors' common acts would constitute the laws of GLSD; second, a primary social convention among the said global actors with respect to the identification and recognition of rules as the laws of GLSD; and third, within the primary social convention, conclusive criteria[36] for the identification and recognition of rules as the laws of GLSD, or in other words, conclusive criteria for distinguishing law from non-law within the context of GLSD.

Before starting to examine whether primary and secondary social conventions of GLSD emerge out of the process leading to the adoption of the SDGs, my initial hypotheses are as follows: First of all, I argue that States, IOs and NGOs—including MNCs, financial institutions, scientific institutions/academia, etc.—are parties to the secondary social convention of GLSD. Secondly, I contend that a primary social convention has emerged among States, IOs and NGOs with respect to the identification and recognition of rules as the laws of GLSD. Thirdly and finally, I sustain that the primary social convention of GLSD includes the following conclusive criteria for the identification and recognition of rules as the laws of GLSD: (1) States-led, (2) inclusiveness, (3) consensus, (4) universality and (5) pluralism.

[34] Tamanaha, "Socio-Legal Positivism and a General Jurisprudence," 8.

[35] Ibid., 9.

[36] Hart, *The Concept of Law*, 94–95.

States-led means that rules—that are adopted and agreed upon to better address the challenges of sustainable development—emerge as a result of an intergovernmental process. Inclusiveness specifies that the said intergovernmental process is to be conducted with full participation of other relevant actors, such as IOs, NGOs, etc. Consensus stipulates that rules are to be adopted and agreed upon by consensus among all actors who are parties to the secondary social convention. Universality provides that rules adopted and agreed upon are applicable at planetary level without jurisdictional limits. And finally, pluralism requires that rules adopted and agreed upon do not seek to contradict any existing rule of international law; rather, they pursue to complement and to coexist in harmony with the existing rules of international law.

At this stage, I must underline the *ratione materiae* limits of my hypotheses. I am only interested in examining law-like quality of global norms/rules in the field of sustainable development. For example, in the field of banking regulations, as the main global actors, there is nothing preventing States, together with other actors, that is, IOs, central banks etc., to agree on another primary social convention with respect to the identification and recognition of rules and norms as laws under the concept of "global banking law." Furthermore, in different fields of globalisation, States and other global actors can come together each time to create other secondary social conventions and agree on a different primary social convention with respect to the identification and recognition of rules and norms as "law" at the global level. This is the reason why I have a legal pluralist approach, and my understanding of law at the global level is at peace with legal pluralism.

4 Embeddedness of the Concept of Law of GLSD into the Existing Literature

GLSD could be considered as one of the sub-categories of global law, such as global administrative law (GAL) or global health law. With respect to the concept of global law, it is still in a stage of "intimations" and it is an "uncharted law" in the sense that our available legal maps are not (yet) able to locate effectively where global law is and what it looks like.[37] The

[37] Neil Walker, *Intimations of Global Law* (Cambridge University Press, 2014); Neil Walker, "Out of Place and out of Time: Law's Fading Co-Ordinates," *Edinburgh Law Review* 14 (2010): 13–46. For example, Walker further notes as follows: "No longer embed-

literature is getting increasingly richer about the notion of global law, but it is not in the scope of this book to provide a coherent analysis of competing propositions about the concept of global law.[38] However, despite the richness of this exponentially growing field, research revealing the underlying concept of law in global law is relatively limited.

For example, Neil Walker does not propose a type of law "identifiable as such by its source or other systemic criteria."[39] Walker's proposition about global law does not have a distinct law-like quality. Certain rules that are already qualified as law in other legal systems are simply considered, according to Walker, as examples of global law based on a content-dependent globality.[40]

For Domingo, global law is a synonym with the "Law of Humanity" and it does not yet constitute a legal order but "it is called to become

ded in the state and so unable to rely on the recognized pedigree of state law as the internal expression of a sovereign authority, and no longer easily accommodated within the parallel category of international law understood in its dominant modern mode as grounded in agreement among sovereign states authorities, global law is uncertainly and insecurely founded." See in Walker, *Intimations of Global Law*, page 151.

[38] The key scholar to bring a crucial understanding to law from a global perspective, without a doubt, is William Twining. William Twining, *Globalisation and Legal Theory* (Cambridge University Press, 2000); Twining, *General Jurisprudence*; William Twining, *Globalisation and Legal Scholarship*, Tilburg Law Lectures Series. Montesquieu Seminars, vol. 4 (Nijmegen: Wolf Legal Publ, 2011); See among many others: Levrat, "Legal Studies and Global Governance"; Gunther Teubner, *Global Law without a State* (Ashgate Publishing Company, 1997); Rafael Domingo, *The New Global Law*, ASIL Studies in International Legal Theory (Cambridge: Cambridge University Press, 2010); Giuliana Ziccardi Capaldo, *The Pillars of Global Law* (Aldershot, Hants, England ; Burlington, VT: Ashgate, 2008); Shavana Musa and Eefje de Volder, *Reflections on Global Law* (Martinus Nijhoff Publishers, 2013); Venzke, I., "Contemporary Theories and International Lawmaking," in *Research Handbooks in International Law*, ed. Brölmann, C. and Radi, Y. (Edward Elgar, 2016); Collins, "The Slipperiness of 'Global Law'"; Cotterrell, "A Concept of Law for Global Legal Pluralism?"; Pierrick Le Golf, "Global Law: A Legal Phenomenon Emerging from the Process of Globalization," *Indiana Journal of Global Legal Studies* 14, no. 1 (August 13, 2007): 119–45.

[39] Collins, "The Slipperiness of 'Global Law,'" 735–36.

[40] Ibid., 726–35. Collins further notes that the specifically global aspect of [Walker's] account of global law—the novel aspect of his legal theory—seems to rely entirely upon a form of content-dependent justification: the importance of accountability under global administrative law, the inherent dignity of the person under global human rights, and so on. In other words, the "globality" of global law—and what precisely that might mean in specific circumstances—would appear to lie entirely in the eye of the beholder and will therefore necessarily remain controversial and contestable in doing so (p. 732).

one."[41] Domingo also sees global law from a positivist perspective.[42] However, Domingo's concept of global law is not a descriptive one, as he consistently makes remarks about how global law should be. He even suggests the following rule of recognition for global law: "*Quod omnes tangit ab omnibus approbetur*: What affects everyone should be approved by everyone."[43] However, in Hartian terms, it is not possible to suggest a rule of recognition, as such a rule emerges as a result of a social convention.

As far as GAL is concerned, Benedict Kingsbury provides a very thorough explanation of the underlying concept of law in GAL.[44] I entirely agree with Kingsbury that Hart's theory of law is a promising starting point for the case of, not only GAL, but also for international law.[45] As mentioned before, I extended and reinforced Hart's theory of law with Tamanaha's non-essentialist legal pluralist perspective. However, my approach differs from Kingsbury's concept of law in GAL, in that Kingsbury prefers to extend Hart's legal positivism with Lon Fuller's views and with the requirement "to adhere to public law norms" or with "publicness."[46] He further considers the observance of this "publicness"

[41] Domingo, *The New Global Law*, 121; See also: Pedro J. Martinez-Fraga, "Book Review, Rafael Domingo, The New Global Law," *McGill Law Journal* 56 (2011 2010): 767–74; Shams Al Din Al Hajjaji, "Review of the New Global Law by Rafael Domingo Review," *Berkeley Journal of International Law* 32 (2014): 268–80; Rafael Domingo, "Global Law and the New Global Human Community," SSRN Scholarly Paper (Rochester, NY: Social Science Research Network, May 11, 2015); Rafael Domingo, "Gaius, Vattel, and the New Global Law Paradigm," *European Journal of International Law* 22, no. 3 (August 1, 2011): 627–47; Rafael Domingo, "The Crisis of International Law," *Vanderbilt Journal of Transnational Law* 42 (2009): 1543–94.

[42] Domingo, *The New Global Law*, pages 122–23. For example, he notes as follows: "In Hart's terms, we could say that the global order, unlike international law, should be formed by primary rules or rules of conduct and by secondary rules – that is, rules for the recognition, change, and adjudication of primary rules."

[43] Ibid., 191–92.

[44] Kingsbury, "The Concept of 'Law' in Global Administrative Law"; For more general explanations about the concept of global administrative law, see especially; Benedict Kingsbury, Nico Krisch, and Richard B. Stewart, "The Emergence of Global Administrative Law," *Law and Contemporary Problems* 68, no. 3/4 (2005): 15–61; Nico Krisch and Benedict Kingsbury, "Introduction: Global Governance and Global Administrative Law in the International Legal Order," *European Journal of International Law* 17, no. 1 (February 1, 2006); Carol Harlow, "Global Administrative Law: The Quest for Principles and Values," *European Journal of International Law* 17, no. 1 (February 1, 2006): 187–214.

[45] Kingsbury, "The Concept of 'Law' in Global Administrative Law," 28.

[46] Ibid., page 30.

requirement as a validity condition for the rules of GAL.[47] Thus, he clearly adopts an inclusive legal positivist[48] approach in his concept of law in GAL,[49] while my understanding of the underlying concept of law in GLSD is rather in accordance with an exclusive legal positivist[50] approach.[51] And, according to the exclusive legal positivist approach, it is not possible to add moral or ethical criteria as a validity condition for considering and qualifying rules as "law."

Last but not least, Benoit Frydman proposes a pragmatic approach to global law.[52] For him, the methodology to be followed for better conceptualising law at the global level is to adapt a micro-legal approach focusing on "unidentified normative objects" in several areas potentially relevant for global law, such as internet regulation, corporate social responsibility, rankings and indicators, financial regulations, climate change, etc.[53] The

[47] In Kingsbury's words: "[...] [T]he rule of recognition is understood as including a stipulation that only rules and institutions meeting these publicness requirements immanent in public law (and evidenced through comparative materials) can be regarded as law. It may thus be possible to be a Hartian positivist, at least in a loose sense, and also to accept these publicness requirements as necessary to law." Ibid., pages 30–31.

[48] Waluchow, *Inclusive Legal Positivism*; Coleman, *The Practice of Principle*; Matthew H. Kramer, *Where Law and Morality Meet* (Oxford University Press, 2008).

[49] Alexander Somek, "The Concept of 'Law' in Global Administrative Law: A Reply to Benedict Kingsbury," *European Journal of International Law* 20, no. 4 (November 1, 2009): pages 988–89.

[50] Joseph Raz, *The Authority of Law: Essays on Law and Morality*, 2nd edition (Oxford; New York: Oxford University Press, 2009); Marmor, *Positive Law and Objective Values.*

[51] Analytical jurisprudence is divided into three sub-categories, and the discussions among the proponents of each of these three approaches constitute one of the main discussions in modern legal theory. In the words of Giudice, the difference among these three sub-categories is as follows: "In contemporary legal philosophy there are three main types of theory from which to choose: Ronald Dworkin's theory of law as integrity (or interpretivism, more generally), which maintains that conformity with moral principles is always a validity condition of law; inclusive legal positivism, which maintains that conformity with moral principles can, under particular conditions, serve as a validity condition of law; and exclusive legal positivism, which maintains that conformity with moral principles can never be a validity condition of law." See in Thomas Schultz, *Transnational Legality: Stateless Law and International Arbitration* (OUP Oxford, 2013), pages 8–9.; See also; Giudice, *Understanding the Nature of Law*, page 113.; Stephen R. Perry, "The Varieties of Legal Positivism," *Canadian Journal of Law and Jurisprudence* 9 (1996): 361–82.

[52] Benoit Frydman, "A Pragmatic Approach to Global Law," SSRN Scholarly Paper (Rochester, NY: Social Science Research Network, August 19, 2013). Benoit Frydman is the President of the Perelman Centre for Philosophy of Law, which hosts a special research program on global law at Université Libre de Bruxelles.

[53] Ibid., pages 3 and 17–18.

methodology that I follow through a case study of the SDGs to discuss the emergence of GLSD is perfectly aligned with Frydman's micro-legal approach. Frydman's approach differs from mine, as he considers that "the value of a norm depends less on its 'pedigree' than on the effects that it produces."[54] With respect to the effects that some of these "unidentified normative objects" produce, Frydman argues that they "potentially operate as 'functional equivalents' of legal rules."[55] It is indeed because of these potential and actual effects that I was particularly curious about their actual and potential law-like quality. Furthermore, contrary to Frydman's assertion, for me, the pedigree of a norm is not necessarily about connecting a norm to an authority. It is rather about connecting a norm to a social convention that the said norm is based upon. As such, the pedigree constitutes the connection between a norm and a society. And the existence of that social convention, which recognizes and identifies valid norms in that society, is the key to distinguishing norms from laws in that society.

Thus, the present book on the emergence of GLSD is well situated in the existing and increasingly growing literature around the issues related to global law. Similar to the concept of law in GAL, the underlying basis of GLSD is Hart's legal positivism. In addition, the methodology I am using in the book in drawing my conclusions matches with Frydman's pragmatic and micro-legal approach to some extent, as the emergence of the concept of law in GLSD is extracted from a specific study of the SDGs. Last but not least, thanks to the legal pluralist essence of GLSD, I am able to capture an interesting and emerging normativity at the global level in the field of sustainable development.[56]

Comparable level of normativity is also present in many other areas affected by globalisation: global finance regulations, global health issues, internet regulation, migration, etc. I believe that it is possible to identify considerable similarities between the relevant actors (secondary social convention) and conclusive criteria of a potential primary social convention in these other areas of globalisation. By bringing forward a simple step-by-step guide for exploring the existence and the components of a rule of recognition within an example of a *prima facie* legal phenomenon at the global level, this book has a great potential to contribute to the broadest

[54] Ibid., 6.
[55] Ibid., 8.
[56] Krisch, "Pluralism in International Law and Beyond," page 10.

understanding of what is law at the global level from a legal positivist and legal pluralist perspective.

This book is much more associated with the methodology of "continuity" of contemporary legal theory.[57] This methodology "emphasizes the value of seeking to understand and pursue relations between diverse approaches to understanding law."[58] Accordingly, legal positivist theories, by following the methodology of continuity, allow other legal theories to provide additional insights into the broadest understanding of law and social reality. In accordance with the methodology of continuity, this book is not an attempt to answer the question of what is law at the global level. Rather, it is a proposition about a method that could be used to achieve the broadest understanding of law at the global level.[59] In other words, this book does not attempt to draw a line between law and other social rules at the global level in the field of sustainable development. It simply points out what would be required for such a line to exist, and it is expected from other legal theorists, social sciences theorists and even moral theorists to debate back and forth, in order to sharpen, enrich, strengthen and consolidate a strong and reliable concept of law for the broadest possible understanding of law at the global level.

[57] For Giudice, "diversity reigns" in contemporary legal theory, which includes "moral, political, or normative theories, descriptive-explanatory theories, social scientific theories of various kinds, and participant or internal as opposed to nonparticipant or external theories of law and legal phenomena." See in Michael Giudice, "Ways of Understanding Diversity Among Theories of Law," *Law and Philosophy* 24, no. 5 (September 1, 2005): page 509. Giudice distinguishes three different methodologies within the methodology of contemporary legal theory, namely "imperialism," "difference" and "continuity". In his words, imperialism is "the attempt to find and demonstrate the truth of a single methodological approach to understanding law. Any theory which does not adopt the method claimed to be the proper one is inadequate." The originality in Giudice's categorisation is that he reveals perfect examples of imperialism among the proponents of competing legal theories. He demonstrates plainly how Posner's social scientific theory, Dworkin's interpretivism, Kelsen's *Pure Theory of Law*, and John Finnis' natural law theory, are all propound to be the only adequate theory of law. The "difference" approach considers that "theories should be distinguished and understood in light of their avowed purposes, such that theories of different types cannot be viewed as competitive if their principal aims are fundamentally different."

[58] Ibid., 510.

[59] Ibid., 542.

CHAPTER 2

The Origins of the Sustainable Development Goals

This chapter first takes the reader back to the UNCHE to better understand the developments that led States to establish the WCED, as well as the practice followed by States with respect to the involvement of CSOs into the discussions on sustainable development. The second section unfolds the efforts of the WCED in merging environmental and development concerns into the concept of sustainable development, as well as its role in establishing a practice about how to proceed to better address the challenges of sustainable development. Based on the practice followed in UNCHE, as well as by the WCED, the third section concludes by noting that, during first DSD, the concept of sustainable development has taken a more concrete shape; that a global perspective emerged with respect to the need to develop a global and systemic approach to address the challenges of sustainable development; and that States have recognised the significance of CSOs by involving them in efforts addressing the challenges of sustainable development.

H. Göksan, *Global Law of Sustainable Development*, Global Issues,
https://doi.org/10.1007/978-3-031-74547-8_2

1 UNCHE: Environmental Concerns Versus Development Concerns

1.1 *Towards the UNCHE: A "States-Led" Initiative*

Following the suggestion of Sweden,[1] in its Resolution 2398 (XXIII) of 1968,[2] the UNGA decided to convene a conference to address "the problems of the human environment." Back then, the challenges related to human environment were not yet considered as global challenges. The word "global" was not used in this UNGA Resolution 2398. However, it will be a central adjective in future resolutions of the UNGA concerning the preparations for the UNCHE. In that sense, international cooperation among States was considered as the only way forward to address the challenges of the human environment back in the 1960s.

The intention to hold a UN Conference was not an everyday idea of Sweden's Government. In fact, it is possible to trace back this idea to the growing environmental concerns of the 1960s. One of the famous references always mentioned as the initial example of growing environmental concerns is Rachel Carson's *Silent Spring*.[3] Although the book's arguments are strongly contested for having negatively impacted the fight against malaria,[4] Carson's book "ignited the environmental movement."[5] Certainly, Carson was not the only environmentalist of the 1960s who tried to raise awareness about the future of the human environment. For example, the World Wildlife Fund (WWF) was also created in 1961, by a group of eminent conservationists and Julian Huxley, the first Director-General of UNESCO, was one of the founding members of the WWF. Hence, the conservationists and environmentalists of the 1960s managed to raise sufficient awareness to incite Sweden to generate a proposition for a UN conference on the environment and to pass a resolution at the UNGA to this end, to wit, UNGA Resolution 2398.

[1] Louis B. Sohn, "Stockholm Declaration on the Human Environment, The," *Harvard International Law Journal* 14 (1973): 424.

[2] "Problems of the Human Environment, UNGA Resolution 2398 (XXIII)," December 3, 1968.

[3] Rachel Carson, *Silent Spring* (Houghton Mifflin Harcourt, 2002).

[4] "Who Was Rachel Carson?," *SafeChemicalPolicy.Org* (blog), March 2, 2007.

[5] Eliza Griswold, "How 'Silent Spring' Ignited the Environmental Movement," *The New York Times*, September 21, 2012, sec. Magazine.

The *Morges Manifesto*, announcing the creation of the WWF, mentions some important civil society actors of the world conservation movement at the time, such as the International Union for Conservation of Nature and Natural Resources (IUCN). Furthermore, one of the preambular paragraphs of Resolution 2398 mentions that it is "aware of the important work being done on the problems of the human environment by [...] [NGOs] such as the [IUCN], the International Council of Scientific Unions and the International Biological Programme[.]"[6] Hence, States were already cognisant of the significance of the role of these CSOs with respect to increasing environmental concerns. This, of course, paved the way for further inclusion of these actors in the process towards the UNCHE.

The initial idea of the UNCHE was to "provide a framework for comprehensive consideration within the United Nations of the problems of the human environment."[7] Accordingly, organizations in the UN system were also considered as being at the centre of the idea of the UNCHE. Indeed, two preambular paragraphs of Resolution 2398 refer to the important work being undertaken by these IOs. These references also suggest a recognition on the part of States with respect to the role of these IOs concerning the challenges of the human environment.

The operative clauses of Resolution 2398 include the decision to convene the UNCHE and request the Secretary-General (SG), in consultation with all the aforementioned actors, to prepare an overall report about the details of the UNCHE.[8] The typical working method of the UNGA in setting up such conferences is to adopt a resolution every year after an initial resolution deciding to convene a conference. Accordingly, the following sections briefly overview these resolutions and, specifically, underline how the issue of development was put forward by developing countries to be considered and addressed together with global environmental concerns. This particularly influenced the emergence of the concept of sustainable development as we know it today.

[6] "UNGA Resolution 2398 (XXIII)."

[7] Ibid.

[8] Ibid., para. 3.

1.2 The Involvement of Actors Other Than States in the Process Leading to the UNCHE

Resolution 2581 (XXIV) (1969)[9] endorsed the SG's report with respect to the purposes and objectives of the UNCHE[10] and set the main purpose of the UNCHE as "to provide guidelines for action [...] to protect and improve the human environment and to remedy and prevent its impairment."[11] Resolution 2581 also established a Preparatory Committee (PrepCom), composed of representatives of certain UN Member States for the preparation of the UNCHE. A Working Group established by the PrepCom was also working "for the preparation of the draft declaration" of the UNCHE.[12] With respect to the adoption of specific guidelines for action at the end of the UNCHE, "the prevailing view [in the PrepCom] was that [...] the Declaration [should] outline broad goals and objectives."[13] With respect to legal effects of the Declaration, the PrepCom noted that the Declaration "should not formulate legally binding provisions."[14]

Given this non-binding character of the envisioned declaration, the participation of other actors to the process towards the UNCHE was facilitated. In this regard, the PrepCom specifically addressed the participation of organizations other than governments, and it was suggested that "a pre-Conference for NGOs should be held at which NGOs could make recommendations to the UNCHE."[15] It is remarkable that back in the beginning of the 1970s, there were 15 IOs and 39 NGOs which participated in the work of the PrepCom.[16]

[9] "United Nation Conference on the Human Environment, UNGA Resolution 2581 (XXIV)," December 15, 1969.

[10] "Problems of the Human Environment: Report of the Secretary-General, E/4667," May 26, 1969, paras. 82–92.

[11] "United Nation Conference on the Human Environment, UNGA Resolution 2581 (XXIV)."

[12] Sohn, "Stockholm Declaration on the Human Environment, The," 426.

[13] "Report of the Preparatory Committee for the United Nations Conference on the Human Environment on Its Second Session, UN Doc. A/CONF.48/PC/9," February 26, 1971, para. 32.

[14] Ibid., para. 33.

[15] "Report of the Preparatory Committee for the United Nations Conference on the Human Environment on Its Second Session, UN Doc. A/CONF.48/PC/9," para. 111.

[16] Ibid., paras. 61–67.

It is also important to underscore at this stage that the non-binding character of the envisioned declaration is not the only factor which paved the way for the emergence of an increasing role and the implications of actors such as IOs and NGOs for norm-making at the global level. To illustrate, in the case of sustainable development, one other reason is the global nature of environmental concerns. As rightly noted, "the politics of global environmental crisis [...] is a politics that defies traditional compromises among states and their industrial partners [and that] pits state industrial interests against community and ecosystem interests."[17] Furthermore, with respect to the emergence of NGOs as global actors due to the global nature of environmental concerns, "NGOs [were] increasingly picking up where governmental action stops or has yet to begin[,] [...] [and] they [were] act[ing] as agents of social learning by linking the biophysical conditions with political concerns while simultaneously acting locally and globally."[18] Thus, these factors created the necessary conditions for the emergence of new global actors other than States, which, in turn, generated a unique momentum in the field of sustainable development for these global actors to come together for the emergence of GLSD.

1.3 Addressing the Concerns of Developing Countries and Ensuring "Consensus"

It is clear in all the reports of the PrepCom of the UNCHE that States, as well as IOs and NGOs involved in the process, were all aware of the global nature of environmental concerns.[19] Notwithstanding, during the meetings, one delegation stated that "the premises for action [...] tended to over-emphasise the global aspects of the environmental problem."[20] In

[17] Matthias Finger, Tom Princen, and Jack Manno, "Nongovernmental Organizations in World Environmental Politics," *International Environmental Affairs* 7, no. 1 (1995): 46.

[18] Ibid., 54.

[19] "Report of the Preparatory Committee for the United Nations Conference on the Human Environment on Its First Session, UN Doc. A/CONF.48/PC/6," April 6, 1970; "Report of the Preparatory Committee for the United Nations Conference on the Human Environment on Its Second Session, UN Doc. A/CONF.48/PC/9"; "Report of the Preparatory Committee for the United Nations Conference on the Human Environment on Its Third Session, UN Doc. A/CONF.48/PC/13," September 30, 1971; "Report of the Preparatory Committee for the United Nations Conference on the Human Environment on Its Forth Session, UN Doc. A/CONF.48/PC/17," March 15, 1972.

[20] "Report of the Preparatory Committee for the United Nations Conference on the Human Environment on Its Second Session, UN Doc. A/CONF.48/PC/9," 39.

that regard, it is important to keep in mind the context of the 1970s and the cold war atmosphere in which the world was ideologically divided. Accordingly, even though the nature of environmental concerns was inherently global, the key global actors at that time was not keen and ready to properly comprehend these environmental problems as "global concerns" and to generate a genuine global agenda for action to address them.

Another division was the one between developing and developed countries. In fact, UNGA Resolution 2657 (XXV) (1970),[21] specifically addresses the concerns of developing countries with respect to environmental policies. However, developing countries were not fully satisfied during this process and with this Resolution 2657. As a result, the following year, there were two parallel resolutions adopted by the UNGA. Resolution 2850 (1971) with the usual title of "UN Conference on the Human Environment"[22] and the alternative Resolution 2849 (1971) entitled "Development and Environment."[23]

Following the criticisms of developing countries, in addition to a number of regional meetings around the world, a special meeting of Panel of Experts on Development and Environment was held at Founex, Switzerland, in June 1971, to better integrate the concerns of developing countries in the preparation of the UNCHE. The recognition in the Founex Report[24] of the fact that environmental problems of developing countries were the result of problems with respect to development and poverty was a crucial step towards the UNCHE. Resolution 2849 (XXVI) also underlined that "development represents at the present stage the best possible solution for most of the environmental problems in the developing countries."[25] With more than 30 NGOs attending the special meeting at Founex, the Founex Report significantly influenced and shaped the outcome of the UNCHE.[26] In addition, the UNCHE was praised for raising

[21] "United Nation Conference on the Human Environment, UNGA Resolution 2657 (XXV)," December 7, 1970.

[22] "United Nation Conference on the Human Environment, UNGA Resolution 2850 (XXVI)," December 20, 1971.

[23] "Development and Environment, UNGA Resolution 2849 (XXVI)," December 20, 1971.

[24] "Founex Report on Development and Environment, 1971," 1971.

[25] "Development and Environment, UNGA Resolution 2849 (XXVI)."

[26] Michele Merrill Betsill and Elisabeth Corell, *NGO Diplomacy: The Influence of Nongovernmental Organizations in International Environmental Negotiations* (MIT Press, 2008), vii. See also the following article with respect to the role played by some of the leading developing countries before and during the Stockholm Conference: Tim E.J. Campbell, "The Political Meaning of Stockholm: Third World Participation in the Environment Conference Process," *Stanford Journal of International Studies* 8 (1973): 138–53.

"the environmental consciousness of the world."[27] Notably, "the [UNCHE] and the simultaneous Environment Forum, together they resulted in one of the largest international gatherings ever held [...] [and] set an important precedent in terms of the pattern of NGOs' involvements in all subsequent such world conferences as well as UN environmental affairs."[28]

Moreover, Maurice Strong, who was appointed as the Secretary-General of both the UNCHE and the UNCED, underlined, in 1999, that the link between development and environment was, in fact, made as a result of informal meetings in Founex.[29] Maurice Strong further noted that the Founex Report was "a seminal milestone in the history of the environmental movement."[30] Accordingly, in Resolution 2849, the UNGA strongly underlined that "the documentation to be submitted to participating States and, in particular, the action plan and the action proposals for each of the main subject areas, as well as the draft Declaration on the Human Environment, be elaborated in such a manner as to take into full account the provisions embodied in the preamble and in the operative paragraphs of the present resolution."[31] As a result, the concerns of developing countries were appropriately integrated into the preparatory process of the UNCHE in order to ensure the realisation of a successful conference in Stockholm.

1.4 *Emerging Practice: No Conference Without NGOs*

Given Resolution 2849, the UNGA further reiterated the importance of integrating the concerns of developing countries into the preparations of the UNCHE.[32] Another point to underline is that articles 58 and 59 of the draft rules of procedure touch upon the participation of intergovernmental

[27] Margaret R. Biswas and Asit K. Biswas, "Environment and Sustained Development in the Third World: A Review of the Past Decade," *Third World Quarterly* 4, no. 3 (1982): 485.

[28] Ibid., 485–86.

[29] Maurice Strong, "The Hunger Project Millennium Lecture Hunger, Poverty, Population and Environment," April 1999.

[30] Ibid.

[31] "Development and Environment, UNGA Resolution 2849 (XXVI)."

[32] "United Nation Conference on the Human Environment, UNGA Resolution 2850 (XXVI)."

organisations (IGOs) and NGOs in the UNCHE as "Observers."[33] Indeed, the increasing role played by civil society actors in multilateral negotiations and their significant role during the preparations leading up to the UNCHE, and the substantial number of IGOs and NGOs which attended meetings of preparatory processes, as well as their particular influence within the framework of the Founex meetings, clarify the fact that the UNCHE and the participation of IGOs and NGOs to the latter was close as the bark to the tree.

Furthermore, had it been proposed by some States to preclude the participation of civil society actors to the UNCHE, it is evident that such a proposition would not have been accepted. This clearly points out, *a contrario*, a significant fact, which is States' recognition of the role of IGOs and NGOs within the framework of conferences addressing the challenges of sustainable development, such as the UNCHE. At that point in time, such a recognition was a segregated event, limited to a specific issue, namely the challenges of sustainable development. However, this specific occurrence repeated itself again throughout the upcoming decades with an ever-increasing role of IGOs and NGOs with respect to global concerns in the field of sustainable development.

1.5 Outcomes of the UNCHE

In addition to States' delegations, 21 UN Agencies, 16 IGOs,[34] and 258 NGO Observers[35] attended the UNCHE, and more than ten resolutions were adopted by the UNGA.[36] The main outcome documents of the UNCHE were the famous "Stockholm Declaration" containing 26 principles, the Action Plan for the Human Environment with 109

[33] "Report of the Preparatory Committee for the United Nations Conference on the Human Environment on Its Third Session, UN Doc. A/CONF.48/PC/13."

[34] "List of Participants, United Nations Conference on the Human Environment, UN Doc. A/CONF.48/INF.5/Rev.1," June 5, 1972.

[35] "List of NGO Observers, United Nations Conference on the Human Environment, UN Doc. A/CONF.48/INF.6," June 5, 1972.

[36] These are UNGA Resolutions from 2994 (XXVII) to 3004 (XXVII).

recommendations[37] and the establishment of the UN Environmental Programme (UNEP) in Nairobi, Kenya.[38]

During the decade preceding the UNCHE, and especially in its aftermath, a crucial development was the emerging understanding among States with respect to the need for international cooperation for better addressing the challenges of both development and environment. This, of course, is not intended to ignore States' bold references to national sovereignty, such as the Principle 21 of the Stockholm Declaration.[39] Nonetheless, it is possible to underscore a collective understanding among States regarding the central role of the UN system in addressing the challenges of the human environment. Precisely, "the effective management of environmental problems require[d] States to cooperate with one another and, at times, to suppress domestic interests to benefit the global environment outside their traditional jurisdictions."[40] Accordingly, the creation of UNEP is the confirmation of such collective understanding.[41] At that stage, the role of UNEP was limited to a facilitator role and it did not have

[37] The Stockholm Declaration is a short political declaration. The Action Plan is detailed and addresses specific issues of development and environment. In terms of format, the Stockholm Declaration and the Action Plan are the equivalent of the Rio Declaration and Agenda 21 that will be adopted 20 years later, in 1992. Rio Declaration is an updated version of the Stockholm Declaration. Given the relationship between Agenda 21 and the MDGs and later the SDGs, the Stockholm Declaration and its Action Plan are the grandfathers of the SDGs' goals and targets.

[38] "Report of the United Nations Conference on Human Environment, A/CONF.48/14/Rev.1," June 5, 1972. For further details about the creation of UNEP, see; Maria Ivanova, "UNEP in Global Environmental Governance: Design, Leadership, Location," *Global Environmental Politics* 10, no. 1 (February 1, 2010): 30–59. See also; Laurence D. Mee, "The Role of UNEP and UNDP in Multilateral Environmental Agreements," *International Environmental Agreements: Politics, Law and Economics* 5, no. 3 (September 1, 2005): 227–63.

[39] Principle 21 reads as follows: "States have, in accordance with the Charter of the United Nations and the principles of international law, the sovereign right to exploit their own resources pursuant to their own environmental policies, and the responsibility to ensure that activities within their jurisdiction or control do not cause damage to the environment of other States or of areas beyond the limits of national jurisdiction."

[40] Jodie Hierlmeier, "UNEP: Retrospect and Prospect - Options for Reforming the Global Environmental Governance Regime," *Georgetown International Environmental Law Review* 14 (2002 2001): 770.

[41] It might be possible that, for developing countries, the location of UNEP was more important than its establishment. In other words, developing countries would not oppose such a secretariat, as long as it took into account their concerns regarding the nexus between development and environment and it was located in a developing country. In this regard, see Ivanova, "UNEP in Global Environmental Governance," pages 34–36, about how Kenya managed to host UNEP Secretariat in Nairobi and how big surprise it was for all.

much executive power[42] for the global environmental action, as "its program initiatives [were] largely implemented by other organizations, with United Nations (UN):United Nations Environmental Programme (UNEP) providing coordination, information and reporting functions."[43] Nevertheless, the establishment of UNEP had a significant implication. It was at the centre of an emerging regime of global environmental governance, which included many other key actors, along with States, in a rather non-hierarchical structure.[44] Afterwards, this momentum increased over the upcoming years and decades and transformed these actors, other than States, into full-fledged global actors.[45]

The understanding among States of the need for international cooperation in order to better address the challenges of the human environment did not, of course, drop out of the sky. Throughout the years preceding the UNCHE, civil society in a broader sense, academics through their publications, scientists through their research, environmentalists through their actions and activities in raising awareness, eminent personalities through their public commitments to environmental cause, etc., together prepared the background and the stage for the emergence of this common understanding. Indeed, the involvement of civil society actors at all stages of the UNCHE, as well as their critical and significant role in the agreement between developing and developed countries at Founex, were the result of the recognition of civil society's contributions. In addition, civil society actors not only attended the whole process of the UNCHE, but they also played a critical role in its success and managed to influence its

[42] Mostafa Kamal Tolba and Programme des Nations Unies pour l'environnement, eds., *The World Environment 1972–1992: Two Decades of Challenge*, Repr. (London ; Glasgow [etc.]: Chapman & Hall, 1993), 745.

[43] Hierlmeier, "UNEP," 771.

[44] Ibid., 770, 774.

[45] It is important to highlight how the concept of networking accelerated this transformation. One example of this is the role of the network of judges in improving the implementation of environmental-related laws. Anne-Marie Slaughter mentions the following: "[UNEP] and the INECE [International Network for Environmental Compliance and Enforcement founded in 1989] – itself a regulators network – organized a Global Judges Symposium in conjunction with the UN Conference on Sustainable Development in Johannesburg [2002]. The symposium brought together over one hundred of the world's most senior judges from over eighty countries to discuss improving the adoption and implementation of environment-related laws." See in Anne-Marie Slaughter, *A New World Order* (Princeton University Press, 2009), 66.

outcome.[46] This paved the way for the transformation of civil society actors into global actors recognized as such by the rest of the global community with respect to the objectives of sustainable development.

In addition to these remarks about the processes through which the UNCHE was prepared and held, the outcomes of the UNCHE were not exceptional. The Declaration was limited in addressing environmental concerns, with 17 out of 26 Principles being related to the questions of development.[47] However, everything that occurred throughout the whole process of the UNCHE has its footprints in the background of the SDGs. Lastly, in terms of substance, the nexus established between environment and development throughout this process is, in fact, the origin of what is referred to today as "sustainable development."

2 World Commission on Environment and Development

2.1 Initiatives Towards the 10th Anniversary of the UNCHE

Towards the 10th anniversary of the UNCHE, the idea to hold a special meeting to review the achievements made in the past decade and to decide on the objectives and prospects for the forthcoming decade in the field of environment was crystallised in UNGA Resolution 35/74 of 1980.[48] Another important aspect of this Resolution 35/74 is that, for the first time, an UNGA resolution referred to the concept of sustainable development. The following year, UNGA Resolution 36/192 introduced the idea to develop a document about the "Environmental Perspective to the Year 2000 and Beyond" (Environmental Perspective).[49] The WCED was, in

[46] Christopher C. Joyner and Nancy D. Joyner, "Global Eco-Management and International Organizations: The Stockholm Conference and the Problems of Cooperation," *Natural Resources Journal* 14, no. 4 (1974): 551–52. The role of civil society actors in international negotiations addressing challenges of sustainable development is only one among countless activities of civil society actors around the world. However, I am mainly interested in the impact of their involvement in the emergence of new norms and rules addressing global challenges. See also: Betsill and Corell, *NGO Diplomacy*, 5–6.

[47] Ibid., 542.

[48] "International Co-Operation in the Field of the Environment, UNGA Resolution, UN Doc. A/RES/35/74," December 5, 1980, paragraphs 13–15.

[49] "International Co-Operation in the Field of the Environment, UNGA Resolution, UN Doc. A/RES/36/192," December 17, 1981, paragraph 6.

fact, established specifically to provide these perspectives for the beginning of the Millennium. In Resolution 36/189, the UNGA, in addition to devoting a single paragraph to inviting ministers dealing with the environment to participate in this session of a special character of UNEP Governing Council, also mentioned and encouraged the participation of NGOs.[50]

The session with a special character of UNEP Governing Council (UNEP's Special Session) was held in Nairobi in May 1982. There were 31 IOs, including UN agencies and specialized agencies, and 113 NGOs.[51] The report of UNEP's Special Session reveals that UNEP repeatedly draws attention to its close relationship and contacts with NGOs and the scientific community. UNEP was rather proud for having these close relationships and cooperation with NGOs. For example, it is underlined in the report of UNEP's Special Session that "[i]n promoting political and resource commitments to match the greater understanding of the environment, UNEP would continue the exercise of its catalytic and coordinating role, under the policy guidance of the Council, both within the [UN] system and through its contacts with [NGOs] and the scientific community."[52] In addition, a specific section with respect to the relationships with NGOs was reserved in the first decision of UNEP's Special Session, and the Executive Director was requested to "further facilitate their participation in the development of the programmes of the UNEP."[53]

As was the case in the UNCHE, a special declaration was also adopted in Nairobi at the end of UNEP's Special Session, namely Nairobi Declaration. Its paragraph 9 mentions that "[NGOs] have a particularly important and often inspirational role to play" in the field of environment.[54] In addition to these references to actors other than States, and their significant role and place with respect to environmental governance, the content and substance of the global approach to the environmental concerns were also improved during the first DSD. Differences of views between the global south and global north were rather surpassed, and the concept of sustainable development was about to become the cornerstone

[50] "Session of a Special Character of the Governing Council of the United Nations Environment Programme, UNGA Resolution, UN Doc. A/RES/36/189," December 17, 1981.

[51] "United Nations Environment Programme: Report of the Governing Council (Session of a Special Character and 10th Session, UN Doc. A/37/25," May 18, 1982, 4.

[52] Ibid., para. 9.

[53] Ibid., para. 85.

[54] Ibid., para. 51.

of global environmental governance.[55] In the same vein, there was also a general agreement during UNEP's Special Session to "begin as soon as possible on a global strategy for sustainable development[.]"[56] Accordingly, in one of the resolutions during UNEP's Special Session, the Governing Council of UNEP recommended the establishment of a special commission "to propose long-term environmental strategies for achieving sustainable development to the year 2000 and beyond."[57] The following UNGA resolutions in 1982 and 1983 took up many of the agreed points during UNEP's Special Session and accordingly established the WCED.

2.2 *The Origins of the SDGs in the UNGA Resolutions of the 1980s*

UNGA Resolution 37/219 of 1982 refers to the Nairobi Declaration as a reiteration of the commitments of the international community made 10 years ago in the UNCHE, and NGOs are mentioned together with governments and intergovernmental institutions for future actions in the field of environment.[58] In addition, the UNGA reiterates its expectations for concrete recommendations for the preparation of a document with respect to the development of the Environmental Perspective.[59]

In 1983, the UNGA established the WCED and the Intergovernmental Inter-Sessional Preparatory Committee (IIPC) regarding the process of preparation of the Environmental Perspective.[60] In fact, given the terms of reference of the WCED, as articulated by the UNGA,[61] the mission of the WCED was essentially to develop the very first version of the SDGs. A comparison between the terms of reference that defined the framework of the upcoming work of the WCED and the SDGs is significantly revealing.

At the outset, in the first article of the terms of reference, the WCED is expected to provide "long-term environmental strategies for achieving sustainable development to the year 2000 and beyond." The same idea and ambition are also present in UNGA Resolution 70/1 adopting the

[55] Ibid., para. 10.
[56] Ibid., para. 13.
[57] Ibid., para. 41.
[58] Ibid., paras. 4–5.
[59] Ibid., para. 8.
[60] "Process of Preparation of the Environmental Perspective to the Year 2000 and Beyond, UNGA Resolution, UN Doc. A/RES/38/161."
[61] Ibid., para. 8.

SDGs. In fact, Resolution 70/1 is entitled "Transforming Our World: The 2030 Agenda for Sustainable Development." The second article of the terms of reference entrusts to the WCED the mission to make recommendations for finding the right balance in order to have goals and objectives for all countries. This point perfectly matches with Goal 17 of the SDGs, entitled "Strengthen the means of implementation and revitalize the Global Partnership for Sustainable Development," and the 19 targets of Goal 17 are all about finding the right balance between the developing and developed countries' respective commitments to achieve sustainable development. In line with the ambitions of this second article of the terms of reference, which highlight it is important to "take account of the interrelationships between people, resources, environment and development," the preamble of Resolution 70/1 clarifies that the SDGs are for people, planet and prosperity.[62]

The third article of the terms of reference invites the WCED to make propositions for more effective ways to deal with environmental concerns. Similarly, the High-Level Political Forum (HLPF) will be created before the adoption of the SDGs with this objective in mind.

The last article of the terms of reference deserves further attention given its wording. It invites the WCED to define (1) "shared perceptions" of long-term environmental issues, (2) "appropriate efforts" needed to deal with environmental problems, (3) a "long-term agenda for action" and (4) "aspirational goals." Such a description perfectly reflects the precise nature of the SDGs. The SDGs are, first of all, the result of shared perceptions of environmental issues among a great diversity of actors at the global level. Secondly, on account of this shared perception that emerged at the global level, the concerned global actors were able to set specific goals, targets and indicators, and the efforts needed to meet these goals and targets were defined with the adoption of the SDGs. Thirdly, the 2030 Agenda for Sustainable Development is evidently a long-term agenda for action.[63] Lastly, one of the main intents of the 17 Goals and 169 targets of the SDGs is to inspire the global community to reach sustainable development for all. In fact, the preamble of Resolution 70/1 indicates that "[a]ll countries and all stakeholders, acting in collaborative partnership, will implement this plan."[64]

[62] Ibid., 2.

[63] Ibid., para. 51.

[64] Ibid., 1.

Consequently, it is important to recall that, back in 1983, had there been no UNCHE or UNEP, it would have been impossible for the UNGA to establish the WCED with such a visionary mission and terms of reference. The developments following the UNCHE effectively paved the way for the UNGA to develop such a proposition. Keeping this in mind, and given the far-sighted terms of reference defined by the UNGA for the WCED, it is clear that UNGA Resolution 38/161 is the origin of the SDGs.

The mission of the WCED was to "consider ways and means" and to "define shared perceptions" for the emergence of the very first version of the SDGs. In this respect, within the framework of such an ambitious project, the roadmap that will be followed by the WCED and the other global actors involved in the process is certainly as significant as the ways and means to be considered and the shared perceptions to be defined. For example, Resolution 38/161 invited the Chairman and the Vice-Chairman of the WCED to consult, in addition to the representatives of governments, "intergovernmental and non-governmental organizations, industry, the scientific community and others concerned with the environment" before electing the members of the WCED.[65] In addition, the wording and the structure of Resolution 38/161 demonstrate the priorities and actors involved. For example, the WCED is called to maintain an exchange of views with the scientific community, environmentalists and those concerned with the environment, before receiving the views of governments.[66] This demonstrates, even back in 1983, not only the significant role played by these actors for bringing environmental concerns to the attention of the international community, but also the recognition of States concerning the importance of their involvement in considering ways and means and in defining shared perceptions for the emergence of the very first version of the SDGs. Furthermore, back in 1983, the necessity to consult a substantial number of different actors while preparing the Environmental Perspective was already evident for the UNGA. This perspective was preserved and emphasised repeatedly and turned into a *conditio sine qua non* for every attempt of norm-making at the global level in the field of sustainable development.

[65] "Process of Preparation of the Environmental Perspective to the Year 2000 and Beyond, UNGA Resolution, UN Doc. A/RES/38/161," para. 6.

[66] Ibid., para. 9.

2.3 Brundtland Report and Environmental Perspective

These two documents were adopted by the UNGA in 1987 and are part of the same process with respect to the challenges of sustainable development. Regarding their respective contents, to start with, one of the most significant contributions of the Brundtland Report is the definition of sustainable development. In its words, sustainable development implies "meeting the needs of the present without compromising the ability of future generations to meet their own needs."[67] The UNGA, in its Resolution 42/187 welcoming the Brundtland Report, further adds that sustainable development "should become a central guiding principle of the United Nations, Governments, and private institutions, organizations and enterprises."[68] In this respect, firstly, the Brundtland Report was a significant step towards this end.[69] Secondly, content-wise, the Environmental Perspective draws upon the Brundtland Report. However, "the Environmental Perspective has sought to delineate, in an organized manner, the elements of shared perceptions, environmental issues, aspirational goals and the agenda for action[.]"[70] The Environmental Perspective represents the origins of the SDGs, as it is possible to identify, in its structure, the triangular concept of goals, targets and indicators. Lastly, both of these documents, and especially the Brundtland Report, constitute a critical step within the process leading to the adoption of the SDGs, as they generated the required momentum in global environmental governance for the UNCED to take place in 1992.

Regarding the procedural aspects of the processes leading to the adoption of these two outcome documents, firstly, the most important characteristic of the WCED was the public hearings it conducted all over the

[67] "Report of the World Commission on Environment and Development, UNGA Resolution, UN Doc. A/RES/42/187."

[68] Ibid.

[69] David Reid, *Sustainable Development: An Introductory Guide* (Routledge, 2013), Introduction; John MacCormick, *The Global Environmental Movement: Reclaiming Paradise* (London: Belhaven Press, 1989), 192–94.

[70] "Environmental Perspective to the Year 2000 and Beyond, UNGA Resolution, UN Doc. A/RES/42/186," December 11, 1987.

world between 1985 and 1987.[71] These open public hearings allowed scientists, experts, research institutes, representatives of industries, civil society members, activists and the general public to contribute to the global mission of the WCED. The Brundtland Report is enriched with tens of testimonies given at these hearings. In addition, more than 500 written submissions were received by the WCED at the occasion of the public hearings.[72] Furthermore, a great number of special advisors assisted the WCED with respect to specific issues on energy, industry and food security.[73] This open, fully participative and inclusive *modus operandi* of the WCED is not a single and isolated event. On the contrary, this practice created a *de facto* precedent with respect to similar global processes to be conducted in the future in the field of sustainable development.

Secondly, despite its independent, open, and participative nature, the WCED was established as a result of a "States-led" initiative through an UNGA resolution. In addition, the Environmental Perspective represents clearly "some shared perceptions of Governments of the nature of environmental issues,"[74] and it was adopted by the UNGA as "a broad framework to guide national action and international co-operation on policies and programmes aimed at achieving environmentally sound development[.]"[75] Accordingly, these features—"States-led" and "inclusiveness"—rigorously observed over decades, eventually will become two of the conclusive criteria of the primary social convention of GLSD.

Thirdly, in her foreword, the Chairman of the WCED, Ms. Brundtland underlines that they produced a unanimous report.[76] In addition, both outcome documents, the Brundtland Report and the Environmental

[71] "Deliberative meetings, site visits, and/or Public Hearings of the Commission were held in Jakarta, Indonesia, 27–31 March 1985; Oslo, Norway, 21–28 June 1985; Sao Paulo and Brasilia, Brazil, 25 October–4 November 1985; Vancouver, Edmonton, Toronto, Ottawa, Halifax, and Quebec City, Canada, 21–31 May 1986; Harare, Zimbabwe, 15–19 September, Nairobi, Kenya. 20–23 September 1986; Moscow, USSR. 6–12 December 1986; and Tokyo, Japan, 23–28 February 1987. Special working group meetings of the Commission were also held in Geneva, Moscow. and Berlin (West)." See "Report of the World Commission on Environment and Development, UN Doc. A/42/427," 349.

[72] Ibid.

[73] Ibid., 349–50.

[74] "Environmental Perspective to the Year 2000 and Beyond, UNGA Resolution, UN Doc. A/RES/42/186."

[75] Ibid., para. 2.

[76] "Report of the World Commission on Environment and Development, UN Doc. A/42/427," 15.

Perspective, were adopted without a vote at the UNGA, in other words, by consensus.[77] Furthermore, from the time of the UNCHE until the adoption of SDGs, global norms/rules addressing the challenges of sustainable development were always adopted by consensus at the global level. As such, the notion of consensus will be another conclusive criterion of the primary social convention of GLSD.[78]

Fourthly, the first remark of Ms. Brundtland in her foreword is her description of the WCED's mission and the scope of their work. She notes that they were asked to formulate "A Global Agenda for Change." It is also clear from the Brundtland Report itself that it intends to be valid and applicable for the entirety of the planet. Given the interconnectedness between the challenges of environment and development, the global agenda was meant to provide a cure not only for developed countries' environmental concerns, but also for developing countries' challenges for a sustainable growth. In their recommendations, the WCED also highlights the challenges to the concept of national boundaries and notes the limits of national policies in resolving environment's challenges without borders.[79] As a result, the Brundtland Report significantly contributed to the emergence of the concept of sustainable development as "the central adage of environmental policies around the globe," and "the environmental discourse has been globalised and transcended national boundaries."[80] UNGA Resolution 42/187 of 1987—welcoming the Brundtland Report—also recognised, "in view of the global character of major environmental problems, the common interest of all countries to pursue policies aimed at sustainable and environmentally sound development."[81] Consequently, the Brundtland Report had "universal reach" in terms of its scope of application with respect to the challenges of sustainable development, even though it is a non-binding and non-legal document. In other

[77] M. J. Peterson, *The UN General Assembly* (Psychology Press, 2006), 74–79. This practice of the GA was not specific to these two resolutions. On the contrary, most of its resolutions are adopted by consensus, especially since 1990s.

[78] With respect to the meaning of "consensus," there is no consensus! See, Dapo Akande, "What Is the Meaning of 'Consensus' in International Decision Making?," *EJIL: Talk!* (blog), April 8, 2013.

[79] "Report of the World Commission on Environment and Development, UN Doc. A/42/427," 307.

[80] Yosef Jabareen, "A New Conceptual Framework for Sustainable Development," *Environment, Development and Sustainability* 10, no. 2 (April 1, 2008): 187.

[81] "Report of the World Commission on Environment and Development, UNGA Resolution, UN Doc. A/RES/42/187," para. 3 of the preamble.

words, it was a document designed to be universally relevant. Accordingly, the notion of universality will also be another conclusive criterion of the primary social convention of GLSD.

Fifthly, it is important to emphasise the fact that the environment recommendations were to be reached in harmony with the international legal system.[82] The WCED notes that "[t]he international legal framework must also be significantly strengthened in support of sustainable development."[83] In addition, one of the significant proposals of the WCED, addressed specifically to the UNGA, is its recommendation for the preparation of a universal declaration and, subsequently, a global convention on sustainable development.[84] To facilitate the preparations of such an initiative, the WCED's group of international legal experts even proposed legal principles as a starting point for eventual negotiations within the UNGA. Furthermore, the WCED also called on States to strengthen and extend existing international conventions and agreements within the context of overall goals of sustainable development.[85]

Therefore, with respect to the means towards achieving sustainable development for all, the common understanding of global actors was to anchor the objectives of sustainable development within the existing framework of international law. A scenario where these objectives would contradict the existing rules of international law was out of the question. Therefore, the notion of pluralism plays a crucial role with respect to the relationship between the rules of international law and rules of GLSD. Accordingly, the rules of sustainable development need to coexist in harmony, and especially should not be in contradiction, with the existing rules of international law. To summarise, in addition to the abovementioned notions of States-led, inclusiveness, consensus and universality, pluralism will be another conclusive criterion of the primary social convention of GLSD.

[82] While establishing the WCED, the UNGA expressly underscored that the WCED's recommendations will not be binding on governments; in other words, they will not constitute rules of international law. Also, the Brundtland Report was not meant to challenge the rules of international law. On the contrary, it was seeking to work in fully harmony with the rules of international law.

[83] "Report of the World Commission on Environment and Development, UN Doc. A/42/427," 307.

[84] Ibid., 324.

[85] Ibid., 322–24.

3 Conclusion

In the 1960s, it was mostly considered that growing environmental concerns could be addressed through international cooperation. Accordingly, the conservationists and environmentalists of the 1960s managed to raise sufficient awareness to incite Sweden to come up with a proposition for an international conference on the environment within the UN framework. During the first DSD, firstly, the concept of sustainable development has taken a more concrete shape. Secondly, a global perspective emerged in the sense that a common understanding was reached with respect to the need to move beyond international cooperation and to develop a global and systemic approach to effectively address the challenges of sustainable development. Thirdly, the role and influence of actors other than States at the "inter-national" level were simply emerging/evolving and were still insignificant before 1972. For example, there was not an IO with a mission with respect to the environmental concerns or challenges of sustainable development. However, with the UNCHE, not only was UNEP created, but also a common understanding emerged with respect to the role and place of IOs in efforts addressing global challenges. In the same vein, States recognised the significance of CSOs by involving them through the UNCHE and paved the way for their further inclusion in efforts addressing the challenges of sustainable development.

In the beginning of the second DSD, it was possible to identify some initial common understandings among States, IOs and CSOs regarding the cornerstones—the five conclusive criteria of the primary social convention of GLSD—of the process to be followed in reaching a global agreement to better address the challenges of sustainable development. The main inquiry in the rest of this book is how these potential conclusive criteria will transform into genuine components of a valid primary social convention of GLSD, and how a secondary social convention will emerge in which the common acts of global actors—States, IOs and CSOs—have the status of law within the framework of GLSD.

CHAPTER 3

Road to Rio: Two Steps Forward, One Step Back?

This first section of this chapter examines the developments towards the UNCED that was organised at the occasion of the 20th anniversary of the UNCHE. I demonstrate that, during this period, actors other than States, especially IOs and NGOs, are *de facto* recognised by States as global actors with respect to the issues related to sustainable development. The second section examines the outcomes of the UNCED and the significance of what is referred to in these documents as "global commitments for sustainable development" as well as "global partnership for sustainable development." In addition, the second section refers to some farsighted scholars who noticed the emergence of a "law of sustainable development" given the developments around the UNCED. Lastly, the third section summarises the progress made during this decade with respect to the secondary and primary social conventions of GLSD.

1 Towards the UN Conference on Environment and Development

UNGA Resolution 43/196 was adopted in 1988, the year after the Brundtland Report and the Environmental Perspective were welcomed by the UNGA.[1] The main idea for the UNCED at this stage was to review

[1] "United Nations Conference on Environment and Development, UNGA Resolution, UN Doc. A/RES/43/196," December 20, 1988.

H. Göksan, *Global Law of Sustainable Development*, Global Issues,
https://doi.org/10.1007/978-3-031-74547-8_3

how environmental concerns have been incorporated into policies since the UNCHE, to assess major environmental problems and risks and to make recommendations for further international cooperation by defining efforts required and associated financial implications.[2] Also, in addition to governments, IOs and NGOs were also invited to submit their views on the objectives, content and scope of the UNCED.

1.1 *Reaffirming the Role of Actors Other Than States*

The SG's report prepared for the purpose of UNGA Resolution 44/228 of 1989 provides the initial perspectives of relevant actors with respect to the idea of holding the UNCED two decades after the UNCHE.[3] The report highlights that there was a general agreement about the timeliness of and necessity for the UNCED and about the objectives, among which were to frame legal instruments and plans of actions and to examine "the evolution of common perceptions of problems and ways and means of dealing with them."[4] With regard to the actors to be involved, the general agreement was to set an "intergovernmental preparatory committee" at the centre of the stage with "appropriate representation or participation of [IOs]."[5] It was also generally agreed that NGOs should play an active part in preparing for the UNCED and participating in it.[6] These notes in the SG's report demonstrate the continuity of general agreements reached among States, IOs and NGOs with respect to the two conclusive criteria of the primary social convention of GLSD, namely, States-led and inclusiveness.

UNGA Resolution 44/228 also stressed that the UNCED should "elaborate strategies and measures to halt and reverse the effects of environmental degradation[.]"[7] For example, in terms of transboundary pollution, its paragraph 7 repeats word by word the Principle 21 of the Stockholm Declaration. Many scholars argue that this principle reflects a

[2] Ibid.

[3] "Report of the Secretary-General, Question of the Convening of a United Nations Conference on Environment and Development, A/44/256 E/1989/66," May 2, 1989.

[4] Ibid., 3.

[5] Ibid., 4.

[6] Ibid.

[7] "United Nations Conference on Environment and Development, UNGA Resolution, UN Doc. A/RES/44/228," December 22, 1989, para. 3.

rule of customary international law.[8] To recall, the Stockholm Declaration is not a binding document of international law. Yet, it served as a basis for the development of certain legal concepts and principles in the field of international environmental law, and some of these principles were later "confirmed and further elaborated, both in the preambular and operative provisions of [...] numerous treaties."[9]

What is the significance of this transformation of non-binding principles articulated in the Stockholm Declaration into actual rules of international law? It proves that the UNCHE was the cradle for the legalisation of environmental principles. However, while some of these principles are admitted to the realm of international law, some were left outside the rules of international law. In the views of international lawyers, this represents a march with one step forward, two steps back.[10] Nevertheless, this blockage at the gates of international law, in turn, triggered a metamorphosis at the global scene and paved the way for the emergence of GLSD.

UNGA Resolution 44/228 also embarks on some sort of collation of major environmental concerns to be addressed at the UNCED in order to maintain the quality of the Earth's environment.[11] At the beginning of the millennium, there were more than 500 international treaties related to the environment, of which more than 300 were from the period after the UNCHE.[12] For example, the UNFCCC, the Vienna Convention for the Protection of the Ozone Layer, the Montreal Protocol on Substances that Deplete the Ozone Layer, the United Nations Convention to Combat Desertification, the Convention on Biological Diversity (CBD), the Basel

[8] Alexandre Kiss and Dinah Shelton, *Guide to International Environmental Law* (BRILL, 2007), 36; Patricia W. Birnie, Alan E. Boyle, and Catherine Redgwell, *International Law and the Environment* (Oxford University Press, 2009), 145.

[9] Marc Pallemaerts, "International Environmental Law in the Age of Sustainable Development: A Critical Assessment of the UNCED Process," *Journal of Law and Commerce* 15 (1996 1995): 626–27.

[10] David A. Wirth, "The Rio Declaration on Environment and Development: Two Steps Forward and One Back, or Vice Versa," *Georgia Law Review* 29 (1995 1994): 599–654. See also Pallemaerts' critical assessment of Rio Conference and his conclusion considering it as "regressive" development of international environmental law rather than being a progressive one in Pallemaerts, "International Environmental Law in the Age of Sustainable Development," 673–76.

[11] "United Nations Conference on Environment and Development, UNGA Resolution, UN Doc. A/RES/44/228," para. 12.

[12] "Report of the Executive Director of UNEP, International Environmental Governance, UNEP/IGM/1/2.," April 4, 2001.

Convention on the Control of Transboundary Movements of Hazardous Wastes and Their Disposal and the UN Convention on the Law of the Sea—dealing with some of the aforementioned major environmental concerns—were in fact, negotiated, signed and ratified before, during or just after the UNCED. The entry in force of all these treaties and their universality in terms of parties are part of the steps forward for the legalisation of international environmental principles on the road to the UNCED and in its aftermath.[13]

Moreover, UNGA Resolution 44/228 established the contours of the UNCED by defining its objectives.[14] One of the objectives provides that the UNCED should promote the development of international environmental law and suggests that the Stockholm Declaration with its 26 principles, is a starting point towards this end.[15] Furthermore, the UNGA added that the UNCED should examine "the feasibility of elaborating general rights and obligations of States in the field of environment."[16]

At first glance, given the significant number of international treaties signed and entered into force, together with the momentum of the UNCED, the UNCED was successful in promoting the development of international environmental law. These developments represent the step forward on the road to the UNCED. Regarding the steps back, "it was only with the utmost reluctance that the [GA] gave [the UNCED] a mandate to study 'the *feasibility* of elaborating general rights and obligations of States in the field of the environment.'"[17]

Another issue addressed in UNGA Resolution 44/228 concerns the preparations for the UNCED, as well as the actors to be involved in the process. Accordingly, the UNGA established a Preparatory Committee (PrepCom) open to all States and also authorised the participation of observers "in accordance with the established practice of [UNGA]."[18] To recall, the established practice of the UNGA with respect to the

[13] Regarding the transboundary air pollution, there was not an international treaty or convention; however, as underlined before, it became a rule of customary international law.

[14] "United Nations Conference on Environment and Development, UNGA Resolution, UN Doc. A/RES/44/228," para. 15 of section I.

[15] Ibid.

[16] Ibid.

[17] Pallemaerts, "International Environmental Law in the Age of Sustainable Development," 628, emphasis added.

[18] "United Nations Conference on Environment and Development, UNGA Resolution, UN Doc. A/RES/44/228," section II, para. 1.

participation of observers is rather limited. It only concerns those organizations which obtained an observer status from the UNGA. For example, Holy See and State of Palestine are presently non-member observer States. In this regard, these observers, and not NGOs, are addressed in this part of Resolution 44/228.[19]

The UNGA respectively requested UNEP and other UN agencies, as well as other IGOs, "to contribute fully to the preparations for the [UNCED]" and all States "to take an active part in the preparations for the [UNCED]" and "to promote [...] broad-based national preparatory processes involving the scientific community, industry, trade unions and concerned [NGOs]." The UNGA further "requested NGOs, in consultative status with the ECOSOC, to contribute to the [UNCED.]"[20] In terms of inclusiveness, it is significant that UNEP and other IOs were requested first, before the States, to fully contribute to the preparations of the UNCED. It is also important to underline the distinction made by the UNGA with respect to the national and international NGOs. Accordingly, States were invited to conduct broad-based national preparatory processes involving the scientific community, industry, trade unions and NGOs, and at the international level, NGOs, in consultative status with ECOSOC, were also requested to contribute to the UNCED.

Regarding the details of the preparatory process, UNGA Resolution 44/228 requested the Secretary-General of the UNCED to prepare a report containing recommendations on an adequate preparatory process.[21] In his report, the Secretary-General of the UNCED strongly underlined the importance of the NGOs' participation in the UNCED and its preparatory process.[22] There were already 11 NGOs, in addition to States and IOs, participating in the "organizational session" of the PrepCom.[23] Based on the aforementioned recommendations of the Secretary-General

[19] Peter Willetts, "From Stockholm to Rio and Beyond: The Impact of the Environmental Movement on the United Nations Consultative Arrangements for NGOs," *Review of International Studies* 22, no. 1 (1996): 71.

[20] "United Nations Conference on Environment and Development, UNGA Resolution, UN Doc. A/RES/44/228," section II, paras. 11–13.

[21] Ibid., section II, para. 7.

[22] "Report of the Secretary-General, Preparatory Process for the United Nations Conference on Environment and Development, UN Doc. A/CONF.151/PC/2," February 23, 1990.

[23] "Report of the Preparatory Committee for the United Nations Conference on Environment and Development on Its Organizational Session, A/44/48," March 16, 1990, 3.

of the UNCED, the PrepCom decided, at the end of the organizational session, that the UNCED Secretariat should suggest arrangements for the participation of NGOs.[24] At the end of heated debates during the first session of the PrepCom, Decision 1/1 was adopted.[25] It is remarkable in terms of inclusiveness that the participation of NGOs was the first concern in advance of the UNCED, and therefore this question was addressed and resolved as the first decision of the PrepCom.

Also, the participation of NGOs was opened not only to NGOs with ECOSOC consultative status, but also to other relevant NGOs, notwithstanding the fact that Resolution 44/228 only mentioned NGOs with ECOSOC consultative status. For that reason, in its Decision 1/1, the PrepCom noted that this would apply only for the first session without prejudice to any decision that may be later taken by the UNGA.[26]

In terms of consensus, with regard to the Tunisian delegation's insistent opposition to the participation of NGOs and how the issue was dealt with, Willetts observes that "there is now a norm that decisions should be taken by consensus at UN conferences."[27] This indeed demonstrates how the idea of consensus was gradually becoming a *sine qua non* part of these global processes. In addition, the PrepCom's reports on its first session and on its organizational session begin by mentioning that the Committee adopted all its decisions by consensus.[28]

1.2 *Enhancing "Inclusiveness": NGOs at the Centre of the UNCED*

In its Resolution 45/211 of 1990, the UNGA "authorize[d] the Preparatory Committee [...] to continue to apply, for the purpose of the preparatory process, the provisional arrangements agreed upon [...]

[24] Ibid., page 14. For further details with respect to the reluctance of developing countries towards the participation of environmental NGOs and their attempt to push for more balanced representation of NGOs, see Willetts, "From Stockholm to Rio and Beyond," 70–76.

[25] "Report of the Preparatory Committee for the United Nations Conference on Environment and Development on Its First Session, A/45/46," August 31, 1990, 22.

[26] "Report of the Preparatory Committee for the United Nations Conference on Environment and Development on Its First Session, A/45/46," 22.

[27] Willetts, "From Stockholm to Rio and Beyond," 74.

[28] See for example: "Report of the Preparatory Committee for the United Nations Conference on Environment and Development on Its First Session, A/45/46," 1; "Report of the Preparatory Committee for the United Nations Conference on Environment and Development on Its Organizational Session, A/44/48," 1.

concerning the participation of [NGOs] in the preparatory process[.]"[29] Accordingly, all NGOs with or without ECOSOC Consultative Status gained the access to the work of PrepCom. The only difference was that NGOs not holding ECOSOC consultative status, in order to be accredited, were required to provide further information and documentation with respect to their relevance and competences in areas relevant to the UNCED.[30] This was also the first decision of the second session of the PrepCom, and it demonstrates that the issue of the participation of NGOs was at the centre.[31] The number of NGOs participating in the preparatory process of the UNCED is also very solid proof to this end. This is the reason why the UNCED was often qualified as "unprecedented" with respect to the participation of NGOs.[32] At its second session, the PrepCom accredited 167 NGOs,[33] and more than half did not have the ECOSOC consultative status.[34] In total, 1378 NGOs were accredited to participate in the work of PrepCom.[35]

At the time of the UNCHE, the main controversial issue was about the balance between environmental and developmental concerns of developed and developing countries. Before the UNCED, it was the participation of NGOs. The developing countries "appeared to think Western environmental concerns would, at best, draw attention away from their development concerns and, at worst, impose restrictions on development. This suspicion about environmentalism found focus for some developing-country governments in antagonism to environmental NGOs."[36] However, NGOs "were well organized right from the beginning of the preparatory process" and they were "far ahead of the governments in bridging the North-South political divide, both by NGOs from North and South

[29] "United Nations Conference on Environment and Development, UNGA Resolution, UN Doc. A/RES/45/211," December 21, 1990.

[30] "Report of the Preparatory Committee for the United Nations Conference on Environment and Development on Its Second Session, A/46/48(Vol.I)," April 5, 1991, 21.

[31] "Report of the Preparatory Committee for the United Nations Conference on Environment and Development on Its Second Session, A/46/48(Vol.I)."

[32] Willetts, "From Stockholm to Rio and Beyond," 57.

[33] "Report of the Preparatory Committee for the United Nations Conference on Environment and Development on Its Second Session, A/46/48(Vol.I)," 22–27, 29.

[34] Willetts, "From Stockholm to Rio and Beyond," 75.

[35] "Reference Document on the Participation of Civil Society in United Nations Conferences and Special Sessions of the General Assembly during the 1990s," August 1, 2001.

[36] Willetts, "From Stockholm to Rio and Beyond," 72.

working together and by environmental and development NGOs working together."[37] Due to the fact that this issue of participation was a heated debate at the UNCED, Resolution 46/168 of 1991 almost exclusively, and in a very detailed manner, addressed who will be invited to the UNCED.[38] At the end of the day, all IGOs and all 1378 NGOs accredited to the work of PrepCom gained access to the UNCED. This was a significant improvement in terms of inclusiveness in the context of UN conferences organised under the auspices of the UNGA.

2 Outcomes of the UNCED

The UNGA, in its Resolution 47/190 of 1992, endorsed the outcome documents of the UNCED by consensus and expressed its satisfaction that the UNCED ensured the active participation of observers, IOs and NGOs and referred to a new "global partnership for sustainable development," highlighting the fact that actors such as IOs and NGOs were gradually becoming stronger candidates to be a party to the secondary social convention of GLSD.[39] Two key outcome documents of the UNCED were the Rio Declaration on Environment and Development (Rio Declaration)[40] and Agenda 21.[41]

2.1 *Towards "(Global) Law of Sustainable Development"*

The importance of the Rio Declaration is better understood once it is examined from a broader perspective in time. In terms of form, it is quite similar to the Stockholm Declaration.[42] Therefore, I rather focus on

[37] Ibid., 72–73.

[38] "United Nations Conference on Environment and Development, UNGA Resolution, UN Doc. A/RES/46/168," para. 9.

[39] "Report of the United Nations Conference on Environment and Development, UNGA Resolution, UN Doc. A/RES/47/190," December 22, 1992.

[40] "Rio Declaration on Environment and Development, Report of the United Nations Conference on Environment and Development, A/CONF.151/26/Rev.1 (Vol.1) Annex I," June 14, 1992.

[41] "Agenda 21, Report of the United Nations Conference on Environment and Development, A/CONF.151/26/Rev.1 (Vol.1) Annex II," June 14, 1992. In addition, two global conventions, the UNFCCC and the Convention on Biological Diversity, were opened for signature and were signed by a large number of States at the UNCED.

[42] An excellent and comprehensive commentary, edited by Jorge E. Viñuales, is available on the Rio Declaration to better grasp the implications of each principle of the Declaration

normative developments at the time of the Rio Declaration and their implications for the concept of law of GLSD.

Viñuales notes that "the concept of sustainable development mainstreamed by the [WCED] and crowned at the UNCED, breathed new life into global environmental governance and triggered a decade of considerable normative developments."[43] Furthermore, by examining four decades of sustainable development from the UNCHE to the UNCSD, Viñuales demonstrates that normative developments in the field of sustainable development reached its peak at the time of the UNCED in 1992.[44]

Furthermore, to better illustrate the architecture of the Rio Declaration, Kiss's model is particularly interesting.[45] Kiss distinguishes legal principles of international environmental law from the principles of "emerging law of sustainable development."[46] Kiss precisely talks about a new body of emerging law, which he distinguishes clearly from the concept of international law. This reveals that, even back in 1992, the density of normative developments in the field of sustainable development was already sending a signal to international lawyers about the emergence of a new concept of law in the field of sustainable development, outside the concept of international law. Kiss notes that the law of sustainable development could challenge the traditional legal approaches.[47] This means that he identified the emergence of a different concept of law in the field of sustainable development at the global level. Kiss also predicted that such a transformation would only be possible as a result of solidarity between states and people and added that such a vision would logically end up with the codification of "international law of sustainable development."[48] Today, this

upon international environmental law. See, Viñuales, *The Rio Declaration on Environment and Development.* Viñuales' examination does not include the SDGs and it is rather a content-wise analyses. I agree with Viñuales that, content-wise, the development of norms/rules to better address the challenges of sustainable development made a significant peak at the UNCED.

[43] Viñuales, The Rio Declaration on Environment and Development, 6.

[44] xxx.

[45] Alexandre Charles Kiss and Stéphane Doumbé-Billé, "Conférence des Nations Unies sur l'environnement et le développement (Rio de Janeiro-juin 1992)," *Annuaire Français de Droit International* 38, no. 1 (1992): 823–43.

[46] Viñuales, The Rio Declaration on Environment and Development, 15, figure 1.3.

[47] Kiss and Doumbé-Billé, "Conférence des Nations Unies sur l'environnement et le développement (Rio de Janeiro-juin 1992)," 842.

[48] Ibid.

makes one think about the 17 Goals, 169 targets and 232 indicators of the SDGs.

Last but not least, Kiss pointed the finger at, already back in 1992, two parallel but significantly interrelated developments.[49] The first one is the emergence of a new concept of law at the global level in the field of sustainable development and the second one is about the emergence of global actors involved in this process. Precisely, for Kiss, NGOs have the potential to be on equal footing with States in the field of sustainable development, given their profound involvement in the process and in the framework of global institutions of sustainable development—such as the Commission on Sustainable Development (CSD)—and in the implementation of the objectives sustainable development.[50] Kiss concludes that these developments prove the recognition of the international community in the role, and the place of NGOs, in the field of sustainable development.[51]

For Pallemaerts, these developments are "nothing less than a change of paradigm."[52] He considers that by not addressing environmental challenges through the existing mechanism of international law but rather doing it through this new "international law of sustainable development," the prescriptive and the normative quality of these norms are being reduced. Pallemaerts mentions in this regard the preference, during the negotiations, not to govern these issues with rules of international law but rather with terms such as "effective, full and prompt implementation" in Chapter 39 of Agenda 21.[53] Kiss expresses the same concerns.[54] In terms of international law, opting for non-legally binding documents such as the Rio Declaration and Agenda 21, and the usage of less prescriptive language in these documents, reveal the preference of States for limited substantive obligations in addressing global challenges of sustainable development.

To sum up, international lawyers were not entirely satisfied with the outcomes of the UNCED because all environmental concerns were not addressed in internationally binding instruments of international law. For

[49] Ibid., 843.

[50] Ibid.

[51] Ibid.

[52] Pallemaerts, "International Environmental Law in the Age of Sustainable Development," 673.

[53] Ibid., 675.

[54] Kiss and Doumbé-Billé, "Conférence des Nations Unies sur l'environnement et le développement (Rio de Janeiro-juin 1992)," 843.

many lawyers and scholars, this was definitely not in line with the objectives of the UNCED about the further development of international law.[55] Nevertheless, this fork in the road back in 1992, distinguishing "law of sustainable development" from international law, was one of the initial steps towards the emergence of GLSD.

2.2 *Agenda 21: Raising of NGOs as Global Actors*

One of the objectives of Agenda 21 is "to set priorities for future law-making on sustainable development," including "an examination of the feasibility of elaborating general rights and obligations of States, as appropriate, in the field of sustainable development."[56] The Rio Declaration contains two different types of principles; namely, principles of international law (new principles and confirmation of principles from the Stockholm Declaration) and principles of "emerging law of sustainable development." In the same vein, according to the priorities set within the framework of Agenda 21, there are two different types of norm-making in the field of sustainable development during the third DSD. While certain rules and principles become rules of international law, others are left outside the realm of international law.

In terms of conclusive criteria of the primary social convention of GLSD, Agenda 21 emphasises that "[a]ny negotiations for the progressive development and codification of international law concerning sustainable development should, in general, be conducted on a universal basis".[57] Similarly, with respect to the criterion of consensus, Agenda 21 "reflects a global consensus and political commitment at the highest level on development and environment cooperation."[58] It is also often repeated in Agenda 21 that "[e]nvironmental measures addressing international

[55] To give a further example, David A. Wirth was hoping that this reference to law of sustainable development was simply illusory: "Future developments may well demonstrate that the apparent tension between the existing international law of the environment on the one hand and the Rio Declaration's allusions to a new international law of sustainable development on the other is illusory." See Wirth, "The Rio Declaration on Environment and Development," 649.

[56] "Agenda 21, Report of the United Nations Conference on Environment and Development, A/CONF.151/26/Rev.1 (Vol.1) Annex II."

[57] Ibid., para. 39.1 (f).

[58] Ibid., para. 1.3.

environmental problems should, as far as possible, be based on an international consensus."[59]

Agenda 21 also provides evidence of the changing landscape of global actors. The emergence of other key actors, in addition to States, is crucial for the crystallisation of the secondary social convention of GLSD. In this regard, a quarter of Agenda 21 addresses only the issues related to the strengthening of the role of major groups. Nine major groups are recognised in Agenda 21 to ensure and facilitate broad participation of all sectors of global society in a more structured manner.[60] A "genuine involvement of all social groups"[61] and "the need for new forms of participation" are emphasised.[62] Furthermore, Agenda 21 adds that "[to] ensure that the full potential contribution of [NGOs] is realized, the fullest possible communication and cooperation between [IOs], national and local governments and [NGOs] should be promoted."[63] Accordingly, one of the key objectives set by Agenda 21 was to strengthen the role of NGOs as "social partners" and "to review formal procedures and mechanisms for the involvement of these organizations at all levels from policy-making and decision-making to implementation."[64]

The aforementioned and other concrete objectives of Agenda 21,[65] together with the unique experience gained at the occasion of the UNCED with respect to the participation of NGOs, triggered the modification of the modalities of the NGOs' participation in the work of the UN through the ECOSOC.[66] An Open-Ended Working Group (OEWG) was

[59] Ibid., para. 39.3 (d).

[60] Major groups referred in Agenda 21 are; women (Chapter 24), children and youth (Chapter 25), indigenous people (Chapter 26), local authorities (Chapter 28), workers and trade unions (Chapter 29), business and industry (Chapter 30), scientific and technological community (Chapter 31) and lastly, farmers (Chapter 32). Regarding Chapter 27, it qualifies non-governmental organizations as "partners for sustainable development" which also include "non-profit organizations representing groups addressed in the [third] section of Agenda 21." See, ibid., para. 27.3.

[61] Ibid., para. 23.1.

[62] Ibid., para. 23.2.

[63] Ibid., para. 27.4.

[64] Ibid., para. 27.6. Furthermore, based on this objective, paragraph 27.9 provides in a very concrete and detailed manner the measures to be taken by the UN system.

[65] See also paragraphs from 38.42 to 38.45 of Agenda 21.

[66] "Review of the Arrangements for Consultation with Non-Governmental Organizations, ECOSOC Decision 1993/214.," February 12, 1993.

established to this end.[67] Even NGOs without the consultative status were allowed to contribute to the work of the OEWG in the same way NGOs were allowed to participate in the UNCED.[68] The review process was completed in 1996, and ECOSOC Resolution 1996/31 was adopted.[69] The most significant change in the arrangements was that national and regional NGOs were now entitled to enter into a consultative relationship with the UN.[70] Consequently, with the ECOSOC Resolution 1996/31, once an NGO has obtained a consultative status, it is entitled to participate in "all conferences convened by any organ of the UN."[71]

Another example of the rise of NGOs as global actors is the UNGA's decision to attribute for the first time an observer status to an NGO, namely, the International Committee of the Red Cross, "in consideration of the special role and mandates conferred upon it by the Geneva Conventions."[72] Despite this exceptional development, after the attribution of observer status to another NGO, namely, the International Federation of the Red Cross and Red Crescent Societies, in 1994, the UNGA blocked—following the United States' reactions[73]—the access to the observer status to NGOs by deciding that "the granting of observer status in the General Assembly should in the future be confined to *States* and to those [IGOs] whose activities cover matters of interest to the Assembly."[74]

Another example that demonstrates how the participation of NGOs was ensured without dismantling Westphalian DNAs of the UN system is

[67] "Review of the Arrangements for Consultation with Non-Governmental Organizations, ECOSOC Resolution, UN. Doc. E/RES/1993/80.," July 30, 1993, para. 1.

[68] Ibid., para. 8. In other words, even the Working Group of the Committee on NGOs of the ECOSOC was inspired by the practice established during the preparations for the Rio Conference with respect to the participation of NGOs to its work.

[69] "Consultative Relationship between the United Nations and Non-Governmental Organizations, ECOSOC Resolution, UN. Doc. E/RES/1996/31.," July 25, 1996.

[70] Peter Willetts, "From Consultative Arrangements to Partnership: The Changing Status of NGOs in Diplomacy at the UN," *Global Governance* 6 (2000): 192; Simone Vromen, "The Council Committee on NGOs: An Analysis of the Reports of the Council Committee on NGOs between 2005 and 2015," *Utrecht Law Review* 13 (2017): 87.

[71] Willetts, "From Consultative Arrangements to Partnership," 196.

[72] "Observer Status for the International Committee of the Red Cross, in Consideration of the Special Role and Mandates Conferred upon It by the Geneva Conventions of 12 August 1949, UNGA Resolution, UN Doc. A/RES/45/6," October 16, 1990.

[73] Willetts, "From Consultative Arrangements to Partnership," 197.

[74] UNGA's Decision 49/426 of 9 December 1994.

where the debates were adjourned to hear from civil society representatives.[75] In other instances, notably during the Habitat II Conference, NGOs participated on equal footing with States in the negotiating process, and they were "allowed to speak in support of their amendments."[76]

All these examples, together with the enthusiasm generated at the UNCED, prepared the background for the adoption of the ECOSOC Resolution 1996/31. Not surprisingly, the text of the ECOSOC Resolution 1996/31 also reflects the influence of the practice established during the preparations for the UNCED. Nevertheless, the ECOSOC Resolution 1996/31 has significant downsides reflecting Westphalian impulses of States. Notably, article 18 of the Resolution underlines that NGOs are participating in the deliberations of the ECOSOC, but only offered "arrangements for consultations."[77] In a significant contradiction with the atmosphere of the 1990s in favour of the NGOs, this article, inherited from the earlier versions of ECOSOC Resolution 1996/31, refers to the distinction made at the time of the adoption of the UN Charter, and thus includes heavy blueprints of States' dominant role in international relations. As clearly illustrated in the abovementioned example about the adjournment of the meeting in order to make room for the intervention of a civil society representative, it is not relatively easy to surpass certain formal barriers of the UN system.

A significant illustration of these formal barriers is what the European Union (EU) went through with respect to its participation in the work of the UN. Originally, the European Economic Community obtained an observer status at the UNGA in 1974.[78] Nevertheless, despite the EU's exclusive competences in various fields relevant to the work of the UN, it was not possible for the EU to obtain a better status at the UNGA until 3 May 2011.[79] Yet, even this status offered much less than what the EU and its Member States had hoped to obtain at the UNGA. As the EU has only an observer status, it is only entitled to take the floor after all the MS have

[75] Willetts, "From Consultative Arrangements to Partnership," 197.

[76] Ibid., 195–96.

[77] "Consultative Relationship between the United Nations and Non-Governmental Organizations, ECOSOC Resolution, UN. Doc. E/RES/1996/31."

[78] "Status of the European Economic Community in the General Assembly, UNGA Resolution 3208 (XXIX)," October 11, 1974.

[79] "Participation of the European Union in the Work of the United Nations, UNGA Resolution, UNGA Resolution, UN Doc. A/RES/65/276," May 3, 2011.

done so, and it is deprived of the right to vote, to co-sponsor draft resolutions or decisions, or to put forward candidates.

All this is to say that, as it would be erroneous to argue that the EU's role in the UN is nothing more than an observer with some additional rights, it would be as erroneous to maintain that the role of NGOs in the UN is limited to some arrangement for consultations. Accordingly, it is primordial to examine in depth the formal/informal developments and arrangements in order to better grasp the level of involvement and the relationship of NGOs with the UN.

2.3 Commission on Sustainable Development: First Global Institutional Mechanism for Sustainable Development

The idea of the CSD was firstly articulated in Agenda 21 "[i]n order to ensure the effective follow-up of [the UNCED] [...] and to examine the progress in the implementation of Agenda 21."[80] Later, the UNGA adopted modalities regarding the functioning of the CSD,[81] and the ECOSOC established the CSD with its Resolution 1993/207.[82] The CSD is composed of 53 MS. Other States, as well as other observers of the UNGA, "may participate in the [CSD] in the capacity of observer."[83] In addition, other IOs and NGOs were allowed to participate in the deliberations of the CSD without the right to vote.[84]

In terms of the primary social convention of GLSD, it is noted in the UNGA's Resolution 47/191 of 1992 that the procedures, "while ensuring the intergovernmental nature of the commission, should allow its members to benefit from the expertise and competence of relevant [IGOs and NGOs]."[85] The term "ensuring the intergovernmental nature" is the emphasis on the "States-led" nature of the CSD, and the "but" following

[80] "Agenda 21, Report of the United Nations Conference on Environment and Development, A/CONF.151/26/Rev.1 (Vol.1) Annex II," para. 38.11.

[81] "Institutional Arrangements to Follow up the United Nations Conference on Environment and Development, UNGA Resolution, UN Doc. A/RES/47/191," December 22, 1992.

[82] "Establishment of the Commission on Sustainable Development, ECOSOC Resolution, UN. Doc. E/RES/1993/207.," February 12, 1993.

[83] "Institutional Arrangements to Follow up the United Nations Conference on Environment and Development, UNGA Resolution, UN Doc. A/RES/47/191," para. 6.

[84] Ibid., para. 7.

[85] Ibid., para. 8.

and referring to other actors to be included is about inclusiveness.[86] Later, the ECOSOC further adopted Decision 1993/215 regarding some procedural arrangements regarding the actors to be involved in the work of the CSD.[87] In principle, when there is a functional commission established under the ECOSOC, "Rules of Procedure of the Functional Commissions of the Economic and Social Council" are applicable, and these rules provide the details of arrangements for the participation of non-members of the commission and for consultation with NGOs.[88] However, as a result of the special role of IOs and NGOs during the preparations of the UNCED, ECOSOC Decision 1993/215 added supplemental arrangements that provided enhanced status for these organizations. For example, Article 76(2) of the Rules of Procedure of the Functional Commissions of the ECOSOC, with respect to the participation of NGOs on the Roster,[89] provides that they may be heard by the CSD. Contrary to this relatively limited arrangement, ECOSOC Decision 1993/215 adds that not only are they entitled to "make written presentations to the [CSD] and its subsidiary organs" but they may also be given "an opportunity to briefly address the meetings of the [CSD] and its subsidiary organs."[90]

Another significant supplemental arrangement regulated with respect to the CSD regards the status of NGOs, which were accredited to the UNCED but were not in a consultative relationship with the ECOSOC. These organizations were invited to apply to the CSD in order to be granted the Roster status.[91] Despite this provision, all interested NGOs were invited to apply for this specific Roster status even though they were not accredited to the UNCED.[92] In total, 550 NGOs—of which 71 were new—applied and obtained the Roster status to contribute to the

[86] See also, paragraphs 38.43 and 38.44 of Agenda 21 highlighting the importance of an expanded role for non-governmental organizations and for major groups within the CSD.

[87] "Procedural Arrangements for the Commission on Sustainable Development, ECOSOC Decision 1993/215.," February 12, 1993.

[88] "Rules of Procedure of the Functional Commissions of the Economic and Social Council, ECOSOC Resolution, UN. Doc. E/5975/Rev.1.," 1983.

[89] There are three categories of status for NGOs at the UN: General, special and roster consultative status. Articles 22–24 of the ECOSOC Resolution 1996/31 defining each of these statuses.

[90] "Procedural Arrangements for the Commission on Sustainable Development, ECOSOC Decision 1993/215.," para. 2(ii), 2(iii).

[91] Ibid., para. (c).

[92] Peter Willetts, ed., "The Conscience of the World": The Influence of Non-Governmental Organisations in the UN System (Washington, D.C: The Brookings Institution, 1996), 57.

work of the CSD.[93] Giving access to this great number of NGOs all at once was so significant that NGOs which were already in a consultative relationship were worried "that their special position might be undermined by the new NGOs" and that the increase in the number of NGOs with access to the UN activities might lead to limitations of NGOs' access in general.[94]

Moreover, regarding the increasing role played by NGOs, at the occasion of the annual conference of NGOs in 1994, Boutros Boutros-Ghali, the then SG, noted that NGOs "are now considered full participants in international life."[95] Truly, the general atmosphere in the 1990s was indeed that NGOs were considered as full participants in international/global life.[96]

3 Conclusion and Progress Appraisal: Second Decade of Sustainable Development

3.1 Secondary Social Convention: Global Actors

During the first DSD, the concept of sustainable development took a more concrete shape, and with the UNCHE, the creation of UNEP, as well as the establishment of WCED, IOs were indeed at the centre of issues related to sustainable development. Furthermore, during the first DSD, an understanding and recognition emerged among States with respect to the role and place of IOs and NGOs in addressing the challenges of sustainable development.

On the road to the UNCED and its aftermath, the role of IOs in the field of sustainable development increased and expanded. The UNCED was one of the most exceptional conferences organised under the auspices of the UNGA. The great number of IOs involved in the whole process

[93] Ibid.

[94] Ibid., 56.

[95] Ibid., 311.

[96] It is important to remember at this juncture that Agenda 21 reiterates repeatedly the idea of partnership among states, IOs and NGOs; *inter alia*, paragraph 27.5 of Agenda 21 provides as follows: "Society, Governments and international bodies should develop mechanisms to allow nongovernmental organizations to play their partnership role responsibly and effectively in the process of environmentally sound and sustainable development." See "Agenda 21, Report of the United Nations Conference on Environment and Development, A/CONF.151/26/Rev.1 (Vol.1) Annex II."

reaffirmed their indispensable role in addressing the challenges of sustainable development. In addition, Agenda 21 considered IOs as part of a new global partnership for sustainable development, and the CSD ensured enhanced mechanisms for the contributions of IOs to its work. All these developments further ascertained the emerging role of the IOs as one of the parties to the secondary social convention of GLSD.

These are not isolated events. In fact, since the beginning of the second half of the twentieth century, the role and place of IOs was exponentially expanding at the international level. Notably, as early as 1949, the ICJ affirmed the UN's international legal personality. Later, the Vienna Convention on the Law of Treaties between States and IOs or between IOs was opened for signatures in 1986. The Convention is not yet in force. Nevertheless, "the Convention is, regardless of its formal status, generally accepted as the applicable law and is widely used as a handy written guide in practice".[97] Therefore, it is not a coincidence that, during the 1980s, IOs reached a significant level of recognition on the part of States regarding the importance of their role and place at the global level.

With regard to NGOs, their interest and involvement in the UNCHE, their firm and constant relationship with UNEP in the aftermath of the UNCHE, and their contributions to the work of the WCED were all significant steps for NGOs during the first DSD. Afterwards, a drastic transformation happened. The interest of NGOs to the UNCED is often described as unprecedented due to the fact that more than a thousand NGOs were accredited to the preparatory process and to the UNCED itself. This great interest of NGOs significantly influenced the outcome documents of the UNCED. Notably, a quarter of Agenda 21 addresses the issues related to the genuine involvement of all social groups as partners of a new global partnership for sustainable development. The exceptional atmosphere of the UNCED also triggered the advancement of the modalities of NGOs' participation in the work of the UN. Furthermore, the adjournment of meetings in UN conferences for the interventions of representative of NGOs; their involvement in certain instances to the negotiations on equal footing with States; and the initiatives for their full participation through supplemental arrangements to the work of the CSD, are all indications with respect to the transformation of NGOs' status at

[97] Karl Zemanek, "Vienna Convention on the Law of Treaties between States and International Organizations or between International Organizations," 2009.

the global level as one of the parties to the secondary social convention of GLSD.

3.2 Primary Social Convention and Conclusive Criteria

It is highlighted in the preamble of Agenda 21 that, "[i]t reflects a global consensus and political commitment at the highest level on development and environment cooperation."[98] This global consensus is evidently a significant footprint of an emerging (primary) social convention at the global level in the field of sustainable development.

To start with the first criterion (States-led), as it was the case within the context of the UNCHE and the WCED, it all started as a result of States' initiatives and with always a strong accent put on the intergovernmental nature. This characteristic has not changed throughout the UNCED and also in the establishment of the CSD.[99] Therefore, this first criterion was reasserted at the end of the UNCED.

In terms of the second criterion (inclusiveness), the UNCHE was a turning point and greatly influenced and contributed to an increasing cooperation with NGOs to better address the challenges of sustainable development. As for the UNCED, it was a paradigm-shifting moment concerning the involvement of NGOs in global affairs. As a result of heated debates among States, a consensus-based agreement was reached with respect to the modalities of NGOs' participation to the UNCED and this agreement shaped the entirety of Agenda 21, as a quarter of the document was entirely dedicated to the role of major groups. Moreover, this agreement also triggered the advancement of the modalities of NGOs' participation to the work of the UN. Last but not least, every remark and indicator about the intergovernmental nature of institutional mechanisms addressing the challenges of sustainable development was always followed by a "but" about the *sine qua non* requirement of inclusiveness. Consequently, this second criterion was also in the picture at the end of the second DSD.

Regarding the third criterion (consensus), as underlined by various commentators, as a result of cumulative experience since the UNCHE, an

[98] "Agenda 21, Report of the United Nations Conference on Environment and Development, A/CONF.151/26/Rev.1 (Vol.1) Annex II," paragraph 1.3.

[99] "Institutional Arrangements to Follow up the United Nations Conference on Environment and Development, UNGA Resolution, UN Doc. A/RES/47/191," para. 8(a).

informal rule has emerged that decisions should be taken by consensus at UN conferences in the field of sustainable development. In addition, relevant UNGA resolutions were all adopted by consensus, including the outcome documents of the UNCHE and the UNCED. Moreover, Agenda 21 was qualified by its authors as reflecting a global consensus.

In terms of the fourth criterion (universality), given the global character of the challenges of sustainable development, since the UNCHE, there are recurrent references to the globality and universality of the issues at stake. Notably, the Brundtland Report was described as a global agenda for change. The same applies to Agenda 21, which reflects a global consensus. Agenda 21 makes many references to the universality of its call for action and underlines that any negotiations for further codification of international law in the field of sustainable development be conducted on a universal basis.[100] Therefore, this fourth criterion of universality was also confirmed at the end of the UNCED.

Regarding the fifth criterion (pluralism), I identified the birthmarks of an emerging concept of law in the field of sustainable development. The unprecedented normative developments in the field of sustainable development during its first two decades inspired legal scholars to put forward the emerging concept of "international law on sustainable development." The reason for distinguishing this new concept from the concept of international law was States' preference for non-binding instruments—in terms of international law—while producing and adopting norms and rules in the field of sustainable development. It is evident that the Rio Declaration, with its 27 principles and Chapter 39 of Agenda 21 on international legal instruments and mechanisms, are both to be understood as key documents in the greater picture of international law. They were designed and adopted to complement and to coexist in harmony with the existing rules of international law, and as such, it is not conceivable for these norms/rules to contradict the existing rules of international law.

In conclusion, despite important signs for the emergence of the secondary social convention of GLSD among States, IOs and NGOs, and despite some significant indicators in order to consider the aforementioned five criteria as conclusive criteria of the primary social convention of GLSD, it was still not possible, at the beginning of the third DSD to talk about the existence of the primary social convention of GLSD. In

[100] "Agenda 21, Report of the United Nations Conference on Environment and Development, A/CONF.151/26/Rev.1 (Vol.1) Annex II," para. 39.1 (f).

order to genuinely confirm the existence of such a primary social convention, one must be able to demonstrate examples of rules adopted in accordance with the criteria of such a convention. However, even though the outcome documents of the UNCED provide significant indicators for the content of a potential primary social convention, it is simply not possible to conclude that these outcome documents were the results of a primary social convention. Notwithstanding the emergence of a primary social convention before the UNCED, a secondary social convention was yet to emerge after the UNCED. Therefore, at this moment in time, despite significant data for the emergence of a secondary social convention among States, IOs and NGOs, a primary social convention among these global actors was yet to emerge.

CHAPTER 4

From Rio to the Millennium Development Goals

This chapter examines the third DSD from Rio Conference until the World Summit of Sustainable Development (WSSD) of 2002. The first section observes the 19th Special Session of the UNGA (Rio+5) organised for an overall review of the implementation of Agenda 21 at its fifth anniversary. This event was historically significant in terms of NGOs' access to the debates within the UNGA as one of the key global actors in the field of sustainable development. In addition, the outcome document of Rio+5, as well as the work of CSD were crucial with respect to the crystallisation of the primary social convention of GLSD. In the second section, I demonstrate how the WSSD contributed to this crystallisation and how the Plan of Implementation of the WSSD ("Johannesburg Plan of Implementation") was another significant step after Agenda 21 towards the development of the substances of the SDGs. In the third section reserved for the Millennium Summit and the MDGs, I argue that the complex and *sui generis* process that led to the emergence of the MDGs is an excellent but *a contrario* affirmation of the five criteria of the primary social convention of GLSD. In addition, following a detailed examination of the MDGs, as well as the Organisation for Economic Co-operation and Development's (OECD) International Development Goals (IDGs), I reveal that, in terms of *style and format*, the origins of the MDGs—as predecessor of the SDGS—are mainly to be found at the OECD's IDGs. The fourth section provides an overview of some of the agreements and

H. Göksan, *Global Law of Sustainable Development*, Global Issues,
https://doi.org/10.1007/978-3-031-74547-8_4

objectives reached in the UN conferences of the 1990s and establishes that, in terms of *substance*, the origins of the MDGs are to be found in these agreements. Lastly, the fifth section examines the progress made during this decade with respect to the secondary and primary social conventions of GLSD.

1 Rio+5 and the CSD

Two key matters were at the centre of the UNGA's attention in the context of Rio+5 for the review of Agenda 21. One was the dissemination of the principles of the Rio Declaration, and the other one was related to the further involvement of major groups in the work of the CSD. With respect to the former, UNGA Resolution 48/190 of 1993 states that Rio Declaration "contains fundamental principles for the achievement of sustainable development, based on a new and equitable global partnership" and "urged all Governments to promote widespread dissemination of the Rio Declaration," as it was crucial to incorporate these principles in the implementation of Agenda 21.[1]

The qualification of the partnership for sustainable development with these three adjectives—new, equitable and global—is first, an indication about the emergence of the secondary social convention of GLSD, within which IOs, NGOs and States are ready and apt to agree on conclusive criteria of the primary social convention of GLSD. Second, the reference to an equitable partnership also reaffirms the secondary social convention of GLSD by highlighting the equality among these global actors. Lastly, the reference to a global partnership is a confirmation of the criterion of universality.

In its Resolution 49/111 of 1994, the UNGA welcomed the submissions made by some governments concerning their "national sustainable development strategies" and action plans for the implementation of Agenda 21 at the national level. Another significant initiative of the CSD praised by the UNGA was its work on the elaboration of "sustainable development indicators."[2] Accordingly, it is possible to trace back the

[1] "Dissemination of the Principles of the Rio Declaration on Environment and Development, UNGA Resolution, UN Doc. A/RES/48/190," December 21, 1993, First preambular paragraph and paragraph 1.

[2] "Report of the Commission on Sustainable Development on Its Second Session, UNGA Resolution, UN Doc. A/RES/49/111," December 19, 1994.

origin of 232 indicators of the SDGs back to the pioneering work of the CSD. Moreover, the UNGA stressed that the role of CSD as a "unique forum for fostering multilateral negotiations" in the field of sustainable development.[3] This emphasis is yet another affirmation that any further negotiations in order to adopt norms/rules in the field of sustainable development must go through the CSD, where norms and regulations are adopted by consensus, as a result of an inclusive and States-led process at the universal level in harmony with international law.

Furthermore, in terms of inclusiveness, the UNGA was not only calling the CSD "to develop close and clear relationships" with IOs, but was also proactively recommending the CSD to cooperate with international institutions, for example, with the newly established World Trade Organization (WTO).[4] In addition, it has become evident already at the second session of the CSD that it was necessary to improve the modalities of the involvement of the major groups in the work of the CSD, especially in view of their critical role in the implementation of Agenda 21. This is the reason why, as early as in 1994, the UNGA noted "the indispensable role that major groups play in the implementation of Agenda 21" and, as a result, this was one of the key matters addressed at Rio+5.

1.1 *Reaffirming "Rio Commitments"*

The first UNGA resolution towards Rio+5 devoted almost half of its text to inviting IOs, IGOs, major groups and other key actors for their contributions[5] and welcomed the decision of the CSD to hold its fifth session in an open-ended manner in order to allow the full participation of all States, in addition to the members of the CSD, for preparatory purposes.[6] Other than these emphases on inclusiveness, the UNGA requested the SG to prepare a report in advance of Rio+5 summarising: the progress achieved since the UNCED; country profiles regarding the implementation of

[3] "Report of the Commission on Sustainable Development on Its Second Session, UNGA Resolution, UN Doc. A/RES/49/111," para. 7.

[4] Ibid., paras. 8, 11.

[5] "Special Session for the Purpose of an Overall Review and Appraisal of the Implementation of Agenda 21, UNGA Resolution, UN Doc. A/RES/50/113," December 20, 1995, paras. 6–12.

[6] Ibid., para. 4.

Agenda 21; emerging trends in the field of sustainable development; and recommendations for the future of the CSD.[7]

With respect to the SG's Report A/50/453, it refers to the conventions signed at the UNCED and to its outcome documents as "Rio commitments."[8] In other words, binding and non-binding documents from the perspective of international law are all referred as part of the Rio commitments. In that sense, it signals a powerful perception about the normativity of outcome documents of the UNCED. After mentioning a number of international conferences held since the UNCED, the SG's Report A/50/453 also notes that "they add substantially to the international understanding and consensus on various critical elements of sustainable development" and that "the comprehensive review of Agenda 21 also needs to take into account the outcomes of these conferences as well."[9]

Moreover, the SG's Report A/50/453 literally refers to the concept of "sustainable development goals."[10] In terms of the substance of the SDGs, it was, of course, not possible back then, to identify 17 specific goals with defined targets and indicators. Yet, the fact that the SG's Report A/50/453 refers to sustainable development goals indicates that the concept was already starting to take a shape back in 1995. In addition, it is important to highlight that the SG's Report A/50/453 is yet another endorsement of my earlier conclusions that States (referred as governments) and IOs and NGOs (referred as major groups) were the key global actors in the field of sustainable development. These three global actors are also mentioned with respect to the implementation of Rio commitments. Consequently, the SG's Report A/50/453 reaffirms, back in 1995, the emergence of the secondary social convention of GLSD.

In its Resolution 51/181 of 1996, the UNGA decided that the fifth session of the CSD be devoted to the preparations of a draft final document to be the basis of further discussions.[11] A first key issue addressed in

[7] Ibid., para. 13.

[8] "Report of the Secretary-General, Proposals on the Format, Scope and Organizational Aspects of the 1997 Special Session of the General Assembly on the Overall Review and Appraisal of Agenda 21, UN Doc. A/50/453," September 20, 1995, para. 5.

[9] Ibid., para. 6.

[10] Ibid., para. 12.

[11] "Special Session for the Purpose of an Overall Review and Appraisal of the Implementation of Agenda 21, UNGA Resolution, UN Doc. A/RES/51/181," December 16, 1996, paragraph 2. This is also another indication about the importance of the existence of institutional mechanisms.

Resolution 51/181 is about the participation of major groups and NGOs to the work of the UNGA during Rio+5. Remember that the UNGA was not keen on allowing NGOs to contribute to its work in the 1990s.[12] In that sense, allowing the involvement of major groups to its work at the occasion of Rio+5 was an enormous step for the UNGA. In principle, the doors of UNGA were closed to NGOs. However, things were different with respect to issues in the field of sustainable development. Notably "the importance of developing a broad-based consensus involving major groups for achieving sustainable development" was repeatedly stressed within the CSD.[13] Furthermore, UNGA recognised "the important role played by major groups, including [NGOs], at the [UNCED] and in the implementation of its recommendations," and also emphasised "the need for their active involvement [...] [and] the need to ensure appropriate arrangements for their contribution."[14]

Instead of providing for the appropriate modalities for the involvement of major groups, the UNGA invited its President to make some propositions about these modalities.[15] This was to make things look less formal concerning these arrangements.[16] As a result, it was agreed that the UNGA President be entitled to extend invitations to representatives of major groups and NGOs to participate in the plenary meeting.[17] As such, "NGOs were allowed for the first time in the history of the UN to take part in the main plenary debate [...] on a daily-basis" and moreover, "one of the key working groups negotiating the final texts was chaired by an NGO leader."[18] Consequently, despite the fact that the note by the President

[12] See, Chap. 3, Sect. 2.2.

[13] "Report of the Secretary-General, Environment and Sustainable Development: Special Session for the Purpose of an Overall Review and Appraisal of Agenda 21, UN Doc. A/51/420," October 1, 1996, para. 9.

[14] "Special Session for the Purpose of an Overall Review and Appraisal of the Implementation of Agenda 21, UNGA Resolution, UN Doc. A/RES/51/181," para. 3.; "Special Session for the Purpose of an Overall Review and Appraisal of the Implementation of Agenda 21, UNGA Resolution, UN Doc. A/RES/50/113," para. 11.

[15] "Special Session for the Purpose of an Overall Review and Appraisal of the Implementation of Agenda 21, UNGA Resolution, UN Doc. A/RES/51/181," para. 3.

[16] Especially, due to the pressure from the United States' delegation. See for further details in Willetts, "From Consultative Arrangements to Partnership," 200–201.

[17] "Note by the President of the General Assembly, Environment and Sustainable Development: Special Session for the Purpose of an Overall Review and Appraisal of Agenda 21, UN Doc. A/51/864," April 7, 1997.

[18] Willetts, "From Consultative Arrangements to Partnership," 200–201.

underlined that this exception "will in no way create precedent for other special sessions of the Assembly,"[19] this historical event not only reaffirmed the role of NGOs as a global actor along with States and IOs in the field of sustainable development, but also stressed the significance of the criterion of inclusiveness. In addition, this practice effectively created precedent, as the UNGA, in the future, always involved the NGOs in its work related to the issues of sustainable development.

The UNGA further emphasised that "there should be no attempt to renegotiate Agenda 21, the Rio Declaration [...] or other internationally recognized intergovernmental agreements in the field of environment and sustainable development[.]"[20] This is a significant indication that Rio+5 was not a negotiating platform, rather it was a discussion about the implementation of previously agreed commitments. In that sense, Rio+5 was not an event of norm-making and was not going to amend any agreement reached with respect to the content of Agenda 21 or the Rio Declaration. Therefore, it is simply not possible to talk about the emergence of the primary social convention of GLSD at the end of Rio+5. However, it is highly important to underscore that Rio+5 was one of the most important building blocks towards the emergence of the primary social convention of GLSD. It is enough to recall in this regard its contribution to the crystallisation of the criterion of inclusiveness. The fact that the negotiations were reserved for discussions on the implementation of the Rio Commitments in no way limits its contributions to the maturing and ripening of the primary social convention of GLSD.

Concerning the dissemination of the principles contained in the Rio Declaration, the UNGA resolution adopted at the end of Rio+5, *inter alia*, emphasised that "[p]rogress has been made in incorporating the principles contained in the Rio Declaration [...] in a variety of international and national legal instruments" and that "much remains to be done to embody the Rio principles more firmly in law and practice."[21] Moreover, in advance of Rio+5, the UNEP Governing Council adopted the Nairobi Declaration on the role and mandate of UNEP with a view to provide

[19] "Note by the President of the General Assembly, Environment and Sustainable Development: Special Session for the Purpose of an Overall Review and Appraisal of Agenda 21, UN Doc. A/51/864."

[20] "Special Session for the Purpose of an Overall Review and Appraisal of the Implementation of Agenda 21, UNGA Resolution, UN Doc. A/RES/51/181," para. 5.

[21] "Programme for the Further Implementation of Agenda 21, UNGA Resolution, UN Doc. A/RES/S-19/2," June 28, 1997, para. 14.

suggestion to the UNGA regarding the enhancement of the role of UNEP in the implementation of Agenda 21.[22] Notably, the Nairobi Declaration also underlined the importance to "further the development of [...] international environmental law aiming at sustainable development," as well as to "advance the implementation of agreed international norms and policies, to monitor and foster compliance with environmental principles and international agreements."[23]

The Nairobi Declaration was endorsed by the UNGA.[24] In this regard, first, the intention to incorporate the principles of the Rio Declaration, a non-binding declaration in terms of international law, into the binding international legal instruments reaffirms the harmonious relationship between the binding rules of international environmental law, as well as previously mentioned emerging law of sustainable development. The principles of the Rio Declaration were designed and adopted to complement and to coexist in harmony with the existing rules of international law. Therefore, this reaffirms the soundness of the criterion of pluralism. Second, it is clear that the Nairobi Declaration also makes the distinction between international environmental law and "emerging law of sustainable development." Precisely, while it refers to the further development of international environmental law, it also remarks the advancement of the implementation of "agreed international norms and policies." In that sense, the reappearance of this distinction five years after the adoption of Agenda 21 reaffirms the conclusions of legal scholars regarding the emergence of "law of sustainable development" as one of the results of the UNCED and strengthens the arguments of the present book. In addition, it establishes that this new concept of law at the global level seeks to coexist in harmony with the existing rules of international law.

Last but not least, a final matter to be underlined is the involvement of other IOs and IGOs to the process towards to Rio+5. It is important to recall at this juncture the establishment of an Inter-Agency Committee on Sustainable Development (IACSD) following the adoption of Agenda 21.[25] In this regard, concerning the activities carried out by the IACSD,

[22] "United Nations Environment Programme: Report of the Governing Council on the Work of Its Nineteenth Session, UN Doc. A/52/25," April 4, 1997, 29–32.

[23] Ibid., 30–31, Nairobi Declaration, paragraph 3.

[24] "Programme for the Further Implementation of Agenda 21, UNGA Resolution, UN Doc. A/RES/S-19/2," para. 123.

[25] "Agenda 21, Report of the United Nations Conference on Environment and Development, A/CONF.151/26/Rev.1 (Vol.1) Annex II," para. 38.16, 38.17;

the SG's Report A/51/420 provides that certain IOs did their own contributions in advance of Rio+5, such as UN Conference on Trade and Development's report on trade and environment, as well as the World Health Organization's world health and environment report.[26] Accordingly, it is clear that IOs were not simply involved in the processes with respect to the goals of sustainable development, but they were, in fact, genuine global actors pointing out their standings in the field of sustainable development.

1.2 Outcome of Rio+5 and the Primary Social Convention of GLSD

There are a number of elements to be highlighted regarding the UNGA Resolution adopted at the end of Rio+5 (UNGA Resolution S-19/2). First, in terms of global actors, UNGA Resolution S-19/2 clearly refers to three global actors as follows: "[W]e—heads of State or Government [...], together with our partners from international institutions and [NGOs]—have gathered to review progress achieved [...] since the [UNCED] and to re-energize our commitment to further action on goals and objectives set out by the [UNCED]."[27] The resolution also reaffirms the criteria of States-led and inclusiveness of the primary social convention of GLSD, as well as its secondary social convention given the reference to "partners."[28] Evidently, States have a central place in the processes towards achieving "Rio commitments." Yet, they act in this direction in an inclusive manner,

"Institutional Arrangements to Follow up the United Nations Conference on Environment and Development, UNGA Resolution, UN Doc. A/RES/47/191," paras. 32–33.

[26] "Report of the Secretary-General, Environment and Sustainable Development: Special Session for the Purpose of an Overall Review and Appraisal of Agenda 21, UN Doc. A/51/420," para. 19.

[27] "Programme for the Further Implementation of Agenda 21, UNGA Resolution, UN Doc. A/RES/S-19/2," para. 1.

[28] The idea of partnership among these three actors could be further investigated with inspiration from the idea of "Multi-Level Governance" developed by Gary Marks in the context of European law. See in this regard, among many others; Gary Marks, "An Actor-centred Approach to Multi-level Governance," *Regional & Federal Studies* 6, no. 2 (June 1, 1996): 20–38; Ian Bache, "Multi-Level Governance in the European Union," in *The Oxford Handbook of Governance*, ed. David Levi-Faur, 2012; Ian Bache, Ian Bartle, and Matthew Flinders, "Multi-Level Governance," in *Handbook on Theories of Governance*, ed. Christopher Ansell and Jacob Torfing, 2016; Simona Piattoni, "Multi-level Governance: A Historical and Conceptual Analysis," *Journal of European Integration* 31, no. 2 (March 1, 2009): 163–80.

together with their global partners, namely, IOs and NGOs. Specifically, UNGA Resolution S-19/2 refers also to the demonstrated involvement and commitment of major groups and IOs.[29]

Second, UNGA Resolution S-19/2 asserts that a new global partnership for sustainable development was launched at UNCED and it was "founded on a global consensus and political commitment at the highest level."[30] Accordingly, the criterion of consensus was also reaffirmed at this occasion of review and appraisal of Agenda 21.

Third, with respect to the criterion of pluralism, UNGA Resolution S-19/2 emphasises that "progress has been made in incorporating the principles contained in the Rio Declaration [...] in a variety of international and national legal instruments."[31] This also reaffirms the criterion of pluralism, even though the primary social convention of GLSD was yet to emerge in 1997.

Fourth, with respect to the criterion of universality, UNGA Resolution S-19/2 also reaffirms global ambitions of Agenda 21. Nevertheless, an important difference is worthy of mention between Agenda 21 and UNGA Resolution S-19/2. There is no reference to the term of globalisation in the 350-page of Agenda 21. However, UNGA Resolution S-19/2 considers that the five years since UNCED have been characterised by globalisation and underlines the importance to "ensure that globalization trends have a positive impact on sustainable development."[32] At the time of UNGA Resolution S-19/2, even though the UNGA simply highlights that the CSD "has a role to play in assessing the challenges of globalisation as they relate to sustainable development," the effects of globalisation will significantly influence the emergence of GLSD.

Regarding the content of Agenda 21, UNGA Resolution S-19/2 and the SDGs, there is an undeniable nexus demonstrating the historical connection in terms of normativity. For example, at the very beginning, UNGA Resolution S-19/2 clearly refers to the goals of sustainable development by indicating that Agenda 21 "aims at preparing the world for the challenges of the next century in order to attain the long-term goals of sustainable development."[33] Specifically, it is possible to find (raw)

[29] "Programme for the Further Implementation of Agenda 21, UNGA Resolution, UN Doc. A/RES/S-19/2," paras. 12, 16.

[30] Ibid., para. 2.

[31] Ibid., para. 14.

[32] Ibid., para. 7.

[33] Ibid., para. 2.

references to each Global Goal in both Agenda 21 and UNGA Resolution S-19/2.[34]

1.3 CSD in Its First Five Years

In terms of substance with respect to the SDGs, the first salient function of the CSD is its role in considering national reports regarding the activities undertaken for the implementation of Agenda 21. In fact, this idea of submitting national reports to the CSD is basically the predecessor of the mechanism of "voluntary national reviews" under Agenda 2030 and the SDGs. In terms of numbers, the CSD was rather successful. One hundred fourteen countries submitted national reports during the first five years of the CSD.[35] In addition, the voluntary submission of national reports is highly interlinked with the provision of Agenda 21 advising the States to adopt national strategies for sustainable development.[36] Agenda 21's simple "should" requirement was strengthened at the occasion of Rio+5 with a specific deadline to adopt national strategies by 2002.[37]

It goes without saying that, in terms of international law, both Agenda 21 and UNGA Resolution S-19/2 are non-binding documents. Nevertheless, as the great majority of MS already adopted such a national strategy, "by 1997 a point had been reached where it would have been difficult for any single country to openly refuse to adopt a national programme for sustainable development or to oppose a corresponding

[34] Goal, corresponding chapter of Agenda 21, and corresponding paragraph of Resolution S-19/2: Goal 1, chapter 3, para 28; Goal 2, chapter 14, paras. 62–63; Goal 3, chapter 6, para. 31; Goal 4, chapter 36, paras. 105–06; Goal 5, chapter 24, para. 27(e); Goal 6, chapter 18, paras. 34–35; Goal 7, chapter 7, paras. 42–46; Goal 8, chapter 2, paras. 25–26 and 29; Goal 9, chapter 7, para. 32; Goal 10, chapter 2, paras. 25–26 and 29; Goal 11, chapter 7, paras. 30 and 32; Goal 12, chapter 4, para. 28; Goal 13, chapter 9, paras. 48–56; Goal 14, chapter 17, para. 36; Goal 15, chapters 11–14, paras. 37–41 and 64–66; Goal 16, N/A, N/A; and Goal 17, chapters 33–40, paras. 76–115. Further details and the origins of many targets of the SDGs might be found in the above-mentioned chapters of Agenda 21 and paragraphs of Resolution S-19/2 of 1997.

[35] Stine Madland Kaasa, "The UN Commission on Sustainable Development: Which Mechanisms Explain Its Accomplishments?," *Global Environmental Politics* 7, no. 3 (August 1, 2007): 113.

[36] "Agenda 21, Report of the United Nations Conference on Environment and Development, A/CONF.151/26/Rev.1 (Vol.1) Annex II," para. 8.7.

[37] "Programme for the Further Implementation of Agenda 21, UNGA Resolution, UN Doc. A/RES/S-19/2," paragraph 24.

decision within the United Nations."[38] More interestingly, Jörgens mentions that this promotion of national sustainable development strategies through "diffusion" paved the way for their subsequent legal harmonisation.[39]

Another significant achievement of the CSD with respect to the substance and origins of the SDGs is the elaboration of sustainable development indicators. Several workshops were held following the third session of the CSD[40] and indicators of sustainable development were made available to States for a "test phase" at the fourth session of the CSD.[41] In that sense, the CSD has played a pioneering role regarding the development of sustainable development indicators and compilation of national reports and these accomplishments "had a positive impact on the CSD's achievements in the area of monitoring and reviewing progress."[42] More importantly, these initiatives significantly shaped the mechanisms in which the SDGs operate.

In terms of the role of global actors within the CSD, the participation of IOs and NGOs to the work of the CSD has already been addressed above. In addition, the UNGA recommended the CSD "[to] receive and analyse relevant input from competent [NGOs], including the scientific and the private sector" and "[to] enhance the dialogue, within the framework of the [UN], with [NGOs] and the independent sector, as well as other entities[.]"[43]

Many scholars agree that the most successful achievements of the CSD are enhancing dialogue with NGOs and building partnership for sustainable development.[44] Following the example of the UN Habitat Conference in 1996, stakeholder dialogue was included in the preparatory process for Rio+5. As a result of the great success of these dialogue sessions, UNGA Resolution S-19/2 held that the CSD should "[s]trengthen its interaction

[38] Jörgens, "Governance by Diffusion," pages 266–67.

[39] Ibid., page 267.

[40] "Report of the Commission on Sustainable Development on Its Third Session, UN Doc. E/1995/32.," April 28, 1995, paragraphs 1–12.

[41] "Report of the Commission on Sustainable Development on Its Fourth Session, UN Doc. E/1996/28.," May 3, 1996, Decision 4/5, page 13.

[42] Kaasa, "The UN Commission on Sustainable Development," page 124. For an in-depth overview, see the following PhD thesis: Eva Mineur, "Towards Sustainable Development : Indicators as a Tool of Local Governance" 2007.

[43] "Institutional Arrangements to Follow up the United Nations Conference on Environment and Development, UNGA Resolution, UN Doc. A/RES/47/191," para. 3.

[44] Kaasa, "The UN Commission on Sustainable Development," 115.

with representatives of major groups, including through greater and better use of focused dialogue sessions and round tables."[45] Furthermore, Kaasa notes that "the multistakeholder dialogues was the most innovative measure to involve major groups [...] [in order] to generate action-oriented dialogue between governments and major groups and identify future policies and actions."[46]

Lastly, in terms of the criteria of the primary social convention of GLSD, Resolution S-19/2 clearly reiterates that the CSD "will continue to provide a central forum [...] for conducting a high-level policy debate aimed at consensus-building on sustainable development (consensus)."[47] In addition, only the States are the members of the CSD (States-led). However, the discussions within the CSD are held in the most inclusive way possible (inclusiveness). UNGA Resolution S-19/2 also indicates that the CSD will continue to provide a central forum "for catalysing action and long-term commitment to sustainable development at all levels" and that it has "a role to play in assessing the challenges of globalization as they relate to sustainable development (universality)."[48] Lastly, the role of the CSD is envisioned alongside the existing rules of international law, and Agenda 21, Rio Declaration and Rio commitments are complementing and aiming to coexist in harmony with those rules (pluralism). Notably, UNGA Resolution S-19/2 provides that "[t]aking into account the provisions of chapter 39, particularly paragraph 39.1, of Agenda 21, it is necessary to continue the progressive development and, as and when appropriate, codification of international law related to sustainable development."[49]

To summarise, the design of and the way the CSD functioned demonstrate the continuing support of the three global actors for the five criteria

[45] "Programme for the Further Implementation of Agenda 21, UNGA Resolution, UN Doc. A/RES/S-19/2," para. 133(e).

[46] Kaasa, "The UN Commission on Sustainable Development," page 115. Kaasa further adds that "NGOs have received credit for contributing to enhancing the quality of the decision-making process, creating attention and pressure on governments, initiating processes, informing the member states and pushing for policies. According to Pietracci, NGOs have advocated certain issues and have tried to influence the states, which is sometimes reflected in the final document through the use of NGO language in some portions of the text." See in ibid., 121.

[47] "Programme for the Further Implementation of Agenda 21, UNGA Resolution, UN Doc. A/RES/S-19/2," para. 130.

[48] Ibid.

[49] "Programme for the Further Implementation of Agenda 21, UNGA Resolution, UN Doc. A/RES/S-19/2," para. 109.

of the primary social convention of GLSD. In this sense, the accomplishments of the CSD were crucial for the evolution of the primary social convention of GLSD. However, as mentioned before, the intention of the global actors was clear about the contours of the roles of the CSD, and the CSD was not designed as a norm-making institutional mechanism. Rather, it was designed as a review and follow-up mechanism for implementation. Furthermore, as clearly underlined by the UNGA, the intention behind Rio+5 was further implementation of Agenda 21 and not to renegotiate its terms. Consequently, I conclude that the primary social convention of GLSD did not come into the existence in 1997. Yet, the experience and achievements of the CSD strongly contributed to the emergence of the primary social convention of GLSD.

2 World Summit on Sustainable Development

2.1 Tightening Steps Towards the Primary Social Convention of GLSD

The WSSD was scheduled to take place just a year after 9/11. This profoundly overshadowed the WSSD and rendered difficult many of its organisational aspects.[50] In terms of participation at the highest level, 104 Heads of State attended this gathering.[51] In the aftermath of Rio+5, in accordance with its outcome, stakeholder dialogue sessions and interactive exchanges were happening between NGOs and States. These sessions were scheduled for the first two days of the CSD's sessions "to enable governments to take serious note of stakeholder views prior to their negotiating of official agreements."[52]

The UNGA resolution providing the details of the WSSD is Resolution 55/199 of 2000.[53] The process leading to the WSSD is quite similar to the process before Rio+5. Therefore, I will not examine it in detail and will only refer to significant developments since 1997, as well as to relevant aspects of the WSSD.

[50] Felix Dodds, Michael Strauss, and Maurice F. Strong, *Only One Earth: The Long Road Via Rio to Sustainable Development* (Routledge, 2012), 95.

[51] Ibid., 96.

[52] Ibid., 77.

[53] "Ten-Year Review of Progress Achieved in the Implementation of the Outcome of the United Nations Conference on Environment and Development, UNGA Resolution, UN Doc. A/RES/55/199," December 20, 2000.

Firstly, novelty in UNGA Resolution 55/199 is the reference to the United Nations Millennium Declaration (Millennium Declaration).[54] The largest number of heads of State and Government ever gathered for a UN meeting was the Millennium Summit.[55] In the context of this book, this new framework will be analysed as a new avenue of commitments in the field of sustainable development, parallel to the path initiated at the UNCED.[56]

Secondly, before the WSSD, there was an increasing awareness about the fragmented picture represented by the booming of UN conferences during the 1990s, each addressing at least some relevant aspects of sustainable development. Despite some similarities among these conferences, the fragmented picture of these norm-making efforts prevented the emergence of the primary social convention of GLSD during the 1990s. Yet, a number of UNGA resolutions were adopted after 1997 to better combine these fragments of various efforts addressing the challenges of sustainable development.[57] Accordingly, in Resolution 55/199, the UNGA noted that the ten-year review of Agenda 21 "should take into account, as appropriate, the results relevant to sustainable development of other [UN] conferences and summits and their follow-up activities."[58]

Thirdly, Agenda 21 and the Rio Declaration were not to be renegotiated and the review was expected to "identify measures for the further implementation of Agenda 21."[59] In that sense, the WSSD was also not planned to be a norm-making exercise. Accordingly, the WSSD was not an instance for the emergence of the primary social convention of GLSD. Nevertheless, the WSSD was a significant step towards the emergence of the primary social convention of GLSD.

Lastly, in terms of global actors to be involved in the process towards the WSSD, UNGA Resolution 55/199 named all the relevant IOs' and

[54] "United Nations Millennium Declaration, UNGA Resolution, UN Doc. A/RES/55/2," September 8, 2000.

[55] Dodds, Strauss, and Strong, *Only One Earth*, 91.

[56] The next section will examine further in depth the Millennium Declaration.

[57] "Enhancing Complementarities among International Instruments Related to Environment and Sustainable Development, UNGA Resolution, UN Doc. A/RES/54/217," December 22, 1999; "International Institutional Arrangements Related to Environment and Development, UNGA Resolution, UN Doc. A/RES/53/186," December 15, 1998.

[58] "Ten-Year Review of Progress Achieved in the Implementation of the Outcome of the United Nations Conference on Environment and Development, UNGA Resolution, UN Doc. A/RES/55/199," para. 11 of the preamble.

[59] Ibid., para. 13 of the preamble.

IGOs' eventual contributions to the review exercise,[60] as well as major groups for their effective contributions at all stages of the preparatory process.[61] Furthermore, in the next resolution with respect to the preparations for the WSSD, the UNGA specifically requested the CSD to organise the details of the "series of events to be held in partnership with stakeholders, the short multi-stakeholder event involving the highest level of representation from major groups and Governments"[62] and reiterated its invitation to "all intergovernmental processes relevant to the Summit to submit their progress reports to the [CSD]."[63] Therefore, it is not possible to notice any backwards steps in terms of global actors in the road to the WSSD.

2.2 *Connecting the Dots in Terms of the Substance of the SDGs*

The two outcome documents of the WSSD were Johannesburg Declaration on Sustainable Development and Johannesburg Plan of Implementation.[64] Both of these documents were welcomed and endorsed by UNGA Resolution 57/253 of 2002.[65] Before examining the two outcome documents, it is worthwhile to refer to certain salient points of UNGA Resolution 57/253.

In terms of substance, the preamble of UNGA Resolution 57/253 reaffirmed "the commitment to achieving the internationally agreed development goals, including those contained in the [Millenium Declaration and in the outcomes of the major [UN] conferences and international agreements since 1992."[66] UNGA Resolution 57/253 is one of the resolutions adopted by the UNGA in the field of sustainable development. However, compared to previous resolutions examined in the present book, this time, in addition to the Rio commitments, there is

[60] "Ten-Year Review of Progress Achieved in the Implementation of the Outcome of the United Nations Conference on Environment and Development, UNGA Resolution, UN Doc. A/RES/55/199," paras. 7–11.

[61] Ibid., para. 12.

[62] "World Summit on Sustainable Development, UNGA Resolution, UN Doc. A/RES/56/226," December 24, 2001, para. 7.

[63] Ibid., para. 14.

[64] "Report of the World Summit on Sustainable Development, UN Doc. A/CONF.199/20," September 4, 2002, 1–5, 6–72.

[65] "World Summit on Sustainable Development, UNGA Resolution, UN Doc. A/RES/57/253."

[66] Ibid., para. 4 of the preamble.

reference to three other categories of commitments, and together with the Rio commitments, they are all presented as parallel lines of the same path of sustainable development. In that sense, the objectives of sustainable development now include the achievement of all these "global commitments," and this is the beginning for the merger of the fragmented efforts in the field of sustainable development.[67]

Another important issue to be underlined in UNGA Resolution 57/253 is the reference to the term "good governance" described as essential for sustainable development.[68] It is important to highlight that this term was almost non-existent before 1997 in UNGA resolutions. However, the term started to be referred to more frequently in many UNGA resolutions, and in UNGA Resolution 57/253, it was described as being essential for sustainable development.

Finally, UNGA Resolution 57/253 highlights that sustainable development is now becoming a key pillar of the UN's global activities and that different categories of global commitments in the field of sustainable development are now part of one, namely, the objectives/goals of sustainable development. UNGA Resolution 57/253 also reaffirms the role and place of the three global actors in the field of sustainable development.[69]

Concerning the Johannesburg Declaration, in terms of substance, the challenges of poverty eradication and human development become central objectives of sustainable development at the WSSD. In the background of this development, there is also the influence of the Millennium Declaration, as poverty eradication is the first one of the MDGs.[70] The Johannesburg Declaration also refers to Agenda 21, the MDGs and the Johannesburg Plan of Implementation as integral parts of one whole of "sustainable development goals and objectives"[71] and uses the term "sustainable

[67] The substance of these different commitments will also be examined further in depth in the upcoming sections.

[68] "World Summit on Sustainable Development, UNGA Resolution, UN Doc. A/RES/57/253," para. 9 of the preamble.

[69] "World Summit on Sustainable Development, UNGA Resolution, UN Doc. A/RES/57/253."

[70] Paragraph 7 of the Johannesburg Declaration reads as follows: "Recognizing that humankind is at a crossroads, we have united in a common resolve to make a determined effort to respond positively to the need to produce a practical and visible plan to bring about poverty eradication and human development (emphasis added)." "Report of the World Summit on Sustainable Development, UN Doc. A/CONF.199/20," page 2, paragraph 7.

[71] Ibid., page 4, paragraphs 20 and 30.

development goals."[72] Accordingly, the WSSD is also one of the key steps leading towards the adoption of the SDGs in 2015.

In terms of the primary social convention of GLSD, in the context of the WSSD, States are also at the centre of the stage. The Johannesburg Declaration—as previous declarations since Stockholm—is a declaration of States. The only difference of the Johannesburg Declaration, instead of "We, heads of State and Government," it begins "We, the representatives of the peoples of the world."[73] In addition to confirming the criterion of States-led, this new wording indicates the start of additional efforts for a deeper level of inclusiveness, up to the involvement of individuals. Precisely, in terms of inclusiveness, the Johannesburg Declaration expressly mentions that the achievement of SDGs and objectives "must be an inclusive process, involving all the major groups and Governments that participated in the historic Johannesburg Summit."[74] The Johannesburg Declaration also underscores that the Summit "has [...] confirmed that significant progress has been made towards achieving a global consensus and partnership among all the people of our planet."[75] Also, the Johannesburg Declaration was adopted by consensus. In terms of universality, in the outcome documents of the WSSD and especially in the Johannesburg Plan of Implementation, the intensity of references to the global dimension of challenges and efforts towards sustainable development is much more on the front.[76] Another interesting novelty is the references to the term of "global society" at the beginning and at the core of the Johannesburg Declaration.[77] These remarks about building a global society to better address "the challenges of poverty eradication and sustainable development confronting all humanity" is a significant step towards the formation of the primary and secondary social convention of GLSD.

Finally, the Johannesburg Declaration contains much more explicit reference in terms of coexistence and harmony with the existing rules of international law.[78] For example, States usually submit interpretative

[72] Ibid., page 5, paragraph 33.

[73] Ibid., paragraph 1.

[74] Ibid., page 5, paragraph 34.

[75] Ibid., page 2, paragraph 10.

[76] Ibid., pages 6–72.

[77] Ibid., page 1, paragraph 2; page 4, paragraph 21.

[78] Paragraph 32 starts as follows: "We reaffirm our commitment to the principles and purposes of the Charter of the United Nations and international law, as well as to the strengthening of multilateralism." Ibid., page 5, paragraph 32.

statements with respect to the adoption of binding rules of international law. In that sense, at the occasion of the adoption of the Johannesburg Plan of Implementation, using the same practice for a non-binding document in terms of international law is an important indication about the nature of these documents that goes beyond being a simple non-binding document in terms of international law. Furthermore, these interpretative statements are also crucial for finding guiding principles about the relationship between the emerging norms/rules of GLSD and the existing rules of international law.[79] The fact that consensus was reached and the outcome documents were adopted despite some important reservations of certain States with respect to the relationship between the outcome documents and existing rules of international law is a reaffirmation of the fifth criterion of pluralism, demonstrating the States' intention for the coexistence of these emerging norms/rules in harmony with the existing rules of international law.

To recapitulate, even though there is no primary social convention of GLSD emerging out of the WSSD, the above explanations demonstrate that the outcome documents were anyway adopted in accordance with the five conclusive criteria of the primary social convention of GLSD. This stability, especially since the UNCED and the UNCHE is highly reassuring and constitutes a significant ground-preparation exercise for the emergence of the primary social convention of GLSD at a later stage.

Finally, in terms of substance, there is a clear nexus between, on the one side, the SDGs and on the other side, the MDGs and the Johannesburg Plan of Implementation.[80] A review of the content of these documents reveals that the origins of the Global Goals and its targets are better traced back to the path coming from the UNCED and passing through Rio+5 and the WSSD, rather than to the path starting from the Millennium

[79] Please refer to the conclusion of the sixth chapter for more insight about the relationship between the rules of international law and of global law of sustainable development.

[80] Goal, corresponding MDG, and corresponding paragraph of Johannesburg Plan of Implementation: Goal 1, MDG 1, para 7; Goal 2, N/A, N/A; Goal 3, MDG 4, 5 and 6, paras. 53–57; Goal 4, MDG 2, para. 62(e); Goal 5, MDG 3, para. 120; Goal 6, Target 10, paras. 8, 25 and 26; Goal 7, N/A, paras. 9 and 20(e); Goal 8, Target 16, paras. 14–24; Goal 9, N/A, paras. 14–24; Goal 10, N/A, para.47; Goal 11, Target 11, para. 11; Goal 12, MDG 7, paras. 15 and 23; Goal 13, N/A, para. 39; Goal 14, N/A, paras. 30–31; Goal 15, N/A, paras. 40 and 45; Goal 16, N/A, para. 5; and Goal 17, MDG 8, paras. 81–136.

Declaration.[81] Such a nexus, in terms of their respective content, between the Johannesburg Plan of Implementation and the SDGs is a significant demonstration about how the efforts to address the challenges of sustainable development at the global level started at the UNCED in 1992, continued at the WSSD in 2002 and until the adoption of the SDGs in 2015.

3 Millennium Summit and Millennium Development Goals

3.1 UN as a Key Global Actor for Sustainable Development

In comparison to the previous sustainable development conferences held in Stockholm, Rio and Johannesburg, one of the main distinctive characteristics of the Millennium Summit was the start of the process. In other UN conferences, the States were at the origin, and the UN was the perfect venue to put the ideas into action. In the case of the Millennium Summit, at the origin, we find a note by the SG.[82] The fact that the idea was the SG's idea is significant in terms of IOs being one of the global actors together with States and NGOs. This was also a personal commitment on the part of the then SG Kofi Annan.[83]

Also, at the origin of the initial draft for the Millennium Summit, there is not a secretariat, a working group or a negotiating body. Instead, there is the SG's report entitled "We the peoples: the role of the United Nations in the twenty-first century" (SG's Report 54/2000) as a basis for further discussions and negotiations.[84] The SG's Report 54/2000 was prepared with contributions from three main sources. The first was a series of informal events organised with UN Members States and NGOs to gather innovative ideas regarding the role of the UN in the twenty-first century;[85] the second was a sort of synthesis report based on the previous UN

[81] This will be further examined and demonstrated in depth in the next section.

[82] "A Millennium Assembly, the United Nations System (Special Commission) and a Millennium Forum: Note by the Secretary-General, UN Doc. A/52/850," March 31, 1998.

[83] David Hulme, "The Millennium Development Goals (MDGs): A Short History of the World's Biggest Promise," SSRN Scholarly Paper (Rochester, NY: Social Science Research Network, September 30, 2009), page 26.

[84] "Report of the Secretary-General, We the Peoples: The Role of the United Nations in the Twenty-First Century, UN Doc. A/54/2000," March 27, 2000.

[85] "A Millennium Assembly, the United Nations System (Special Commission) and a Millennium Forum: Note by the Secretary-General, UN Doc. A/52/850," paragraph 6.

conferences;[86] and the third source was the result of consultations made with other IOs.[87] The last chapter of the SG's Report 54/2000 is a summary of goals and targets—approximately 25 targets—to be considered at the Millennium Summit.[88] Even though the SG's Report 54/2000 was envisioned as a starting point for further discussions, certain important goals and targets agreed in previous UN conferences were not included.[89]

With respect to the scope of the SG's Report 54/2000, 25 proposed targets also addressed—in addition to development, poverty eradication and protection of the environment—the challenges related to human rights, democracy, peace and security, and disarmament, as well as the reform of the UN.

In terms of actors involved in the preparations of the Millennium Summit, a week-long "Millennium Forum" was organised with the participation of "1350 representatives of over 1000 [NGOs] and other [CSOs] from more than 100 countries."[90] Moreover, the Declaration entitled "We the Peoples Millennium Forum Declaration and Agenda for Action: Strengthening the United Nations for the twenty-first century" adopted at the end of the Forum was issued and circulated as an official document of the UNGA.[91] This is a striking development considering the reluctance of the UNGA, less than five years ago, in allowing NGOs to contribute to its work. Also, a representative of the Millennium Forum was included in the list of speakers for the plenary meeting of the Millennium Summit.[92]

[86] Ibid., paragraph 7.

[87] Ibid., paragraphs 8–12.

[88] Ibid., pages 55–57.

[89] For example, goals with respect to reducing child and infant mortality as well as maternal mortality that were agreed upon by all MS—notably in the World Summit for Children, 1990, the International Conference on Population and Development, Cairo, 1994, and the World Conference on Women, Beijing, 1995—were omitted. Hulme, "The Millennium Development Goals (MDGs)," 28–29.

[90] "Millennium Forum, Note by the Secretariat, UN Doc. A/54/959," August 8, 2000, page 2.

[91] "Millennium Forum, Note by the Secretariat, UN Doc. A/54/959." Remember the reluctance of the GA a few years ago in allowing the non-governmental organizations to contribute its work. Less than five years later, the agreement reached by the non-governmental organizations are issued as a GA document.

[92] "Organization of the Millennium Summit of the United Nations, UNGA Resolution, UN Doc. A/RES/54/281," August 11, 2000, para. 11. In total, 149 heads of State or Government, five Vice-Presidents, six representatives from the observers of UNGA, and two representatives from civil society addressed the plenary meeting of the Summit. See, Jerome

At the end of the day, despite positive indications regarding the involvement of the CSOs into the process leading to the Millennium Declaration, the practice preceding the Millennium Summit did not match the threshold established at the UNCED. In previous UN conferences, there was always a preparatory committee composed of MS and with the access open to other actors, such as IOs and NGOs. In the SG's practice preceding the Millennium Summit, it was his office and his team who played the role of the preparatory committee. Accordingly, the involvement of other actors in the process towards the Millennium Summit was limited compared to the practice and threshold established at the UNCED.

3.2 Millennium Declaration and the MDGs

The Millennium Declaration was adopted by consensus at the UNGA in September 2000.[93] I emphasise that the MDGs were not part of the Millennium Declaration. The foremost idea of the SG with this gathering was, "at the dawn of a new millennium, to reaffirm [...] faith in the [United Nations] and its Charter as indispensable foundations of a more peaceful, prosperous and just world."[94] The scope of the Millennium Declaration was well beyond sustainable development. Its first section was reserved for fundamental values that are "essential to international relations in the twenty-first century";[95] the second section was about peace, security and disarmament; there were chapters on human rights, democracy, good governance, refugees, and special needs of Africa, as well the reform of the UN. Only two sections, namely, development and poverty reduction and protecting our common environment, were directly relevant with respect to the challenges of sustainable development. Thus, the Millennium Declaration is not a significant outcome document for the emergence of GLSD, and no primary social convention of GLSD emerged out of the Millennium Summit.

Rather, what is relevant for GLSD is how the MDGs emerged following the Millennium Summit. In fact, there was not a formal adoption process of the MDGs within the UNGA. The MDGs were simply agreed

C. Glenn, Elizabeth Florescu, and Theodore J. Gordon, "Analysis of United Nations Millennium Summit Speeches," April 2001, 1.

[93] "United Nations Millennium Declaration, UNGA Resolution, UN Doc. A/RES/55/2."

[94] Ibid., paragraph 1.

[95] Ibid., paragraph 6.

upon and included as an annex to a report of the SG circulated in 2001 (SG's Report 56/326).[96] To better understand how the MDGs emerged following the Millennium Declaration, it is necessary to go back to the year 1995, during which the idea of the IDGs of the OECD's Development Assistance Committee (DAC) came to light.

A *Groupe de Réflexion* was established in 1995 within the framework of the OECD's ministerial event "to review the future of development aid and the role of DAC."[97] Initially, the *Groupe de Réflexion* gathered a coherent list of agreements reached at the previous UN summits.[98] However, "[t]he DAC meetings were of small numbers of people, did not involve 'shadowing' or 'lobbying' from NGOs and social activists, and [...] the idea of setting targets [...] appealed to the US, UK, Germany and Norway[.]"[99] Thus, the process at the OECD in reaching agreements in terms of goals was significantly different than the UNCED's practice in terms of inclusiveness. A year later negotiations have been finalised,[100] and the IDGs were published in 1996,[101] years before the Millennium Summit.

Six out of eight of the MDGs were, in fact, proposed already with the IDGs, as were the targets associated to these six goals. Therefore, the origins of most of the key MDGs and targets were to be found at the OECD's IDGs. In the upcoming years, the IDGs gained a greater publicity, support and recognition, especially thanks to the efforts of the famous "Utstein Group."[102] This was a group of four women, who were all ministers for international development in their respective countries.[103] Given

[96] "Report of the Secretary-General, Road Map towards the Implementation of the United Nations Millennium Declaration, UN Doc. A/56/326," September 6, 2001, Annex, Millennium development goals, pages 55–58.

[97] Hulme, "The Millennium Development Goals (MDGs)," 13–14.

[98] Ibid., page 14.

[99] Ibid.

[100] "The DAC is a subsidiary body of the OECD. It comprises of a committee, of the representatives of its member governments, and a secretariat to service the committee. Its highest level of decision making is its council, comprised of the Ministers for International Development (or their equivalent). However, for historical reasons the DAC has more autonomous standing than any of the other OECD committees. It has a permanent Chair, who can express their opinions without gaining the approval of the OECD Council." See ibid., page 15, footnote 19.

[101] "Shaping the 21st Century: The Contribution of Development Co-Operation" (OECD, May 6, 1996).

[102] Hulme, "The Millennium Development Goals (MDGs)," 25.

[103] Dutch Minister for Development Co-operation, Ms Eveline Herfkens, British Minister for International Development, Ms Clare Short, German Minister of Economic Co-operation

the success of this group and the IDGs, a "twin track process" was inevitable at the global level, as result of competing sustainable development visions of the UN and the OECD for the twenty-first century.[104] Hulme explains that this difference was the result of: (1) different audiences addressed by these organisations—for the UN, it is all MS as well as all IOs and NGOS, and for the OECD, it is only developed countries that are OECD's members—and, (2) their respective methodologies—for the UN, global conferences with follow-up and review mechanisms; for the OECD, "new public management" techniques of "what works" with specific and measurable targets.[105]

By 2000, the DAC improved the IDGs, especially by adding specific indicators and prepared an updated version entitled "A Better World for All: Progress towards the International Development Goals" (IDGs).[106] In addition to the IMF and the World Bank, the then SG Kofi Annan also endorsed the IDGs. In his words, "it is the product of an unprecedented collaboration among four major multilateral organizations [OCED, IMF, World Bank, UN][,] [a]nd it responds to a specific request from the G-8 countries [...] to help monitor progress in the reduction of poverty worldwide and to guide them in their partnership with developing countries."[107] Annan was heavily criticised for having endorsed the IDGs, especially by NGOs. I recall that the great majority of the IDGs are identical to those of the MDGs. As such, content-wise, there were no downsides for the SG to endorse the IDGs. But, in the opinion of CSOs, associating the UN with the Bretton Woods Institutions, who were perceived by CSOs as the main obstacle to eradicating poverty globally, was not acceptable.

A close comparison of the IDGs and the MDGs reveals the great similarities between all the goals, targets and indicators. Specifically, 6 out of 8 of the MDGs, 6 out of 18 targets and 19 out of 48 indicators of the MDGs were entirely identical to corresponding goals, targets and indicators of the IDGs. Furthermore, the OECD has never intended to have a

and Development, Ms Heidemarie Wieczorek-Zeul, and Norwegian Minister of International Development, Ms Hilde F. Johnson.

[104] Hulme, "The Millennium Development Goals (MDGs)," page 21.

[105] Ibid.

[106] "Better World for All: Progress Towards the International Development Goals" (International Monetary Fund, June 26, 2000).

[107] "Transcript of Press Conference Given by Secretary-General Kofi Annan and Other Officials to Launch Joint Report 'A Better World for All', UN Doc. SG/SM/7466," United Nations Press Release, June 26, 2000.

goal such as the MDG 8. Accordingly, if the MDG 8, and its 7 targets and 17 indicators, are not included in the comparison, 6 out of 7 of the MDGs, 6 out of 11 targets and 19 out of 31 indicators of the first 7 MDGs were entirely identical to corresponding goals, targets and indicators of the IDGs. Accordingly, in addition to most of the goals and targets, most of the MDGs' indicators originate as well from the IDGs' indicators. Consequently, the MDGs circulated in 2001 as an annex to the SG's Report 56/326 are originating from the IDGs rather than the Millennium Declaration, which was adopted by consensus by all MS after considerable and significant inputs of NGOs as a result of the Millennium Forum.

3.3 *Breaking the "Consensus": NGOs and the Emergence of the Primary Social Convention of GLSD*

CSOs were part of the process leading to the Millennium Declaration, even though they were not fully satisfied about the level of their involvement. Things were worse concerning the MDGs. Bissio notes that "the MDGs [were] still largely unknown by [CSOs] at the national level, and there [was not] the same feeling of 'ownership' as citizen groups have over 'Agenda 21'."[108] There was also the unease between CSOs and international financial institutions (IFI). NGOs' declaration adopted in advance of the Millennium Summit emphasises that "[a] single-minded focus on economic growth [...] combined with the [...] policies of [IFI] controlled by the rich creditor nations, are crippling many national economies, exacerbating poverty, eroding human values and destroying the natural environment."[109] Thus, it was shocking for CSOs to witness the SG endorsing the IDGs.[110]

CSOs were also unsatisfied with having the Millennium Declaration altered through the SG's Report 56/326. They argued that "the MDGs were not democratically formulated but put together by bureaucrats and

[108] Roberto Bissio, "Civil Society and the MDGs," *Development Policy Journal* 3, no. April 2003 (April 2003): 153–54.

[109] "Millennium Forum, Note by the Secretariat, UN Doc. A/54/959," page 2, paragraph 4.

[110] See for example, the letter of the General-Secretary of the Geneva-based World Council of Churches to the SG. "Geneva 2000: WCC General Secretary Writes to UN Secretary-General Kofi Annan, WCC Press Release, PR-00-18, of 20 June 2000," United Nations Press Release, June 28, 2000.

agreed on among governments without wider consultation."[111] CSOs were also not satisfied with the final listing of the MDGs, for example, the omission of the issue of reproductive health.[112] Reproductive health goals have been endorsed in previous UN conferences—especially in Cairo, 1994 and in Beijing, 1995—and it was one of the IDGs. Yet, an alliance among the Holy See and some conservative members of the G77 from the Muslim World ensured that the SG crossed off this goal from the Millennium Declaration and later, from the MDGs.[113] Nevertheless, things will change in 2005 and after the 2005 World Summit, the issue of reproductive health entered into the MDGs as a target under MDG 5 together with four new indicators.[114]

This modification of the MDGs years after is significantly telling about the cost of the failure to act in accordance with the criteria, namely inclusiveness and consensus, for adopting rules at the global level in the field of sustainable development. It indicates that, failing to meet these criteria would only result in having incomplete norms and rules, and would require amendments. This change is also telling about the attribute of CSOs as global actors, as they were able to push other global actors to step back with respect to these issues and have them included in the MDGs.

Another significant criticism of CSOs with respect to the content of the 2001 version of the MDGs is about Goal 8 and its targets. In this respect, a plain reading of the targets of Goal 8 reveal that these were the targets for the developed countries and that they were "systematically" worded not to include quantitative and time-bound targets, such as "achieve, by 2015, the target of ..." that were used in defining the first six goals.[115] Furthermore, a footnote was added at the end of the list of the MDGs with respect to the seven indicators of Goal 7, and 17 indicators of Goal 8

[111] Sakiko Fukuda-Parr and David Hulme, "International Norm Dynamics and the 'End of Poverty': Understanding the Millennium Development Goals," *Global Governance: A Review of Multilateralism and International Organizations* 17, no. 1 (February 15, 2011): page 26.

[112] Ibid., page 27.

[113] For a detailed account of this issue, see David Hulme, "Reproductive Health and the Millennium Development Goals: Politics, Ethics, Evidence and an 'Unholy Alliance,'" SSRN Scholarly Paper (Rochester, NY: Social Science Research Network, February 1, 2010).

[114] Ibid., page 23.

[115] Hulme, "The Millennium Development Goals (MDGs)," 41; Fukuda-Parr and Hulme, "International Norm Dynamics and the 'End of Poverty,'" 28.

providing that they were "subject to further refinement."[116] Hulme notes that "[t]hese were the goals that most affected what the rich world was promising to achieve and it wanted some flexibility!"[117]

Notwithstanding countless criticisms, "[f]or all stakeholders, the danger of appearing to object to pulling people out of abject poverty was a position to be avoided."[118] Therefore, with respect to the substance of the MDGs, there was nothing for CSOs to object to. The MDGs were simply not ambitious enough. Accordingly, the CSOs' contestations were not primarily about the substance of the MDGs. It was rather about the process leading to the adoption of the MDGs. Consequently, the MDGs slowly entered into the field of "international development," and they started to be considered as a key component of various policy documents. Yet, the fact remains that one of the key global actors, namely CSOs, were not in agreement with States and IOs with respect to the process leading to the adoption of the MDGs. Furthermore, it is even questionable whether there was even a process. Rather, "the making of the MDGs was an on-going process with no precise beginning and end and without clear 'stages' for identification, formulation, assessment and implementation."[119] Consequently, given the CSOs critics and opposition to the process leading to the adoption of the MDGs, I conclude that the primary social convention of GLSD did not emerge among the three global actors at the time of the Millennium Declaration.

3.4 *Formulating the MDGs: A Sui Generis Process*

Following the Millennium Declaration, UNGA Resolution 55/162 of 2000 with respect to the implementation of the Millennium Declaration was adopted.[120] Resolution 55/162 stressed the need to translate

[116] "Report of the Secretary-General, Road Map towards the Implementation of the United Nations Millennium Declaration, UN Doc. A/56/326," 58.

[117] Hulme, "The Millennium Development Goals (MDGs)," page 40. One of the persons interviewed by Fukuda-Parr and Hulme also noted that the experts who come up with the final version of the Millennium Development Goals "engaged in self-censorship" by avoiding to define specific targets for developed countries given the already limited support of some of them, such as the United States. See Fukuda-Parr and Hulme, "International Norm Dynamics and the 'End of Poverty,'" 28.

[118] Ibid., 26.

[119] Hulme, "The Millennium Development Goals (MDGs)," 43.

[120] "Follow-up to the Outcome of the Millennium Summit, UNGA Resolution, UN Doc. A/RES/55/162," December 14, 2000.

commitments agreed in the Millennium Declaration into concrete action and establishment of a framework for the implementation of the Declaration.[121] Accordingly, the SG was urgently requested "to prepare a long-term 'road map' towards the implementation of the Millennium Declaration."[122] On the other hand, for the OECD, there was "no reason to drop the IDGs it had been working with for five years."[123] The targets and indicators were crucial with respect to the implementation and follow-up processes at the global level. Consequently, in order to avoid a confusing, disorganised and complex reporting and follow-up process, it was indispensable for all to have the Millennium Declaration merged with the IDGs. In this respect, a series of meetings was convened by the World Bank in Washington in March 2001.[124] The participants were specialists from numerous IOs, such as World Bank, IMF, OECD, UN Agencies, delegates from governments, etc.[125]

The Millennium Declaration was substantially modified during these "technical meetings."[126] For example, one of the first-degree goals (para. 19) in the Millennium Declaration—the goal about providing "special assistance to children orphaned by HIV/AIDS"—was totally downgraded to the level of indicators in the MDGs. Similarly, the goal about safe drinking water and slum dwellers were also downgraded to the level of targets in the MDGs.

In addition, UNGA Resolution 55/162 is significantly telling in demonstrating how limited the role was of CSOs in the process leading to the Millennium Declaration and the MDGs. Specifically, while UNGA Resolution 55/162 invited the Bretton Woods institutions "to become involved actively in the implementation of and follow-up to the Summit," NGOs were only cited after the WTO and national parliaments "to ensure their contribution to the implementation of the Declaration."[127] They were also other paragraphs in UNGA Resolution 55/162 addressing the

[121] Ibid., preamble.

[122] Ibid., paragraph 18.

[123] Hulme, "The Millennium Development Goals (MDGs)," 37.

[124] I think it is important to note that, even the venue of this meeting is significantly telling in demonstrating the driving actor behind the content of the MDGs.

[125] Hulme, "The Millennium Development Goals (MDGs)," 37.

[126] Ibid., 40.

[127] "Follow-up to the Outcome of the Millennium Summit, UNGA Resolution, UN Doc. A/RES/55/162," paras. 12–14.

Bretton Woods institutions, WTO etc., while the NGOs were only addressed once.

After the agreement on the MDGs in Washington, the MDGs were officially annexed to the SG's Report 56/326.[128] The SG indicated that the SG's Report 56/326 aimed to "harmonize reporting on the development goals in the Millennium Declaration and the [IDGs]" following the "consultations [...] held among members of the [UN] Secretariat and representatives of IMF, OECD and the World Bank."[129] No reference was made about the involvement of the CSOs, as they were excluded from taking part in the consultations. Nevertheless, the SG did not omit to add a clause with respect to the authoritative value of the MDGs, as follows: "The list of [MDGs] does not undercut in any way agreements on other goals and targets reached at the global conferences of the 1990s."[130] In terms of formality, the UNGA adopted UNGA Resolution 56/95, where it took note of the SG's Report 56/326 and recommended that "[it] be considered as a useful guide in the implementation of the Millennium Declaration by the [UN] system, and invite[d] Member States, as well as the Bretton Woods institutions, the [WTO] and other interested parties [no direct mention of NGOs] to consider the [SG's Report 56/326] when formulating plans for implementing goals related to the [Millennium] Declaration."[131]

Thus, this is actually how the MDGs were born! It is quite striking that they were not even part of a UNGA resolution. For example, the Millennium Declaration was adopted by the UNGA, by consensus (A/RES/55/2). The same goes for the SDGs (A/RES/70/1). Even the indicators of the SDGs were adopted as a UNGA resolution (A/RES/71/313). However, with respect to the MDGs, there is no UNGA resolution listing or mentioning the goals and the targets of the MDGs, let alone their indicators. They were simply annexed to SG's Report 56/326, and this has been simply taken note by the UNGA. Afterwards, 48 indicators of the initial version of the MDGs for monitoring progress of the implementation of the goals entered in force(!) on 8 September 2003. Despite the fact that most of the MS gradually recognised the MDGs and

[128] "Report of the Secretary-General, Road Map towards the Implementation of the United Nations Millennium Declaration, UN Doc. A/56/326."

[129] Ibid., 55.

[130] Ibid.

[131] "Follow-up to the Outcome of the Millennium Summit, UNGA Resolution, UN Doc. A/RES/56/95," December 14, 2001.

referred to them in national policy documents, the United States was not on board.[132] This is the reason behind the fact that the reference to the MDGs in the resolutions of the UNGA was systematically avoided, and, instead, the formulation "internationally agreed development goals, including those in the Millennium Declaration" was always preferred. In other words, none of the UNGA resolutions even included the term of "Millennium Development Goals" until September 2005. As late as 26 August 2005, just weeks in advance of the 2005 World Summit, the US Ambassador to the UN not only demanded hundreds of modifications to the draft of the 2005 World Summit Declaration,[133] but also stated that the MDGs "are solely a Secretariat product, which member states never formally adopted."[134]

Given the US's approach and reservations to the MDGs, I conclude that, in addition to CSOs, there were also significant actors among States, who systematically contested, even until the 2005 World Summit, the process leading to the establishment of the MDGs.[135] This is also another significant evidence revealing that a consensus among global actors was not reached with respect to the process leading to the creation of the MDGs.[136]

[132] Hulme, "The Millennium Development Goals (MDGs)," 42.

[133] Julian Borger, "Bolton Throws UN Summit into Chaos," *The Guardian*, August 26, 2005.

[134] John Bolton, "Letter from Amb. Bolton on Millennium Development Goals," United States Mission to the United Nations, August 26, 2005.

[135] "2005 World Summit Outcome, UNGA Resolution, UNGA Resolution, UN Doc. A/RES/60/1," September 16, 2005. Even the following wording in this resolution with respect to the MDGs signals the absurdness with respect to the origins of the MDGs: "We strongly reiterate our determination to ensure the timely and full realization of the development goals and objectives agreed at the major United Nations conferences and summits, including those agreed at the Millennium Summit that are described as the Millennium Development Goals, which have helped to galvanize efforts towards poverty eradication" (para. 17). Even though the goals agreed in the Millennium Summit are quite different that the MDGs, the resolution ignores that and notes that they are simply ***described*** as MDGs.

[136] Similar reactions were also present among some leading international organisations: To give an example, Fukuda-Parr and Hulme notes the following with respect to the position of the International Labour Organization: "Reportedly, the top management of the [ILO] was dismissive of the IDGs and MDGs exercises. They advised staff that such lists were "a passing fad, we don't need to get mixed up with them ... this is not the only game in town." The ILO position changed in the early 2000s and, by 2005, it was effectively advocating for decent work to become an MDG target." See Fukuda-Parr and Hulme, "International Norm Dynamics and the 'End of Poverty,'" pages 27–28.

3.5 *Table 1: Comparing the MDGs and the IDGs*

Millennium Development Goals (MDGs) Goals, Targets and Indicators	*International Development Goals (IDGs) Goals, Targets and Indicators*
Goal 1: Eradicate extreme poverty and hunger	**Goal 1: Reducing extreme poverty***
Target 1.A: Halve, between 1990 and 2015, the proportion of people whose income is less than one dollar a day	*The proportion of people living in extreme poverty in developing countries should be reduced by at least one-half between 1990 and 2015**
1.1 Proportion of population below $1.25 (PPP) per day	People living on less than $1 a day*
1.2 Poverty gap ratio	Incidence times depth of poverty*
1.3 Share of poorest quintile in national consumption	Poorest fifth's share of national consumption*
Target 1.B: Achieve full and productive employment and decent work for all, including women and young people	
1.4 **Growth rate of GDP per person employed**	
1.5 **Employment-to-population ratio**	
1.6 **Proportion of employed people living below $1.25 (PPP) per day**	
1.7 **Proportion of own-account and contributing family workers in total employment**	
Target 1.C: Halve, between 1990 and 2015, the proportion of people who suffer from hunger	Proportion of children under 5 who are underweight*
1.8 Prevalence of underweight children under-five years of age	
1.9 Proportion of population below minimum level of dietary energy consumption	
Goal 2: Achieve universal primary education	**Goal 2: Universal primary education***
Target 2.A: Ensure that, by 2015, children everywhere, boys and girls alike, will be able to complete a full course of primary schooling	*There should be universal primary education in all countries by 2015**
2.1 Net enrolment ratio in primary education	Net enrolment in primary education*
2.2 Proportion of pupils starting grade 1 who reach last grade of primary	Completion of 4th grade of primary education*
2.3 Literacy rate of 15–24-year-olds, women and men	Literacy rate of 15–24-year-olds*

(continued)

(continued)

Millennium Development Goals (MDGs) Goals, Targets and Indicators	*International Development Goals (IDGs) Goals, Targets and Indicators*
Goal 3: Promote gender equality and empower women	**Goal 3: Gender equality***
Target 3.A: Eliminate gender disparity in primary and secondary education, preferably by 2005, and in all levels of education no later than 2015 3.1 Ratios of girls to boys in primary, secondary and tertiary education 3.2 Share of women in wage employment in the non-agricultural sector 3.3 Proportion of seats held by women in national parliament	*Progress towards gender equality and the empowerment of women should be demonstrated by eliminating gender disparity in primary and secondary education by 2005** Ratio of girls to boys in primary and secondary education* Ratio of literate females to males (15–24-year-olds)
Goal 4: Reduce child mortality	**Goal 4: Reduce infant and child mortality***
Target 4.A: Reduce by two-thirds, between 1990 and 2015, the under-five mortality rate 4.1 Under-five mortality rate 4.2 Infant mortality rate 4.3 Proportion of 1-year-old children immunised against measles	*The death rates for infants and children under the age of five years should be reduced in each developing country by two-thirds between 1990 and 2015** Under-5 mortality rate* Infant mortality rate*
Goal 5: Improve maternal health	**Goal 5: Reduce maternal mortality***
Target 5.A: Reduce by three quarters, between 1990 and 2015, the maternal mortality ratio 5.1 Maternal mortality ratio 5.2 Proportion of births attended by skilled health personnel	*The rate of maternal mortality should be reduced by three-quarters between 1990 and 2015** Maternal mortality ratio* Births attended by skilled health personnel*
Target 5.B: Achieve, by 2015, universal access to reproductive health 5.3 **Contraceptive prevalence rate** 5.4 **Adolescent birth rate** 5.5 **Antenatal care coverage** 5.6 **Unmet need for family planning**	

(*continued*)

(continued)

Millennium Development Goals (MDGs) Goals, Targets and Indicators	*International Development Goals (IDGs) Goals, Targets and Indicators*
Goal 6: Combat HIV/AIDS, malaria and other diseases	**Goal 6: Reproductive health*** *Access should be available through the primary healthcare system to reproductive health services for all individuals of appropriate ages, no later than 2015** Contraceptive prevalence rate*
Target 6.A: Have halted by 2015 and begun to reverse the spread of HIV/AIDS	HIV prevalence in 15–24-year-old pregnant women*
6.1 HIV prevalence among population aged 15–24 years	
6.2 Condom use at last high-risk sex	
6.3 Proportion of population aged 15–24 years with comprehensive correct knowledge of HIV/AIDS	
6.4 Ratio of school attendance of orphans to school attendance of non-orphans aged 10–14 years	
Target 6.B: Achieve, by 2010, universal access to treatment for HIV/AIDS for all those who need it	
6.5 **Proportion of population with advanced HIV infection with access to antiretroviral drugs**	
Target 6.C: Have halted by 2015 and begun to reverse the incidence of malaria and other major diseases	
6.6 Incidence and death rates associated with malaria	
6.7 **Proportion of children under 5 sleeping under insecticide-treated bed nets**	
6.8 **Proportion of children under 5 with fever who are treated with appropriate anti-malarial drugs**	
6.9 Incidence, prevalence and death rates associated with tuberculosis	
6.10 Proportion of tuberculosis cases detected and cured under directly observed treatment short course	

(*continued*)

(continued)

Millennium Development Goals (MDGs) Goals, Targets and Indicators	*International Development Goals (IDGs) Goals, Targets and Indicators*
Goal 7: Ensure environmental sustainability *Target 7.A: Integrate the principles of sustainable development into country policies and programmes and reverse the loss of environmental resources* ***Target 7.B: Reduce biodiversity loss, achieving, by 2010, a significant reduction in the rate of loss*** 7.1 Proportion of land area covered by forest 7.2 CO_2 emissions, total, per capita and per $1 GDP (PPP) 7.3 **Consumption of ozone-depleting substances** 7.4 **Proportion of fish stocks within safe biological limits** 7.5 **Proportion of total water resources used** 7.6 **Proportion of terrestrial and marine areas protected** 7.7 **Proportion of species threatened with extinction**	**Goal 7: Environment*** *There should be a current national strategy for sustainable development, in the process of implementation, in every country by 2005, so as to ensure that current trends in the loss of environmental resources are effectively reversed at both global and national levels by 2015** Forest area as a percentage of national surface area* Carbon dioxide emissions per capita* Countries with effective processes for sustainable development Energy efficiency: GDP per unit of energy use Biodiversity: protected land area*
Target 7.C: Halve, by 2015, the proportion of people without sustainable access to safe drinking water and basic sanitation 7.8 Proportion of population using an improved drinking water source 7.9 Proportion of population using an improved sanitation facility *Target 7.D: By 2020, to have achieved a significant improvement in the lives of at least 100 million slum dwellers* 7.10 Proportion of urban population living in slums	Population with access to an improved water source*
Goal 8: Develop a global partnership for development	Not part of the IDGs.

Targets and indicators that are bold in the first column are the targets and indicators that were added to the original list of the MDGs. Three new targets and 18 new indicators were added to the MDGs. In the previous version, Goal 6 on reproductive health of the IDGs was not part of the MDGs. In the updated version of the MDGs, the issue of reproductive health was one of the three new targets. Accordingly, all seven goals of the IDGs became part of the MDGs in 2005.[137] IDGs' goals, targets and indicators with an asterisk indicate the existence of an identical, goal, target or indicator in the list of the MDGs. In addition of the seven goals of the IDGs, all seven targets of the IDGs were also part of the updated version of the MDGs. With respect to the IDGs' indicators, except three of them,[138] they were all part of the MDGs.

4 UN Conferences of the 1990s

It is outside the scope of this book to review all the major UN conferences of the 1990s to examine whether some of the agreements reached in these conferences made their way to the MDGs. However, it is important to have at least some perspectives with respect to the relationship between these conferences and the MDGs, as despite the contrary arguments of some CSOs,[139] the SG and other heads of IOs involved in the preparations of the MDGs consistently argued that both the MDGs and the IDGs were prepared in accordance with the outcome of these UN conferences.[140] The following are the key UN summits and conferences held in the field of sustainable development during the 1990s:[141]

- Global Conference on the Sustainable Development of Small Island Developing States, April/May 1994, Barbados (Barbados Conference);
- International Conference on Population and Development, September 1994, Cairo (Cairo Conference);

[137] Six goals of the IDGs as goals of the MDGs, one goal of the IDGs as a target of the MDGs.

[138] The following are the 3 indicators of the IDGs that were not part of the MDGs: Ratio of literate females to males (15–24-year-olds); Countries with effective processes for sustainable development; and Energy efficiency: GDP per unit of energy use. It is worth mentioning that the ratio of literate females to males was part of the original version of the MDGs' list but was deleted with the modifications following the 2005 World Summit.

[139] See Chap. 4, Sect. 3.4.

[140] See Chap 4, Sects. 3.3 and 3.5.

[141] The IDGs were first issued in May 1996, only the conferences before that are relevant for the IDGs.

- World Summit for Social Development, March 1995, Copenhagen (Copenhagen Conference);
- Fourth World Conference on Women: Action for Equality, Development and Peace, September 1995, Beijing (Beijing Conference);
- United Nations Conference on Human Settlements, June 1996, Istanbul (Istanbul Conference);
- 21st Special Session of the UNGA, June/July 1999 (ICPD+5);
- 22nd Special Session of the UNGA, September 1999 (Barbados+5);
- 23rd Special Session of the UNGA, June 2000 (Beijing+5);
- 24th Special Session of the UNGA, June 2000 (Copenhagen+5);
- 25th Special Session of the UNGA, June 2001 (Istanbul+5);
- 26th Special Session of the UNGA, June 2001, Commitment on HIV/AIDS.

One of the key practices established after the UNCED was to organise subsequent conferences every five years in order to review the implementation of the commitments made. This practice became the key component of all the UN conferences of the 1990s related to the issues of sustainable development. This practice started with the UNCED and Rio+5. This demonstrates also how significant the influence of the UNCED was in terms of standard setting with respect to the process related to global mechanisms in the field of sustainable development.[142]

The Target 8.C of the MDGs that reads:

> Target 8.C: Address the special needs of landlocked developing countries and small island developing States (through the Programme of Action for the Sustainable Development of Small Island Developing States and the outcome of the twenty-second special session of the GA)

Accordingly, the Programme of Action of the Barbados Conference,[143] and the outcome of Barbados+5 are both fully part of the MDGs.[144] Thus,

[142] See and also recall Chap. 3, Sect. 2.3 where we demonstrated that, how even the Working Group of the Committee on Non-Governmental Organizations of the ECOSOC was inspired by the practice established during the preparations for the Rio Conference with respect to the participation of non-governmental organisations to its work.

[143] "Report of the Global Conference on the Sustainable Development of Small Island Developing States, UN Doc. A/CONF.167/9," May 6, 1994.

[144] "Declaration and State of Progress and Initiatives for the Future Implementation of the Programme of Action for the Sustainable Development of Small Island Developing States, UNGA Resolution, UN Doc. A/RES/S-22/2," September 28, 1999.

at the origin of this Target 8.C, there is the Barbados Conference and Barbados+5. This means that, parallel to the efforts concretised with "Rio commitments" in 1992 and continued with Rio+5 and the WSSD, other global efforts in some other aspects of sustainable development were being concretised at other venues, such as the Barbados Conference. And these "Barbados commitments" were further concretised under the MDGs, establishing a reaffirmation of these commitments by global actors through the MDGs.

The MDG 2 aims to achieve universal primary education and its target 2.A provides: "Ensure that, by 2015, children everywhere, boys and girls alike, will be able to complete a full course of primary schooling." The MDG 3 promotes gender equality and empower women and its target 3.A provides: "Eliminate gender disparity in primary and secondary education, preferably by 2005, and in all levels of education no later than 2015." The MDG 4 aims to reduce child mortality and its target 4.A provides: "Reduce by two-thirds, between 1990 and 2015, the under-five mortality rate." Similarly, the outcome document of the Cairo Conference provides the goals of "universal primary education in all countries before the year 2015," "the widest and earliest possible access by girls and women to secondary and higher levels of education" (para. 4.18), as well as "reduction in infant and under-5 child mortality rates by one third" (para. 8.13).[145]

With respect to the targets of the MDGs on reproductive health and HIV/AIDS, the Programme of Action of the Cairo Conference also provides "the goal [...] to ensure universal availability of and access to high-quality reproductive health and family-planning services" (para. 13.22).[146] Similar references exist also in the outcome document of the Beijing Conference of 1995.[147]

[145] "Report of the International Conference on Population and Development, UN Doc. A/CONF.171/13," October 18, 1994; See also; "Key Actions for the Further Implementation of the Programme of Action of the International Conference on Population and Development, UNGA Resolution, UN Doc. A/RES/S-21/2," July 2, 1999.

[146] "Report of the International Conference on Population and Development, UN Doc. A/CONF.171/13," 99.

[147] "Report of the Fourth World Conference on Women, UN Doc. A/CONF.177/20," October 17, 1995, paragraph 80(b), page 31; See also; "Further Actions and Initiatives to Implement the Beijing Declaration and Platform for Action, UNGA Resolution, UN Doc. A/RES/S-23/3," June 10, 2000; "Report of the Fourth World Conference on Women, UN Doc. A/CONF.177/20," paragraph 106(i), page 42.

The Programme Action of the Copenhagen Conference includes almost all the goals and targets of the MDGs, with the exception of the MDG 8.[148]

The Target 7.D of the MDGs provides: "By 2020, to have achieved a significant improvement in the lives of at least 100 million slum dwellers." Similarly, the UNGA Resolution adopted after Istanbul+5 "reiterate[d] the aim of the 'Cities without Slums' initiative to make a significant improvement in the lives of at least 100 million slum dwellers by 2020."[149]

It follows that, even though the goals and targets agreed upon in UN conferences are not exactly identical to those that are listed in the MDGs, it is obvious that there is a significant nexus between them. Accordingly, it is possible to conclude that, ***in terms of substance and content***, the origins of the MDGs are mainly to be found in the agreements reached at the UN summits and conferences of the 1990s. This means that the MDGs were simply representing a reaffirmation of these goals of sustainable development agreed to by global actors at previous UN Conferences of the 1990s. In other words, notwithstanding a highly different format, the MDGs were simply a reiteration of formerly and globally agreed goals of sustainable development.

Yet, what would be the significance of this conclusion with respect to the nexus between the MDGs and the IDGs? Regarding their style and format, they are (1) concrete and simple; (2) with quantified time-bound targets; (3) short enough to fit into a single PowerPoint slide; and (4) measurable with specifically designed indicators.[150] Thus, I conclude that, ***in terms of style and format***, the MDGs' origins are to be found in the IDGs.

[148] "Report of the World Summit for Social Development, UN Doc. A/CONF.166/9," April 19, 1995, paragraph 36, pages 50–52; See also; "Further Initiatives for Social Development, UNGA Resolution, UN Doc. A/RES/S-24/2," July 1, 2000.

[149] "Declaration on Cities and Other Human Settlements in the New Millennium, UNGA Resolution, UN Doc. A/RES/S-25/2," June 9, 2001, paragraph 46, page 8; See also; "Report of the United Nations Conference on Human Settlements, UN Doc. A/CONF.165/14," August 7, 1996.

[150] Fukuda-Parr and Hulme, "International Norm Dynamics and the 'End of Poverty,'" page 23.

5 Conclusion and Progress Appraisal—Third DSD (1992–2002)

5.1 Secondary Social Convention—Actors

First of all, during this third DSD, the outcome documents of the UNCED were described and referred to as a new and unique global partnership among the three global actors to achieve the objectives of the sustainable development.

Secondly, despite the UNGA's reluctance in allowing NGOs to contribute to its work in the beginning of the 1990s, thanks to the performance of NGOs at the meetings of the CSD, especially during the stakeholder dialogues held in advance of the CSD's sessions, it was clear that, in the eyes of all other global actors, the involvement of NGOs in the work of the UNGA during Rio+5 was a one-way street for achieving sustainable development at all levels. This led to an historical development and opened the doors for NGOs to participate in the UNGA's plenary debate. Even though this exception was not supposed to create a precedent, the practice of holding stakeholder dialogues with NGOs before major UN conferences became a *sine qua non* feature of every global conference in the field of sustainable development. Indeed, this practice established at the sessions of the CSD is what is behind the idea of Millennium Forum held before the Millennium Summit.

Thirdly, until the beginning of 1990s, IOs were rather considered as subjects of the global commitments made in the field of sustainable development. Accordingly, they were primarily expected to support States to achieve these commitments, and, where it is relevant, to integrate such commitments into their internal processes. However, the novelty of third DSD is that IOs started to make their own contributions to the substance of the objectives of sustainable development and they have become active and genuine actors at the global level. A notable example of this development is the initiative taken by the SG to organise the Millennium Summit that eventually gave birth to the MDGs.

Fourthly, in UNGA Resolution 57/253 about the implementation of the outcomes of the WSSD, the UNGA urged States, IOs and CSOs, in other words, all three of the global actors, to ensure the effective implementation of and follow-up to the Johannesburg Declaration and its plan of action.[151]

In conclusion, it would be impossible to provide an exact time of birth for the secondary social convention of GLSD; especially due to its nature—being a social convention and not a formal agreement among some global actors. Nevertheless, I conclude that the secondary social convention of GLSD was fully operational, at the latest, at the beginning of the new millennium. In the framework of this book, the existence of such a secondary social convention among three global actors signifies that the adoption of any sort of rules of sustainable development at the global level would require the common endorsement of these three global actors. In other words, only commonly adopted acts by these three global actors would potentially have the status of laws of GLSD. The question whether these common acts have such a status depends on the existence of a primary social convention among these three global actors.

5.2 *Primary Social Convention and Conclusive Criteria*

I have already identified five potential conclusive criteria for the primary social convention of GLSD, namely, (1) States-led, (2) inclusiveness, (3) consensus, (4) universality and (5) pluralism. I concluded that, at the end of the second DSD, it was still not possible to talk about the existence of the primary social convention of GLSD that is composed of these conclusive criteria agreed among the three global actors.

Regarding the progress during the third DSD, first, the CSD was designed to be the key institution regarding the implementation of Agenda 21 and objectives of sustainable development. Its design fully represents all the features of the five criteria: only States are entitled to be members of the CSD (States-led). However, it makes its deliberations in the most inclusive way. Recall the significant role played by the EU in the CSD, as well as stakeholder dialogues with IOs and CSOs (inclusiveness). Its decisions are adopted by consensus, and actors other than States are informally and impliedly part of this consensus. The CSD deals with global concerns in the field of sustainable development (universality), and it observes the rules of international law (pluralism). Similarly, the process leading to the

[151] "World Summit on Sustainable Development, UNGA Resolution, UN Doc. A/RES/57/253," para. 4.

adoption of the outcome documents of the WSSD was also conducted in accordance with these five potential conclusive criteria.

Despite the presence of all these potential conclusive criteria in the framework of the CSD and the WSSD, the third DSD was an exceptional period with respect to a variety of major UN conferences held during this decade. These major UN conferences addressed different aspects of sustainable development throughout the 1990s, and the fragmented picture of these norm-making efforts prevented the emergence of the primary social convention of GLSD.

With respect to the Millennium Summit and the MDGs, there were many obstacles to even considering the adoption of the MDGs as an exemplary norm-making exercise for the identification and recognition of rules as the laws of GLSD. At the global actors' level, in addition to open contestations of the NGOs, the United States kept contesting the MDGs until September 2005. Thus, not only was there no agreement among the three global actors with respect to the process leading to the establishment of the MDGs, but criteria such as inclusiveness and consensus were also not fulfilled. It is important to underline that the fact that the United States succeeded in preventing any reference to the MDGs in the resolutions of the UNGA from September 2001 until September 2005, proves, *a contrario*, the validity of the criterion of consensus as one of the conclusive criteria for the existence of the primary social convention of GLSD. Consequently, no primary social convention of GLSD emerged out of the process leading to the MDGs.

In conclusion, despite the reaffirmation of our five potential conclusive criteria in the context of distinct and separate processes, the primary social convention of GLSD was yet to emerge at the beginning of the fourth DSD (2002–2012).

5.3 *Substance*

To begin with, in terms of origins of the SDGs, it is fascinating to see that the appearance of the term of "goals of sustainable development" in the UNGA resolutions on the implementation of Agenda 21 during the period before the WSSD. The term was mentioned in some of the SG's reports before 1995. What is remarkable is that the term almost became part of the usual vocabulary of the UNGA resolutions regarding the implementation of Agenda 21 establishing the strong nexus between the two.[152]

Moreover, States were invited to voluntarily submit their national reports to the CSD regarding their implementation of Rio commitments. This idea is basically the predecessor of the "voluntary national reviews" mechanism under the SDGs. Likewise, the idea of using indicators for a better review and appraisal process has existed since the CSD, and it gained further momentum with the MDGs.

In addition, considering the fact that each one of the outcome documents of major UN conferences, as well as the resolutions adopted at the end of the special sessions of the UNGA, contain hundreds of pages, they offer much richer content than the MDGs. This is the reason why the origins of SDGs are better traced back to the path coming from the UNCED and passing through Rio+5 and the WSSD, rather than the path starting from the Millennium Declaration and the MDGs.

Furthermore, to better understand the evolution of the MDGs into the SDGs, I conclude that, ***in terms of substance and content***, the origins of the MDGs were mainly to be found in the agreements reached at major UN conferences held during the third DSD, and ***in terms of style and format***, they were mainly to be found in the OECD's IDG.[153] In the same vein, I conclude that the origins of the SDGs are to be found, ***in terms of substance and content***, in the outcome documents of the UNCED, Rio+5 and the WSSD—and also from the outcome documents of all other major

[152] "Implementation of and Follow-up to the Outcome of the United Nations Conference on Environment and Development and the Nineteenth Special Session of the General Assembly, UNGA Resolution, UN Doc. A/RES/54/218," December 22, 1999, paras. 5–6, third preambular paragraph; "Implementation of and Follow-up to the Outcome of the United Nations Conference on Environment and Development and the Nineteenth Special Session of the General Assembly, UNGA Resolution, UN Doc. A/RES/53/188," December 15, 1998, para. 3, of the preamble.

[153] The role of OECD countries led by the US cannot be underestimated in the rise of managerialist perspectives to law at the global level. See in Mikhail Xifaras, "The Global Turn in Legal Theory," *Canadian Journal of Law and Jurisprudence* 29 (2016): page 219. For other perspectives in this respect, see; Anne van Mulligen, "Framing Deformalisation in Public International Law," *Transnational Legal Theory* 6, no. 3–4 (October 2, 2015): 635–60; David Restrepo Amariles, "Supping with the Devil? Indicators and the Rise of Managerial Rationality in Law," *International Journal of Law in Context* 13, no. 4 (December 2017): 465–84; Friedrich Kratochwil, "How (Il)Liberal Is the Liberal Theory of Law? Some Critical Remarks on Slaughter's Approach," *Comparative Sociology* 9, no. 1 (January 1, 2010): 120–45.

UN conferences of the 1990s—and, ***in terms of style and format***, in the MDGs.

Last but not least, the level of evolution from the MDGs to the SDGs is enormous. For example, only in terms of numbers, while there are only 8 goals, 21 targets and 60 indicators in the case of MDGs, the SDGs are much more sophisticated and are composed of 17 goals, 169 targets and 232 indicators. For example, in the MDGs, eradication of extreme poverty and hunger is part of the same goal, Goal 1, and there is only one target and three indicators with respect to the objective for the eradication of poverty. However, in the case of SDGs, the objective for the eradication of poverty is one of the 17 goals and has its own 7 specific targets and 12 indicators. Therefore, given the SDGs' nexus with the MDGs, the outcome documents of major UN conferences of the 1990s, and the crucial contribution of all these processes in providing a unique process of trial and error, the SDGs represent today a much more sophisticated framework in order to achieve the objectives of sustainable development.

CHAPTER 5

Back to Rio After 20 Years: For the Sake of Sustainable Development

Starting from 2002, the "Rio commitments," the commitments to achieve the MDGs and the commitments in the outcomes of the major UN conferences of the 1990s were described as one and they were all part of "global commitments" to achieve the objectives of sustainable development. Thus, firstly, in this chapter, how these global efforts on sustainable development have been merged will be examined. Secondly, the most significant event of this fourth DSD, is of course, the UNCSD. As such, the significance of the UNCSD with respect to the emergence of the primary social convention of GLSD will also be addressed.[1]

[1] The CSD kept its sessions until 2012, and its reports provide important insight with respect to the efforts in implementing global commitments in the field of sustainable development. However, it is not necessary to examine in depth every step of implementation during the period from 2002 to 2012. Instead, where it is relevant, references will be made to the work of the CSD, especially in the context of the preparations of the Rio+20, regarding its implications for the emergence of the primary social convention of GLSD.

H. Göksan, *Global Law of Sustainable Development*, Global Issues,
https://doi.org/10.1007/978-3-031-74547-8_5

1 Merging Global Efforts on Sustainable Development Around the MDGs

1.1 Period Before the World Summit of 2005

Recall that the nexus between the major UN Conferences of the 1990s and the Millennium Declaration/the MDGs was quite significant, especially in terms of the substance of their respective outcome documents. Consequently, holding plus-five, plus-ten review conferences for each of the major UN conferences of the 1990s and for the Millennium Declaration would constitute significant overlaps and would overshadow the efforts for the implementation of the outcomes of all these conferences.

Also recall that the UNCED was the first one of the major UN conferences of the 1990s. The conferences in Barbados, Cairo, Copenhagen, Beijing and Istanbul followed suit. The WSSD was organised as a ten-year review exercise of the UNCED and it was already planned before the Millennium Summit. Normally, similar ten-year reviews would have been held for other major UN conferences. Nevertheless, given the significant overlaps between the outcome of these conferences and the Millennium Declaration, the ECOSOC—as the principal organ responsible for the follow-up of these conferences—recommended the GA to examine "how best to address the reviews of the implementation of the outcomes of the major [UN] conferences […] of the 1990s, including their format and periodicity[.]"[2] Following this suggestion, the UNGA included this issue in its agenda[3] and requested the SG to submit a report "ensuring full integration between the review and follow-up processes of the Millennium Summit and of other conferences."[4]

Another novelty of the UNGA's close follow-up of the Millennium Declaration is the approach followed with respect to the review of the

[2] "Integrated and Coordinated Implementation of and Follow-up to the Outcomes of the Major United Nations Conferences and Summits, UN. Doc. E/RES/2001/21.," July 26, 2001, para. 4.

[3] "Integrated and Coordinated Implementation of and Follow-up to the Outcomes of the Major United Nations Conferences and Summits in the Economic and Social Fields, UNGA Resolution, UN Doc. A/RES/56/211," December 21, 2001.

[4] "Integrated and Coordinated Implementation of and Follow-up to the Outcomes of the Major United Nations Conferences and Summits, UN. Doc. E/RES/2001/21.," para. 7; "Integrated and Coordinated Implementation of and Follow-up to the Outcomes of the Major United Nations Conferences and Summits in the Economic and Social Fields, UNGA Resolution, UN Doc. A/RES/56/211," para. 3.

implementation process. The review process of the UNCED has been done through the CSD. However, in the case of the Millennium Declaration, in its Resolution 56/95 of 2001, the UNGA requested the SG "to prepare an annual report and a comprehensive report every five years on progress achieved by the [UN] system and Member States towards implementing the Millennium Declaration."[5] In other words, the tasks of the ECOSOC functional commissions, such as the CSD, were to be assumed by the SG in the case of the Millennium Declaration. Accordingly, the usual three-tiered system for the follow-up of the UN conferences—carried out by the functional commissions, the ECOSOC and the UNGA—were replaced, in the context of the Millennium Declaration, by close follow-up of the UNGA through the annual reports and five-year comprehensive reports of the SG. Given the significant nexus between the outcomes of the major UN conferences and the Millennium Declaration, there was a clear overlap in the tasks assigned to the SG and to the functional commissions.[6] Furthermore, in this new structure, the role of the ECOSOC was vanishing as the SG was playing the role of the functional commissions and was reporting directly to the UNGA.

A first step was made by the UNGA in its Resolution 57/144 of 2002 towards a better coordination of the review processes for the implementation of the outcomes of the major UN conferences.[7] Accordingly, it was agreed to attach more importance, coherence and visibility to the implementation of the Millennium Declaration and its review process. Thus, the UNGA's intention was to mainstream the MDGs, and the MDGs took the stage in the field of sustainable development in its entirety.

Other steps made by the UNGA for a better coordination were to establish an ad hoc working group to "produce concrete

[5] "Follow-up to the Outcome of the Millennium Summit, UNGA Resolution, UN Doc. A/RES/56/95," para. 3.

[6] The Secretary-General, in his report about the coordination of the implementation processes, politely and positively mentions this overlap as follows: "The goals and targets of the Millennium Declaration are closely linked with the key objectives agreed upon at major United Nations conferences and summits. The follow-up process to the Millennium Summit thus creates new opportunities to reinforce the key objectives of other conferences and to accelerate momentum for their implementation." See "Report of the Secretary-General, Integrated and Coordinated Implementation of and Follow-up to the Outcomes of the Major United Nations Conferences and Summits, Including the Millennium Summit UN Doc. A/57/75-E/2002/57," May 7, 2002, para. 10.

[7] "Follow-up to the Outcome of the Millennium Summit, UNGA Resolution, UN Doc. A/RES/57/144," December 16, 2002, para. 7.

recommendations to ensure an integrated and coordinated follow-up to the outcomes of the [UN] conferences" and to put on hold the decisions on "follow-up to conferences whose ten-year anniversaries [were] imminent."[8] By putting the decisions about these review exercises on hold, the UNGA implicitly decided to integrate these review exercises into the framework of the 2005 World Summit.[9] With respect to the efforts for a better road map for an integrated and coordinated implementation of and follow-up to the outcomes of the major UN conferences, despite the work of ad hoc working group, a concrete way forward was yet to be found even after the 2005 World Summit.

1.2 2005 World Summit

Regarding the MDGs, things have changed with the 2005 World Summit. There were clear and direct references to the MDGs in the 2005 World Summit Outcome.[10] In addition, three new targets were added to the goals and one target was moved from Goal 8 to Goal 1 with some modification in the wording.[11] Later, following the SG's Report A/61/1 of

[8] "Integrated and Coordinated Implementation of and Follow-up to the Outcomes of the Major United Nations Conferences and Summits in the Economic and Social Fields, UNGA Resolution, UN Doc. A/RES/57/270," December 20, 2002, paragraphs 3 and 6. See also the resolution adopted on the report of the ad hoc working group; "Integrated and Coordinated Implementation of and Follow-up to the Outcomes of the Major United Nations Conferences and Summits in the Economic and Social Fields, UNGA Resolution, UN Doc. A/RES/57/270 B," June 23, 2003.

[9] "Follow-up to the Outcome of the Millennium Summit and Integrated and Coordinated Implementation of and Follow-up to the Outcomes of the Major United Nations Conferences and Summits in the Economic and Social Fields, UNGA Resolution, UN Doc. A/RES/58/291," May 6, 2004.

[10] For example, paragraph 17 provides: "We strongly reiterate our determination to ensure the timely and full realization of the development goals and objectives agreed at the major United Nations conferences and summits, including those agreed at the Millennium Summit that are described as the Millennium Development Goals, which have helped to galvanize efforts towards poverty eradication." See "2005 World Summit Outcome, UNGA Resolution, UNGA Resolution, UN Doc. A/RES/60/1," paragraph 17.

[11] Target 16 of Goal 8, "in cooperation with developing countries, develop and implement strategies for decent and productive work for youth" was replaced with Target 1.B, Goal 1 "Achieve full and productive employment and decent work for all, including women and young people." Three new targets were:

- Target 5.B: Achieve, by 2015, universal access to reproductive health

2006, further technical works were conducted. Consequently, some indicators were reformulated, 18 new indicators were added to the MDGs and 6 indicators were removed;[12] the final official list of MDGs indicator became "effective" on 15 January 2008.

As Rio+5 was the plus-five and the WSSD was the plus-ten review exercise of the UNCED, the 2005 World Summit was the plus-five review exercise of the Millennium Summit. As such, it was not envisioned to be a norm-making exercise by global actors. The idea was also not to renegotiate the agreements reached at the Millennium Summit. However, due to the very puzzled itinerary followed for the establishment of the MDGs, some reformulations and updates were indispensable to fix certain "bugs" for having an updated version of the MDGs. Consequently, the 2005 World Summit was not an appropriate instance for the emergence of the primary social convention of GLSD.

1.3 Period Before the UNGA's High-Level Plenary Meeting of 2010

Recall that the key question with respect to an integrated and coordinated implementation of and follow-up to the outcomes of the major UN conferences was about the role of the ECOSOC, given the new role assumed by the UNGA in exercising a close follow-up for the implementation of the MDGs. Accordingly, in the outcome document of the 2005 World Summit (UNGA Resolution 60/1), the UNGA stressed that "the

- Target 6.B: Achieve, by 2010, universal access to treatment for HIV/AIDS for all those who need it
- Target 7.B: Reduce biodiversity loss, achieving, by 2010, a significant reduction in the rate of loss

For official sources of these modifications, see "Report of the Secretary-General on the Work of the Organization, UN Doc. A/61/1," August 16, 2006, paragraph 24; "2005 World Summit Outcome, UNGA Resolution, UNGA Resolution, UN Doc. A/RES/60/1," paragraphs 47, 57(c), 57(d) and 57(g).

[12] The following are the six indicators that were removed: 10. Ratio of literate women to men, 15–24 years old; 22. Proportion of population in malaria-risk areas using effective malaria prevention and treatment measures; 26. Ratio of area protected to maintain biological diversity to surface area; 27. Energy use (kg oil equivalent) per $1 GDP (PPP); 29. Proportion of population using solid fuels; 45. Unemployment rate of young people aged 15–24 years, each sex and total.

organization of work, the agenda and the current methods of work of the [ECOSOC] should be adapted."[13]

Later, UNGA Resolution 60/265 of 2006 clearly stated the goals and objectives agreed to at the major UN conferences, and the MDGs are basically understood as one.[14] Furthermore, given the style and format of the MDGs with short, concrete and simple goals, quantified time-bound targets and sophistically developed indicators to precisely measure the level of implementation, and given the momentum the MDGs gathered after the 2005 World Summit, the implementation of and the follow-up to the major UN conferences were going to be simply merged into the implementation and follow-up efforts of the MDGs.

In addition, despite the work of an ad hoc working group,[15] a concrete way forward was yet to be found after the 2005 World Summit.[16] Later, in November 2006, the UNGA adopted Resolution 61/16 with respect to the improvement of the methods of work of the ECOSOC and clarified the role of the ECOSOC in reviewing progress made in the implementation of the outcomes of the major UN conferences, including the MDGs and other internationally agreed development goals, and their follow-up processes.[17] Consequently, global efforts in the field of sustainable development were practically merged around the MDGs, and the ECOSOC was assigned to hold "annual ministerial-level substantive reviews" during which States were recommended "to make voluntary national presentations," the functional commissions were urged "to contribute, in accordance with their mandates and taking into account their specificity, to the assessment."[18]

The 2010 High-level Plenary Meeting was a plus-ten review exercise of the Millennium Summit. Accordingly, the 2010 High-level Plenary Meeting was also not envisioned to be a norm-making exercise by global actors. The idea was also not to renegotiate the agreements reached at the Millennium Summit. As it is clear from the outcome document of the

[13] "2005 World Summit Outcome, UNGA Resolution, UNGA Resolution, UN Doc. A/RES/60/1," paragraph 156.

[14] Ibid., paragraph 1.

[15] Summarised in the UNGA's Resolution 57/270 B of 2002.

[16] Ibid., page 10. (as indicated in paragraph 53 of Resolution 60/265—which was adopted in June 2006)

[17] "Strengthening of the Economic and Social Council, UNGA Resolution, UN Doc. A/RES/61/16," November 20, 2006, para. 8.

[18] Ibid.

2010 High-level Plenary Meeting, it was especially about "[k]eeping the promise: united to achieve the Millennium Development Goals."[19] This global action plan included commitments made by States, IOs, NGOs and private sector to achieve the MDGs by 2015. Consequently, the 2010 High-level Plenary Meeting was not an appropriate instance for the emergence of the primary social convention of GLSD.

2 The United Nations Conference on Sustainable Development

2.1 Return to the "Inclusiveness" and "Consensus" Based Practice

Following the WSSD, the UNGA adopted each year a resolution entitled "Implementation of Agenda 21, the Programme for the Further Implementation of Agenda 21 and the outcomes of the [WSSD]" and closely monitored the work of the CSD with respect to the implementation of the objectives of sustainable development.[20] In its Resolution 63/212 of 2008, the UNGA invited MS to express their views about holding a UN conference on sustainable development.[21] Different views were expressed by MS, but Brazil's proposition took the lead.[22] Thus, in its Resolution 64/236 of 2009, the UNGA decided to organise the UNCSD in 2012.[23] The objectives of the UNCSD were threefold: (1) to secure renewed political commitment for sustainable development, (2) to assess the progress to date and the remaining gaps in the implementation

[19] "Keeping the Promise: United to Achieve the Millennium Development Goals, UNGA Resolution, UN Doc. A/RES/65/1," September 22, 2010.

[20] These resolutions are the followings: A/RES/58/218, A/RES/59/227, A/RES/60/193, A/RES/61/195, A/RES/62/189, A/RES/63/212, A/RES/64/236, A/RES/65/152, A/RES/66/197.

[21] "Implementation of Agenda 21, the Programme for the Further Implementation of Agenda 21 and the Outcomes of the World Summit on Sustainable Development, UNGA Resolution, UN Doc. A/RES/63/212," December 19, 2008, paragraph 5.

[22] For other options proposed by Member States, see "Report of the Secretary-General, Implementation of Agenda 21, the Programme for the Further Implementation of Agenda 21 and the Outcomes of the World Summit on Sustainable Development, UN Doc. A/64/275," August 10, 2009, pages 40–41.

[23] "Implementation of Agenda 21, the Programme for the Further Implementation of Agenda 21 and the Outcomes of the World Summit on Sustainable Development, UNGA Resolution, UN Doc. A/RES/64/236," December 24, 2009, paragraph 20.

of the outcomes of the major summits on sustainable development and (3) to address new and emerging challenges.[24] The main themes to be discussed were "a green economy in the context of sustainable development and poverty eradication and the institutional framework for sustainable development."[25]

In terms of actors to be involved in the preparatory process of the UNCSD, there is no need to provide a detailed examination given the fact that I already concluded that the secondary social convention of GLSD had emerged at the time of the millennium. Yet, I note that, in its Resolution 64/236, the UNGA established the PrepCom for the UNCSD, and it was decided that the PrepCom would operate in the way the CSD was functioning in terms of actors involved.[26] Thus, it is clear that the PrepCom would operate in accordance with the primary and secondary social conventions of GLSD.

In addition, there was a clear return to the "inclusiveness" and "consensus" based practice established at the UNCED, as all major groups were invited "to provide ideas and proposals reflecting their experiences" along with international financial institutions and other UN agencies.[27] It is in that sense that the unease between IFIs and the NGOs was not anymore as rough as it had been. In other words, NGOs would not oppose anymore, in principle, a partnership with IFIs for achieving sustainable development. Also, the first paragraph of the outcome document of the UNCSD, "The Future We Want" (UNGA Resolution 66/288) was crystal clear that the CSOs fully participated in the adoption process of UNGA Resolution 66/288.[28]

2.2 *"The Future We Want": Primary Social Convention of GLSD*

Recall that the main function of a primary social convention is to distinguish what is law from ordinary social norms. In the case of GLSD, it would be about distinguishing rules of law of GLSD from all other social norms at the global level. The following paragraphs will demonstrate that

[24] Ibid., paragraph 20(a).

[25] Ibid.

[26] Ibid., paragraph 23.

[27] Ibid., paragraph 22.

[28] "The Future We Want, UNGA Resolution, UN Doc. A/RES/66/288," July 27, 2012, paragraph 1.

UNGA Resolution 66/288 is precisely the document containing the conclusive criteria of the primary social convention of GLSD.[29]

2.2.1 States-Led

UNGA Resolution 66/288 contains a sub-section entitled "Sustainable Development Goals" under its chapter 5. This brief one-and-a-half-page sub-section establishes the road map to be followed by global actors towards the adoption of the SDGs. In that sense, it comprises all essential information with respect to the primary social convention of GLSD. Concerning the first conclusive criterion, paragraph 248 in this sub-section provides:

> 248. We resolve to establish an inclusive and transparent intergovernmental process on sustainable development goals that is open to all stakeholders, with a view to developing global sustainable development goals to be agreed by the GA. An open working group shall be constituted [...] and shall comprise thirty representatives, nominated by Member States[.] At the outset, this open working group will decide on its methods of work, including developing modalities to ensure the full involvement of relevant stakeholders and expertise from civil society, the scientific community and the United Nations system in its work, in order to provide a diversity of perspectives and experience. It will submit a report, to the Assembly at its sixty-eighth session, containing a proposal for sustainable development goals for consideration and appropriate action.[30]

As was the case since the UNCHE, all relevant norm-making at the global level in the field of sustainable development was designed as an intergovernmental process. The States were always at the centre stage and the key and predominant constituent of these exercises. And, in UNGA Resolution 66/288, this has been again reaffirmed and States were designated to formally overview the preparations of the SDGs—through an

[29] It will also be demonstrated that "The Future We Want" was also adopted by these three global actors in accordance with the five conclusive criteria of the primary social convention at the global level in the field of sustainable development. However, "The Future We Want" cannot be considered as the first legal document adopted within the context of global law of sustainable development because the beginning of the preparatory process for the UNCSD goes back to 2009, and back then, the primary social convention in question was yet to emerge.

[30] "The Future We Want, UNGA Resolution, UN Doc. A/RES/66/288," page 47, paragraph 248.

Open Working Group (OWG). Even though there are only 30 members in the OWG, the fact that it is an "open" working group means that all MS are entitled to fully participate and contribute to its work. Furthermore, the MS also agreed that the OWG's membership seats could be shared by more than one State. As a result, the great majority of seats were shared by two, three, even four States and this ensured the participation of 70 States as members of the OWG.[31] Accordingly, this practice of having an intergovernmental process and having the UNGA as an overarching institution to formally overview this process is, as demonstrated throughout this book, continuously followed since the UNCHE. Thus, three recognised global actors,[32] by stipulating that the SDGs must be adopted through an intergovernmental process and under the overall supervision of the UNGA, instituted the first conclusive criterion for the recognition and identification of rules of law of GLSD. In other words, this signifies that rules of GLSD would only be adopted as a result of a "States-led" process.

This is not the only reference to the criterion of "States-led" process in UNGA Resolution 66/288. Paragraphs 84 and 86 of UNGA Resolution 66/288 establishing the HLPF to replace the CSD and to become the global institutional mechanism to follow up on the implementation of the SDGs also designed the HLPF as an intergovernmental forum.[33]

2.2.2 *Inclusiveness*

Paragraph 24 of UNGA Resolution 66/288 provides that an intergovernmental process is initiated for producing the SDGs, but it had to be (1) inclusive, (2) transparent and (3) open to all stakeholders. Accordingly, the content of the criterion of inclusiveness is hereby clarified. Inclusiveness

[31] "The Open Working Group was established on 22nd of January 2013 by decision 67/555 of the GA." For further details, see "Open Working Group on Sustainable Development Goals," available at https://sustainabledevelopment.un.org/owg.html.

[32] Recognized in the sense that there exists a (secondary) social convention about the entitlement of these three global actors to commonly adopt rules of 'law' at the global level in the field of sustainable development, namely global law of sustainable development.

[33] "The Future We Want, UNGA Resolution, UN Doc. A/RES/66/288," pages 16–17, paragraphs 84–86. There are many other references throughout UNGA Resolution 66/288 with respect to intergovernmental arrangements for sustainable development. See especially paragraphs 77–86. For example, in paragraph 80, "the role and authority of the UNGA on global matters of concern to the international community" has been reaffirmed.

also signifies a transparent process open to all stakeholders. Furthermore, the OWG is required to "ensure the full involvement of relevant stakeholders and expertise from civil society, the scientific community and the United Nations system in its work, in order to provide a diversity of perspectives and experience."[34] Concerning the contributions of IOs to the work of the OWG, the UNGA requested the SG "to ensure all necessary input and support to this work from the [UN] system."[35]

Furthermore, UNGA Resolution 66/288 comprises a sub-section about the engagement of major groups and other stakeholders.[36] Recall that nine major groups were recognised in Agenda 21 to ensure and facilitate broad participation of all sectors of global society in a more structured manner. At the UNCSD, "other stakeholders, including local communities, volunteer groups and foundations, migrants and families, as well as older persons and persons with disabilities" were also recognised to participate in a more structured manner to the process towards the adoption of the SDGs.[37] As a result, starting from 2012, all references to major groups in UN documents was replaced with "major groups and other stakeholders."[38]

Also, with respect to the role and place of IOs within the field of sustainable development, paragraph 54 of UNGA Resolution 66/288 recognises "the central role of the [UN] [...] [as well as] the contributions of other relevant [IOs], including [IFIs] and multilateral development banks."[39] Regarding IFIs, it is clear that they are also fully part of the global partnership for sustainable development. However, compared to the way they were involved for the creation of the MDGs, it is clear that, this time, their involvement was not at the expense of exclusion of NGOs.

[34] "The Future We Want, UNGA Resolution, UN Doc. A/RES/66/288," page 47, paragraph 248.

[35] "The Future We Want, UNGA Resolution, UN Doc. A/RES/66/288," page 47, paragraph 249.

[36] Ibid., paragraphs 42–55.

[37] Ibid., page 8, paragraph 43.

[38] It is important to clarify that these major groups and stakeholders are basically groups of CSOs. In that sense, when the UNGA refers to the major groups or stakeholders, it refers to these groups of CSOs. Where the UNGA refers, as is the case above, both to stakeholders and CSOs, it refers to both, to NGOs that are already categorised in a major group or in another group of stakeholders, and to other CSOs that are not categorised in a specific group. In practical terms, the categorisation of some sectors of NGOs in major groups or as stakeholders meant to facilitate their involvement and contributions to the UN's activities.

[39] Ibid., page 10, paragraphs 53–54.

Accordingly, a genuine observance of the criterion of inclusiveness significantly contributed to the emergence of the primary social convention of GLSD at the end of the UNCSD.

2.2.3 *Consensus*

The criterion of consensus was also observed while adopting UNGA Resolution 66/288. First of all, all the UNGA resolutions adopted in the field of sustainable development and mentioned throughout this book, if not specified otherwise, were adopted by consensus. Also, in paragraph 247 of its Resolution 66/288, the UNGA aspires that the SDGs be universally applicable. Furthermore, the OWG also decided, in the context of its methods of works, that its "work shall be guided by the principles of openness, transparency, inclusiveness and consensus" and that it would "adopt its report and recommendations by consensus, reflecting different options, if necessary."[40]

Thus, the criterion of consensus is an indispensable requirement for every decision-making at the global level in the field of sustainable development. This was the case within the CSD throughout its two-decade lifetime and it was the case for the HLPF. In that sense, in its Resolution 67/290 of 2013 establishing the format and organisational aspects of the HLPF, the UNGA decided that "in all meetings of the forum, every effort shall be made to reach consensus."[41] I therefore conclude that rules of GLSD can only be adopted by consensus and as a result of a States-led and inclusive process.

2.2.4 *Universality*

In UNGA Resolution 66/288, the UNGA decided with respect to scope, form, style and characteristics of the SDGs that they should be "global in nature and universally applicable to all countries."[42] In other words, already back in 2012, the vision was clear for global actors: developing global goals and ensuring that they are universally applicable to all. Recall that one of the key criticisms of CSOs about the MDGs was that they were only goals for developing countries and not for the developed countries.

[40] "Methods of Work, Open Working Group on Sustainable Development Goals," 2013.

[41] "Format and Organizational Aspects of the High-Level Political Forum on Sustainable Development, UNGA Resolution, UN Doc. A/RES/67/290," July 9, 2013, paragraph 5.

[42] "The Future We Want, UNGA Resolution, UN Doc. A/RES/66/288," page 47, paragraph 247.

Thus, it is clear that it was the UNGA's intention to address this point in the process towards the adoption of the SDGs.

In addition, UNGA Resolution 66/288 reaffirmed "the central position of the [UNGA] as the chief deliberative, policymaking and representative organ of the [UN]" as well as its role and authority in that quality "on global matters [such as sustainable development] of concern to the international community."[43] Lastly, with respect to the establishment of the HLPF on sustainable development, the UNGA repeatedly emphasised the "universal" nature of the Forum.[44] Thus, it follows that rules of GLSD must be adopted by consensus, following a States-led and inclusive process, and they must aspire to universal applicability.

2.2.5 *Pluralism*

Recall that States, while agreeing on some legally binding treaties and conventions on some occasion, also opted for legally non-binding instruments for certain agreements. For example, while some of the outcome documents such as the Rio Declaration and Agenda 21 were legally non-binding in terms of international law, legally binding conventions, such as the UNFCCC and the CBD were also signed by numerous States at the UNCED. Yet, neither States nor other global actors that were involved in the process for the adoption of legally non-binding agreement ever envisioned these agreements to be inconsistent with international law. In that sense, these new global commitments in the field of sustainable development are complementing and aiming to coexist in harmony with the existing rules of international law.

Also, paragraph 246 of UNGA Resolution 66/288 emphasises that "a set of SDGs [to be developed] [...] are consistent with international law."[45] In addition to this specific requirement clarifying that SDGs are aiming to coexist in harmony and be consistent with international law, there are many other references in UNGA Resolution 66/288 confirming this aim to coexist in harmony.[46] It follows that together with the adoption of UNGA Resolution 66/288, global actors commonly agreed that rules

[43] Ibid., page 15, paragraphs 80–81.

[44] Ibid., page 16, paragraph 84.; "Format and Organizational Aspects of the High-Level Political Forum on Sustainable Development, UNGA Resolution, UN Doc. A/RES/67/290," paragraph 2.

[45] "The Future We Want, UNGA Resolution, UN Doc. A/RES/66/288," page 47, paragraph 246.

[46] Ibid., pages 11 and 39.

of GLSD must cumulatively fulfil the requirements of five criteria; namely, (1) States-led, (2) inclusiveness, (3) consensus, (4) universality and (5) pluralism.

3 Conclusion and Progress Appraisal—Fourth DSD (2002–2012)

The fact that UNGA Resolution 66/288 represents the emergence of the primary social convention of GLSD is a hypothesis, and Resolution 66/288 does not include a text where it says, "the following five criteria are hereby declared as conclusive criteria for the identification and recognition of rules as laws of GLSD." Yet, UNGA Resolution 66/288 sets out clearly an outline to be followed by the OWG with respect to the adoptions of the SDGs. Notably, the UNGA states that (1) the SDGs must be based on Rio commitments, Agenda 21 and Johannesburg Plan of Implementation; (2) they must build upon commitments made in all major UN summits in the field of sustainable development; and (3) they "should address and incorporate in a balanced way all three dimensions of sustainable development and their interlinkages."[47] The UNGA further adds that the SDGs "should be action-oriented, concise and easy to communicate, limited in number, aspirational, global in nature and universally applicable to all countries [.]"[48] These are clear directions for the OWG to take into consideration while preparing their proposition for the UNGA. Nevertheless, the fact that the UNGA, at this occasion, indicated certain conditions to be respected concerning the substance and format of the SDGs, does not mean that these conditions are part of the conclusive criteria of the primary social convention of GLSD. To reach such a conclusion requires more than one UNGA resolution. In the present book, in order to genuinely establish the existence of certain conclusive criteria as part of the primary social convention of GLSD, I have described a four-decade-long practice enhanced with a significant amount of clear and convincing evidence.

Therefore, besides the five conclusive criteria that I have identified, other directions given by the UNGA to the OWG with respect to the substance and format of SDGs cannot be considered as part of the primary social convention of GLSD. In other words, if I recall Hart's terminology,

[47] Ibid., page 47, paragraph 246.
[48] Ibid., page 47, paragraph 247.

five conclusive criteria that I have identified basically constitute the rule of recognition of GLSD. A rule of recognition is a "rule about rules." The UNGA's directions about SDGs being action-oriented, concise, limited in number etc., are simple instructions about the content and format of the rules to be adopted and are not rules about rules.

Moreover, one can simply remark on the increasing number of references to the involvement of private sector and scientific community to achieve sustainable development. In this regard, a question that may come to mind is why not consider these other actors as part of the secondary social convention of GLSD. In fact, these other actors are also part of it under NGOs category. Recall that both "business and industry" and "scientific and technological communities" were recognised as one of the nine major groups in Agenda 21. Accordingly, the UN's civil society database provides that there were more than 1757 organisations accredited to the CSD as part of the major group "business and industry" and 1756 organisations as part of the major group "scientific and technological communities."[49] Accordingly, all these organisations representing the private sector and scientific community, as well as all other organisations registered as part of major groups and other stakeholders, are also NGOs and they constitute an integral part of the secondary social convention of GLSD.

I thus conclude that, at the end of the fourth DSD, the global stage was ready for the adoption of the very first rules of GLSD. On the one hand, since the beginning of the millennium, the secondary social convention of GLSD was present. On the other hand, with the adoption of UNGA Resolution 66/288 as an outcome document of the UNCSD, the primary social convention of GLSD with five precise conclusive criteria has taken shape. In light of these developments, the next chapter examines whether SDGs are the very first rules of GLSD.

[49] "United Nations – Civil Society Database" available at United Nations Civil Society Participation – Sustainable Development.

CHAPTER 6

Towards Global Law of Sustainable Development

In 2010, a High-Level Meeting of the UNGA was organised in order to review the progress in the implementation of the MDGs as a ten-year review before the 2015 deadline. Back then, the question of what will happen after 2015 in the field of sustainable development was already on the table. Accordingly, in the last paragraph of the outcome document of the 2010 High-Level Meeting, the UNGA requested the SG to make recommendations "for further steps to advance the United Nations development agenda beyond 2015."[1] This is the official beginning of the Post-2015 Development Agenda and the efforts intensified, especially, following UNCSD. The initiative taken by the SG following his mandate from the 2010 High-Level Meeting and initiatives emerging from the UNCSD, such as the OWG, constitute rather a twin-track process within the UN's Post-2015 Development Agenda.

Given the scope of this book, I will only provide some indispensable information about these initiatives and only examine whether the five conclusive criteria were observed by global actors while formulating the SDGs. Thus, I will first mention the SG's initiatives as part of his mandate for the UN's Post-2015 Development Agenda. Later, I will move to the aftermath of the UNCSD and describe the significance of the HLPF in the context of the SDGs. Afterwards, before moving into the work of the

[1] "Keeping the Promise: United to Achieve the Millennium Development Goals, UNGA Resolution, UN Doc. A/RES/65/1," paragraph 81.

H. Göksan, *Global Law of Sustainable Development*, Global Issues,
https://doi.org/10.1007/978-3-031-74547-8_6

OWG, I will briefly mention the Special Event organised by the President of UNGA in 2013 as a last global event on the MDGs.

1 SG's Initiatives in the Context of the UN

To begin with, in July 2012, the SG announced the 26 members of the High-Level Panel of Eminent Persons on Post-2015 Development Agenda (High-Level Panel) "to advise him on a bold and at the same time practical development agenda beyond 2015."[2] The High-Level Panel was therefore established right after the UNCSD. The Report of the High-Level Panel indicates that the High-Level Panel was informed by a broad consultative process at national, regional and global levels. In addition, the scientific and academic communities, hundreds of civil society organisations and business leaders, as well as online consultations, contributed to the deliberations of the High-Level Panel.[3] In terms of substance, the High-Level Panel provided the SG with 12 illustrative goals and 54 associated targets and underlined the importance of identifying indicators to better measure whether the targets are met or not.

Secondly, the SG requested the United Nations Global Compact (UNGC) to bring the perspective of the private sector to the Post-2015 Development Agenda. Initially, the UNGC and the World Business Council for Sustainable Development prepared a joint report with the support of the World Economic Forum to be submitted to the High-Level Panel (Joint Report). The Joint Report indicates that, back in the beginning of the Millennium, the private sector was essentially not part of the process for the formulation of the MDGs. The Joint Report mentions two factors for this lack of cooperation: one is the unease about the role of the private sector in socio-economic matters between the international development community and the business community; the second is the lack of interest on the part of the business community to the challenges of

[2] "Secretary-General Assembles High-Level Panel on Post-2015 Development Agenda, Appointing 26 Members of Government, Civil Society, Private Sector, UN Doc. SG/A/1364-DEV/2949," United Nations Press Release, July 31, 2012; For the terms of reference of the high-level panel, see; "Secretary-General Appoints High-Level Panel on Post-2015 Development Agenda," United Nations Press Release, July 31, 2012.

[3] "A New Global Partnership: Eradicate Poverty and Transform Economies Through Sustainable Development, The Report of the High-Level Panel of Eminent Persons on the Post-2015 Development Agenda," May 2013, page 59.

sustainable development.[4] This comparison is quite insightful in demonstrating how the global community and the interactions between different actors at the global level evolved over just a bit more than a decade.

In addition to this submission to the High-Level Panel, the UNGC also submitted its own report to the SG entitled "Corporate Sustainability and the United Nations Post-2015 Development Agenda" (UNGC Report).[5] In terms of the extent of the consultations conducted and inputs gathered, the UNGC Report states that 43 national consultations were conducted through local networks, that the UNGC's leadership platform comprised of 56 multinational corporations convened several discussion forums, including the Corporate Sustainability Forum organised at the occasion of the UNCSD, and that the views of 1712 companies from over 100 countries were integrated to the UNGC Report.[6] The UNGC Report also came up with its proposal for the SDGs containing 9 goals and 49 targets.

Another critical initiative of the SG was the establishment of the UN System Task Team (UNSTT) on the Post-2015 Development Agenda. This was established "to coordinate system-wide preparations for the agenda, in consultation with all stakeholders," bringing together "senior experts designated by the Principals of over 50 UN system entities and other international organizations" (UNSTT Report).[7] The UNSTT Report circulated just before the UNCSD reveals, based on the shortcomings and achievements of the MDGs, how a general agreement emerged at the occasion of the UNCSD to pursue a States-led, inclusive process to generate, through consensus, global goals that are universally applicable. Remarkably, the UNSTT Report touches upon the significance of all the aforementioned criteria for an appropriate Post-2015 Development Agenda. Manifestly, all these criteria are strongly related to the five conclusive criteria of the primary social convention of GLSD. In addition to the UNSTT Report, the UNSTT Report prepared two other specific reports,

[4] "Joint Report to the High-Level Panel on the Post-2015 Development Agenda, The UN Global Compact and the World Business Council for Sustainable Development," March 2013.

[5] "Corporate Sustainability and the United Nations Post-2015 Development Agenda, UN Global Compact's Report to the UN Secretary-General," June 2013.

[6] Ibid., page 4.

[7] "Realizing the Future We Want for All, UN System Task Team's Report to the UN Secretary-General," June 2012.

one about the global partnership of the Post-2015 Development Agenda[8] and the other about monitoring and indicators.[9]

The SG also commissioned the creation of the Sustainable Development Solutions Network (SDSN), a network of research centres and universities. The SDSN comprises more than a thousand institutions, including universities, research centres, NGOs and foundations.[10] The SDSN also created 12 thematic groups for "global expertise to identify critical pathways to sustainable development in twelve priority areas."[11]

Lastly, the SG has initiated a global online conversation on 11 issue areas with individuals from all around the world—www.worldwewant2030.org—and launched "My World" survey[12] [...] reach[ing] more than a million people."[13]

To summarise, these initiatives roughly picture a glimpse of countless undertakings and inputs of a very diverse range of actors' contributions to the Post-2015 Development Agenda. The common denominator in all of these inputs and contributions is that there is an overarching consensus around the idea of adopting goals, targets and indicators for the Post-2015 Development Agenda. In addition, universality of these goals, and a States-led but fully inclusive and transparent process towards their adoption and the necessity of consensus-building are definitely genuine features and backbones of the Post-2015 Development Agenda without which the SDGs would not see the light of day.

[8] "A Renewed Global Partnership for Development, UN System Task Team's Report," March 2013.

[9] "Statistics and Indicators for the Post-2015 Development Agenda, UN System Task Team's Report," July 2013.

[10] See at https://www.unsdsn.org/sdsn-members.

[11] "A Framework for Sustainable Development, The Sustainable Development Solutions Network," December 2012.

[12] See at http://vote.myworld2015.org/.

[13] "Report of the Secretary-General, A Life of Dignity for All: Accelerating Progress towards the Millennium Development Goals and Advancing the United Nations Development Agenda beyond 2015, UN Doc. A/68/202," July 26, 2013, paragraph 76.

2 High-Level Political Forum on Sustainable Development

2.1 *First Institution of GLSD*

Following the adoption of its Resolution 66/288, the UNGA concentrated on the follow-ups, especially, the establishment of the HLPF as a successor to the CSD. In this regard, the UNGA recommended the CSD to hold its last session before the first session of the HLPF and requested the SG to submit a report on lessons learned from the CSD, "compiling relevant existing information in consultation with [MS] and benefiting from the inputs of major groups and other stakeholders."[14] The aim of this report was to better contribute to the negotiation process about the establishment of the CSD, and it provides a quite useful appraisal of the CSD's weaknesses and achievements since 1992.[15]

Furthermore, with respect to the format and organisational aspects of the HLPF, the UNGA adopted Resolution 67/290 in 2012. In terms of observance of the five conclusive criteria of GLSD, UNGA Resolution 67/290 emphasised several times the intergovernmental character of the Forum in accordance with paragraph 84–86 of UNGA Resolution 66/288. Furthermore, by deciding to convene the HLPF every four years under the auspices of the UNGA and every year under the auspices of the ECOSOC, the States-led feature of the Forum has been underscored as a central aspect.

In terms of inclusiveness, UNGA Resolution 67/290 noted that the arrangements established for the CSD should also apply to the HLPF and further detailed the participation of IOs and NGOs and allowed their representatives: (1) to attend all official meetings of the HLPF; (2) to have access to all official information and documents; (3) to intervene in official meetings; (4) to submit documents and present written and oral contributions; (5) to make recommendations; and (6) to organise side events and

[14] "Implementation of Agenda 21, the Programme for the Further Implementation of Agenda 21 and the Outcomes of the World Summit on Sustainable Development and of the United Nations Conference on Sustainable Development, UNGA Resolution, UN Doc. A/RES/67/203," December 21, 2012, paragraphs 3–4.

[15] For further details, see "Report of the Secretary-General, Lessons Learned from the Commission on Sustainable Development, UN Doc. A/67/757," February 26, 2013.

round tables.[16] In this regard, Strandenaes concluded that "no other UN resolution has granted so far-reaching rights and privileges to major groups, NGOs, civil society and other stakeholders than the resolution establishing the HLPF."[17]

In terms of consensus, not only was UNGA Resolution 67/290 adopted by consensus, but it was also decided that "in all meetings of the [HLPF], every effort shall be made to reach consensus."[18] Fourthly, together with its intergovernmental character, UNGA Resolution 67/290 underlined several times the universal character of the HLPF. It was noted that "all meetings of the [HLPF] shall provide for the full and effective participation of all States Members of the United Nations and States members of specialized agencies."[19] For example, even though the HLPF was to be convened every year under the auspices of the ECOSOC and to adopt a ministerial declaration, these "are not subject to review by the 54-member ECOSOC, because the HLPF has universal membership, [as such, they] are forwarded directly to the [UNGA]."[20]

In terms of harmony with the existing rules of international law, it is important to note that the HLPF was not mandated with any norm-making mission. Its role consists of providing "political leadership, guidance and recommendations," reviewing "progress in the implementation of sustainable development commitments," enhancing "the integration of the three dimensions of sustainable development [...] at all levels" and having "a focused, dynamic and action-oriented agenda, ensuring the appropriate consideration of new and emerging sustainable development challenges."[21] Even its political and ministerial declarations are forwarded to the UNGA for its considerations. Therefore, there is no need to look for the observance of this criterion and there is also nothing in international law preventing the establishment of such a forum at the global level.

[16] "Format and Organizational Aspects of the High-Level Political Forum on Sustainable Development, UNGA Resolution, UN Doc. A/RES/67/290," paragraphs 14–17.

[17] Jan-Gustav Strandenaes, "Participatory Democracy - HLPF Laying the Basis for Sustainable Development Governance in the 21st Century," March 2014, page 68.

[18] "Format and Organizational Aspects of the High-Level Political Forum on Sustainable Development, UNGA Resolution, UN Doc. A/RES/67/290," paragraph 5.

[19] Ibid., paragraph 4.

[20] Kenneth W. Abbott and Steven Bernstein, "The High-Level Political Forum on Sustainable Development: Orchestration by Default and Design," *Global Policy* 6, no. 3 (2015): page 225.

[21] "Format and Organizational Aspects of the High-Level Political Forum on Sustainable Development, UNGA Resolution, UN Doc. A/RES/67/290," paragraph 2.

Consequently, it follows that the HLPF was specifically designated as the universal institution to follow up and review progress in the implementation of the SDGs. Recall in this regard paragraphs 86 and 248 of UNGA Resolution 66/288. Both called for an intergovernmental, open, transparent and inclusive negotiation process to establish the HLPF and to adopt the SDGs. Therefore, it is possible to conclude that the establishment of the HLPF is an integral part of the process towards the adoption of the SDGs. In that sense, the HLPF is essentially the first product of this process. In other words, the global actors, before adopting the very first rules of GLSD, created the very first institution of this emergent body of global law.[22]

2.2 *The Launch and Functioning of the HLPF*

In 2013, an inaugural session of the HLPF was convened under the auspices of the UNGA. In accordance with UNGA Resolution 67/290, "on an extraordinary basis and only for the purpose of that meeting, the outcome of the meeting [consisted] of the summary of the President."[23] Before the adoption of the SDGs in September 2015, the first and second session of the HLPF was held under the auspices of the ECOSOC in 2014 and 2015.[24]

As it will be recalled, with UNGA Resolution 61/16 adopted in November 2006, the methods of work and the role of the ECOSOC were

[22] With respect to uniqueness of the HLPF and its role in the field of sustainable development at the global level, Abbott and Bernstein noted as follows: "[T]he circumstances of its creation, its universal, high-level structure and its unique dual links to the GA and ECOSOC should make the HLPF 'focal,' a natural leader of the sustainable development policy domain. These features should also give the HLPF greater 'political weight' than the CSD, addressing one of the latter's fundamental flaws." See Abbott and Bernstein, "The High-Level Political Forum on Sustainable Development," page 226.

[23] "Format and Organizational Aspects of the High-Level Political Forum on Sustainable Development, UNGA Resolution, UN Doc. A/RES/67/290," paragraph 27. For the summary of the meeting, see; "Note by the President of the General Assembly, Summary of the First Meeting of the High-Level Political Forum on Sustainable Development, UN Doc. A/68/588," November 13, 2013.

[24] For the reports of the first two sessions of the HLPF under the auspices of the ECOSOC, see "Report of the First Meeting of the High-Level Political Forum on Sustainable Development Convened under the Auspices of the Economic and Social Council, UN Doc. E/HLPF/2014/2," October 15, 2014; "Report of the Second Meeting of the High-Level Political Forum on Sustainable Development Convened under the Auspices of the Economic and Social Council, UN Doc. E/HLPF/2014/4," August 18, 2015.

improved in order to better review progress made in the implementation of sustainable development commitments. Accordingly, back then, global efforts in the field of sustainable development were merged around the MDGs, and the ECOSOC was assigned to hold "annual ministerial reviews" during which States were making voluntary national presentations. In order to further improve the work of the ECOSOC and to better integrate the context of the SDGs, in accordance with UNGA Resolution 67/290, it was decided to replace the ECOSOC's annual ministerial reviews with the meetings of the HLPF—held under the auspices of the ECOSOC—as from 2016.[25] Similarly, voluntary national presentations made during the annual ministerial reviews were also replaced by "Voluntary National Reviews" under the SDGs.[26]

Consequently, the ECOSOC was further empowered through the HLPF's annual sessions held under its auspices to follow up and review progress in the implementation of SDGs. With respect to the UNGA, its overview of the SDGs' implementation gained a regular and structured process with the HLPF's quadrennials sessions under its auspices. Therefore, at the end of a two-decade long process of trial and error, with respect to the follow up and review mechanisms of the sustainable development commitments at the global level, significant experience accumulated through the Rio commitments, Agenda 21, the CSD, the MDGs, etc., genuinely shaped the very first institution of this emergent body of GLSD and its organisational aspects to follow up and review progress in the implementation of the SDGs.

[25] "Format and Organizational Aspects of the High-Level Political Forum on Sustainable Development, UNGA Resolution, UN Doc. A/RES/67/290," paragraph 7(a).

[26] Ibid., paragraph 8(d). In Resolution 70/1 adopting the SDGs, the mechanism of voluntary national reviews is described as follows: "The high-level political forum, under the auspices of the Economic and Social Council, shall carry out regular reviews, in line with GA resolution 67/290 of 9 July 2013. Reviews will be voluntary, while encouraging reporting, and include developed and developing countries as well as relevant United Nations entities and other stakeholders, including civil society and the private sector. They shall be States-led, involving ministerial and other relevant high-level participants. They shall provide a platform for partnerships, including through the participation of major groups and other relevant stakeholders." See "Transforming Our World: The 2030 Agenda for Sustainable Development, UNGA Resolution, UN Doc. A/RES/70/1," paragraph 84.

3 Special Event of the President of the UNGA for the MDGs

A one-day special event was organised by the President of the UNGA in order to give one last impulse to all actors in order to reach the MDGs by 2015. The outcome document of this special event was adopted in UNGA Resolution 68/6 of 2013.[27] The relevance of this event with respect to the SDGs is that it was at this occasion the UNGA determined the precise timeline and negotiation process for the adoption of the SDGs. Accordingly, the negotiations were going to start in September 2014. In addition, the OWG was going to accomplish its work before September 2014, and the SG was requested to "synthesize the full range of inputs" before September 2014.[28]

4 The Open Working Group on Sustainable Development Goals

There are many interesting aspects of the work of the OWG for researchers. For example, the negotiation process at the OWG was an exceptional one in comparison to other negotiations in UN settings. However, given the scope of this book, I will limit my examination to whether the five conclusive criteria were observed while formulating the first official proposal for the SDGs.[29]

To begin with, the OWG was designed in the UNCSD as a working group with 30 members. However, at the end of six months of the negotiation process, the MS agreed that membership seats could be shared by

[27] "Outcome Document of the Special Event to Follow up Efforts Made towards Achieving the Millennium Development Goals, UNGA Resolution, UN Doc. A/RES/68/6," October 9, 2013.

[28] Ibid., paragraphs 22–26.

[29] For further details about the exceptional nature of the negotiation process, see Pamela S. Chasek and Lynn M. Wagner provide an excellent overview of the OWG's two-year-long negotiation process. In fact, both of the authors followed all the 13 sessions of the OWG and also conducted several interviews with Co-Chairs of the OWG as well as with many other participants of the negotiations. See; Pamela S. Chasek and Lynn M. Wagner, "Breaking the Mold: A New Type of Multilateral Sustainable Development Negotiation," *International Environmental Agreements: Politics, Law and Economics* 16, no. 3 (June 1, 2016): 397–413. For a more general overview on the negotiation of the SDGs, see; Felix Dodds, Ambassador David Donoghue, and Jimena Leiva Roesch, *Negotiating the Sustainable Development Goals: A Transformational Agenda for an Insecure World* (Taylor & Francis, 2016).

more than one State. That ensured the participation of 70 States as members of the working group.[30] Yet, as the process was designed to be inclusive and transparent, all MS were entitled to participate in the work of the OWG. Accordingly, the intergovernmental nature of the OWG was one of its main characteristics, as per the criterion of "States-led."

Secondly, from its first session in March 2013 to its last session in July 2014, the OWG held 13 sessions. The first eight sessions were organised as "a 'stocktaking' process to create a common space, based on scientific evidence, and allow everyone to have the same terms of reference, to achieve a substantive rather than a political outcome."[31] In terms of the extent of inclusiveness during these sessions, I note that "[e]ach of the stocktaking sessions involved early-morning meetings with representatives of civil society [...], panel presentations by experts, question and answer periods, and opportunities for the troikas and others to give statements."[32] Another specific example with respect to the involvement and influence of the NGOs is about the inclusion of the fight against the anti-microbial resistance to the paragraph 26 of UNGA Resolution 70/1 on the SDGs just before the end of the negotiations.[33] "This had been something that a number of organizations tried to have a target on in the SDG without success."[34] Regarding the IOs' inputs to the negotiations within the OWG, the UNSTT was created by the SG and brought together senior experts from more than 50 IOs. "The [UNSTT] would play an important role in producing twenty-nine issue briefs [...] for the [OWG]. [...] These briefs had a vital role in what would be the [OWG] outcome."[35]

Thirdly, in terms of the process leading to the consensus within the OWG, the last five sessions of the OWG were reserved for negotiations. At the outset, the Co-Chairs circulated a brief starting point outlining 19 focus areas to be discussed by the OWG. These 19 focus areas correspond largely to do the 17 goals of sustainable development. Following the OWG's meetings in its ninth session, the Co-Chairs enriched their starting document with more than hundreds of targets proposed. This document became a "working document" for the 11th session of the OWG in May 2014 and, after that, it became a "zero draft" with 17 Goals and 212

[30] Dodds, Donoghue, and Roesch, *Negotiating the Sustainable Development Goals*, page 31.

[31] Chasek and Wagner, "Breaking the Mold," page 406.

[32] Ibid.

[33] Dodds, Donoghue, and Roesch, *Negotiating the Sustainable Development Goals*, page 62.

[34] Ibid.

[35] Ibid., page 56.

targets for further negotiations at the OWG's 12th session in June 2014. Finally, on 19 July 2014, the OWG agreed by consensus on the proposal for the SDGs containing 17 Goals and 169 targets.[36]

Fourthly, the outcome of the UNCSD was sufficiently clear about the universality of the goals to be formulated. The proposal of the OWG was also quite clear in noting that the SDGs would be universally applicable.[37] For example, the OWG ensured the observance of the requirement of universality by eliminating proposals for targets that were not universally applicable.[38]

Lastly, in terms of harmony and consistency with the existing rules of international law, there was nothing against the requirements established in UNCSD in the OWG's proposals. On the contrary, there are many direct and indirect indications in the proposed goals and targets demonstrating the aim for a harmonious relationship with the rules of international law. For example, the proposed Goal 13 acknowledges that the UNFCCC as the primary international, intergovernmental forum for negotiating the global response to climate change. Target 5 of Goal 14 reads as follows: "By 2020, conserve at least 10 per cent of coastal and marine areas, consistent with national and international law and based on the best available scientific information." In conclusion, the five conclusive criteria of the primary social convention of GLSD were thoroughly observed by the OWG and its proposal for the SDGs was adopted and transmitted to the UNGA accordingly.

5 Secretary-General's Synthesis Report and Intergovernmental Negotiations

On 10 September 2014, the UNGA decided that "the proposal of the [OWG] on [SDGs] [...] shall be the main basis for integrating [SDGs] into the post-2015 development agenda, while recognizing that other

[36] For further details and documents with respect to each session of the OWG, see; "Open Working Group on Sustainable Development Goals." See also; Chasek and Wagner, "Breaking the Mold," pages 407–10. For the official submission of the OWG to the GA, see; "Report of the Open Working Group of the General Assembly on Sustainable Development Goals, UNGA Resolution, UN Doc. A/68/970," August 12, 2014.

[37] "Report of the Open Working Group of the General Assembly on Sustainable Development Goals, UNGA Resolution, UN Doc. A/68/970," paragraph 18.

[38] Dodds, Donoghue, and Roesch, *Negotiating the Sustainable Development Goals*, 36.

inputs will also be considered."[39] This resolution was rather a surprise, as it placed the OWG's proposal on the SGDs at the centre of the upcoming intergovernmental negotiations process even before the submission of the SG's synthesis report. In fact, the SG submitted his synthesis report on the Post-2015 Development Agenda on 4 December 2014.[40] This was to avoid the disruption of the fragile consensus reached within the OWG.[41]

The difference in this second step of negotiations from the negotiations within the OWG is that all 193 MS were fully part of the process. The Co-Chairs of the OWG were also appointed as Co-Facilitators of this intergovernmental negotiations process (INP). Accordingly, this was a "States-led" process. In terms of inclusiveness, the UNGA noted that the negotiations be "open, inclusive and transparent intergovernmental consultations."[42] Accordingly, the INP was launched in January 2015, and it started with a stocktaking exercise with CSOs in January 2015. In addition, a two-day informal stakeholders hearing was organised in May 2015 to gather stakeholders' views and perspective before the adoption of the Post-2015 Development Agenda in September 2015. Without getting into further details, inclusive, universal and pluralist characteristics were also preserved throughout the INP.[43] Finally, on 2 August 2015, a

[39] "Report of the Open Working Group on Sustainable Development Goals Established Pursuant to General Assembly Resolution 66/288, UNGA Resolution, UN Doc. A/RES/68/309," September 10, 2014, paragraph 2.

[40] "Synthesis Report of the Secretary-General on the Post-2015 Sustainable Development Agenda, The Road to Dignity by 2030: Ending Poverty, Transforming All Lives and Protecting the Planet, UN Doc. A/69/700," December 4, 2014.

[41] Dodds, Donoghue, and Roesch, *Negotiating the Sustainable Development Goals*, pages 70–72.

[42] "Organization of the United Nations Summit for the Adoption of the Post-2015 Development Agenda, UNGA Resolution, UN Doc. A/RES/69/244," December 29, 2014, paragraphs 14–15.

[43] For all further details about all aspects of the intergovernmental negotiations process, please refer to the excellent review of Felix Doods, Ambassador David Donoghue – who was one of the Co-Chairs of the OWG and Co-Facilitators of the intergovernmental negotiations process - and Jimena Leiva Roesch in Dodds, Donoghue, and Roesch, *Negotiating the Sustainable Development Goals*, pages 70–112.

consensus was reached over the final text circulated by the Co-Facilitators.[44] This text became the first resolution of the 70-year-old UN, Resolution 70/1, for "Transforming Our World: The 2030 Agenda for Sustainable Development."[45]

6 Conclusion and the Relationship Between International Law and GLSD

I determined that, at the end of the second DSD, the significant increase in the roles of NGOs and IOs as key global actors together with States in the field of sustainable development. During the third DSD and at the latest, at the time of the Millennium, the secondary social convention of GLSD took a clearer shape. This brand-new secondary social convention among three global actors meant that a global agreement emerged providing that common acts of these actors might constitute the rules of GLSD. To this end, a primary social convention was also needed. And finally, at the end of the fourth DSD, with the adoption of the outcome of the UNCSD, global actors agreed on five conclusive and cumulative criteria with respect to the identification and recognition of their common acts as the laws of GLSD. Accordingly, during a three-year long negotiation process, these five criteria were thoroughly observed, and, at the end of this unprecedented process, the very first rules of GLSD were adopted.

For the time being, the only rules of GLSD are the SDGs. In that sense, potential answers to the extent of this relationship between international law and GLSD are to be found in the SDGs. Notably, there are many references to the existing rules of international law in the SDGs, such as Goal 13, targets 3.a, 3.b, 10.a, 13.a, 14.c, as well as Indicator 14.c.1. In addition to these references, there exists several references to several soft law

[44] Ibid., page 111.

[45] "Transforming Our World: The 2030 Agenda for Sustainable Development, UNGA Resolution, UN Doc. A/RES/70/1."

instruments,[46] some global standards and index,[47] as well as certain international negotiations.[48]

This demonstrates that global actors were not adopting the SDGs in isolation from existing rules of international law, as well as from other global soft law instruments or standards. This confirms once again the fifth criterion with respect to the harmonious and co-existential relationship between the rules of international law and GLSD. Secondly, it is clear from the above references that global actors were sufficiently alert to bring clarifications in the SDGs with respect to some potential overlaps between the SDGs and the existing rules of international law.

Accordingly, the extent of the relationship between international law and GLSD is to be found in the above references. These references confirm the fifth criterion and make some further clarifications with respect to certain potential overlaps. For example, Goal 13 of the SDGs makes it clear that global response to climate change is to be negotiated within the framework of the UNFCCC, and, as it is clear from its targets, Goal 13 is rather about implementation and "taking urgent action" in accordance with the outcome of the negotiations under UNFCCC. This is again a perfect example with respect to harmonious relationship and a great demonstration about global actors' preferences and practice in clarifying the relationship between the rules of international law and GLSD.

[46] Such as Sendai Framework for Disaster Risk Reduction 2015–2030 (Target 11.b and Indicators 1.5.3, 11.b.1 and 13.1.2.), Doha Declaration (Target 3.b), Programme of Action of the International Conference on Population and Development and the Beijing Platform for Action (Target 5.6), 10-Year Framework of Programmes on Sustainable Consumption and Production (Targets 8.4 and 12.1), and Global Jobs Pact of the International Labour Organization (Target 8.b).

[47] Such as FAO's Food Insecurity Experience Scale (Indicator 2.1.2), WHO's Child Growth Standards (Indicator 2.2.1) as well as Agriculture orientation index for government expenditures (Indicator 2.a.1), Global food loss index (Indicator 12.3.1), Index of coastal eutrophication and floating plastic debris density (Indicator 14.1.1), Mountain Green Cover Index (Indicator 15.4.2), Red List Index (Indicator 15.5.1).

[48] Precisely, Doha Development Agenda (Targets 2.b and 17.10) even though the negotiations were abandoned.

CHAPTER 7

Concluding Remarks and the Promise of the GLSD

This book started with the following hypothesis: Would it be possible to consider the SDGs as rules of law at the global level in the field of sustainable development? But what is law at the global level or what is law? This is the question of general jurisprudence that legal theorists and legal philosophers have been trying to answer for centuries. As it is not an exact science, many different answers are available in the literature. In this volume, the concept of law in GLSD has been inspired from Hart's theory of law, especially, his union of primary and secondary rules thesis and social rule thesis.

According to Hart's social rule thesis, primary rules constituting a social practice would be qualified as law if they are supported by secondary rules. In Hart's theory, secondary rules are rules for recognising (rule of recognition) (1), changing (rule of change) (2), and adjudicating (rule of adjudication) (3) primary rules. Even though all three of these secondary rules are necessary for a legal system, the existence of the rule of recognition is sufficient in order to qualify primary rules as law. Thus, the existence of a rule of recognition is the key in order to qualify social rules as law. Nevertheless, in Hart's theory of law, it is not crystal clear how to pinpoint a rule of recognition. For this reason, the way Hart initially explained the existence of a rule of recognition was adapted and contextualised for the case of GLSD.

H. Göksan, *Global Law of Sustainable Development*, Global Issues, https://doi.org/10.1007/978-3-031-74547-8_7

Another difficulty in attempting to identify a new concept of law at the global level is related to the emerging nature of GLSD. It is not possible to be certain about the existence of GLSD.[1] However, it is possible to envision a concept of law in an emerging context given the social nature of Hart's rule of recognition. In Hart's theory, a rule of recognition is essentially a social convention and the existence of a social convention does not depend on the existence and validity of an associated legal system because the existence of a social convention is a matter of fact.[2] Accordingly, uncertainties about the existence of GLSD has no bearing on the existence of a social convention for the identification and recognition of rules as laws of GLSD.

In conceptualising GLSD, Hart's theory had its limits because his understanding of law is based on state law and this essentialist vision was not convenient for a concept of law at the global level. Therefore, in this volume "law" was rather understood from a legal pluralist perspective in accordance with Tamanaha's "non-essentialist legal pluralist perspective."[3] For Tamanaha, law has no essence and it is impossible to capture the essence of law. He proposes that "law is whatever we attach the label law to." Accordingly, what we label as law at the global level might be entirely different than what we label as law at municipal level. That is why law has no essence. Similarly, for Tamanaha, the identification criteria of law in different contexts might be different.

In this book, not only the concept of law in GLSD was understood differently than it is envisioned in Hart's theory of law, but Hart's rule of recognition was also revised with inspirations from Tamanaha's "non-essentialist legal pluralist perspective." In fact, Tamanaha brilliantly explains and demonstrates that "Hart's ultimate rule of recognition requires a co-ultimate social convention regarding whose actions have the

[1] Evidently, it would be entirely normal for many lawyers to be quite uncertain about the existence of such a type of "law." For example, regarding the concept of transnational law, Giudice notes as follows: "[S]ome theorist of transnational law are uncertain about whether there is such a thing as transnational law, or that the phenomena they are observing amount to a distinct kind or form of law at all. Here, questions about transnational law ask about the emergence of prima facie legal phenomena for which no settled convention yet exists. In fact, I think many of the new forms of normative order which now exist (at local, national and global levels) are interesting precisely because their emergence tends to precede any settled linguistic convention about their nature." See in Giudice, *Understanding the Nature of Law*, 64.

[2] d'Aspremont, 'Herbert Hart in Post-Modern International Legal Scholarship', 18.

[3] Tamanaha, 'A Non-Essentialist Version of Legal Pluralism'.

status of law."[4] Accordingly, I renamed Hart's ultimate rule of recognition as "primary social convention" and Tamanaha's co-ultimate social convention as "secondary social convention" in the context of GLSD.

With respect to a secondary social convention, my starting question was: "Whose acts might have the status of law at global level in the field of sustainable development?" I concluded that States, IOs and NGOs—including MNCs, financial institutions, scientific institutions/academia, etc. —are parties to the secondary social convention of GLSD. I reached this conclusion in two steps. Initially, I argued that States are by far the most important actors whose acts have the status of law beyond national boundaries, especially, in the context of international law. In addition, content-wise, there was a great analogy among global norms of sustainable development and the rules of international law. Moreover, some of these norms of sustainable development were later adopted as rules of international law.[5] Based on these arguments, I concluded that States were one of the global actors whose acts, together with other actors, might have the status of law at global level in the field of sustainable development. I also added IOs and civil society at large are potential global actors together with States, based on their involvement in norm-making at the global level in the field of sustainable development and States' recognition about their status as such global actors. In the second step, I demonstrated how a secondary social convention emerged by the beginning of the millennium and how these actors mutually recognised each other's respective "legislative" roles in the field of sustainable development.

Parallel to my search for global actors and the emergence of a secondary social convention, I also searched for the foundations of a possible primary social convention. I determined five potential conclusive criteria of a possible primary social convention for the identification and recognition of rules as laws of GLSD. These were (1) State-led, (2) inclusiveness, (3) consensus, (4) universality and (5) pluralism. Based on a comprehensive review covering more than a four-decade-long period of norm-making efforts at the global level in the field of sustainable development, I concluded that, together with the adoption of the outcome document of the Rio+20 Conference in 2012, a primary social convention among the

[4] Tamanaha, 'Socio-Legal Positivism and a General Jurisprudence', 9.

[5] For example, the Stockholm Declaration, when adopted back in 1972, was not a binding document of international law. However, it served as a basis for the development of certain legal concepts and principles in the field of international environmental law.

global actors took a clear shape with respect to the identification and recognition of rules as laws of GLSD. And finally, as a result of a three-year-long process, on 25 September 2015, the SDGs were commonly adopted by global actors and in full accordance with their primary social convention as the very first rules of GLSD.

This is how I explored the four-decade journey of sustainable development from its birth as a simple concept to being the "key element of the overarching framework for United Nations activities" and becoming: (i) in practical terms, a globally recognised guidebook and homework for sustainable development with goals, targets and indicators, and (ii) in theocratical terms, a new concept of law at the global level, namely, GLSD.

The reason for my quest into the SDGs and subsequent finding of the SDGs as the rules of GLSD is significantly related to the global actors', especially States', long-time commitment to sustainable development. Legal bindingness is the most significant indicator of commitment in terms of rules. Given the planetary nature of the concept of sustainable development, the ideal candidate for legal bindingness of any rule at the global level is to be a binding rule of international law. This is a high threshold to reach. The next available option is to be part of myriad examples of soft law.

The challenge in attempting to place the SDGs in one of these two available categories is that, although it is clear that the SDGs are not legally binding in terms of international law, their categorisation as another example of soft law is also unfit. Considering soft law and international law are at the opposite ends of the "commitment spectrum" of global norms, global actors', especially States' serious and decades-long commitments to the SDGs warrants that the SDGs are better placed around the middle of this spectrum, in a position closer to international law than to soft law.

Back in 1983, when the UNGA adopted Resolution 38/161—where I found the origin of the SDGs—the GA could not help but underscore that the Brundtland Report would not be binding on Governments.[6] In other words, UN Member States were simply emphasising that they would not be legally obliged—in terms of international law—to follow the recommendations of the WCED. Legal bindingness, within the framework of international law, can be described as a key concept with respect to the

[6] 'Process of Preparation of the Environmental Perspective to the Year 2000 and Beyond, UNGA Resolution, UN Doc. A/RES/38/161', para. 13.

"validity of a rule and its membership to the international legal order."[7] Accordingly, the UNGA legally meant that the Brundtland Report would not constitute rule(s) of international law and it would not be part of the international legal order.

This oversimplification of international rules and norms through this binary understanding of "legally binding" and "legally non-binding" in the context of international law has been thoroughly contested by international lawyers and scholars.[8] However, after having provided an overview of different ways in which many approach and methods of international law has been trying to discredit this ontological character of bindingness, Aspremont concludes that the concept of bindingness turned out to be quite resilient and argues that "international lawyers have found that, in spite of those refreshing experiments on the genetic code of the discipline, their role was inextricably bound to be centred on the mastery (and deployment) of those techniques that allow an autonomous distinction between the "legally binding" and the "legally non-binding" as well as a determination of the content of the former."[9]

The topic of sources of international law is, in fact, at the centre of this binary understanding of "legally binding" and "legally non-binding" in the context of international law. Aspremont, Samantha Besson and Sévrine Knuchel edited a very comprehensive handbook on the sources of international law.[10] After having provided a summary of the contestations of international lawyers and scholars against this binary understanding of legal bindingness in international law, they note: "For better or worse, sources of international law remain nowadays deeply entrenched, not only in the practice and theory of international law, but also in the consciousness of international lawyers."[11] Nevertheless, they also added that many

[7] d'Aspremont, 'Bindingness', 4.

[8] For an overview, see; d'Aspremont, 'Towards a New Theory of Sources in International Law'. See also; Peters and Pagotto, 'Soft Law as a New Mode of Governance'. For a more recent and very comprehensive overview of key debates on the sources of international law—which is, in fact, the topic that is at the centre of this binary understanding of "legally binding" and "legally non-binding" in the context of international law, see; d'Aspremont, Besson, and Knuchel, *The Oxford Handbook of the Sources of International Law*. I have to mention that choosing Escher's Waterfall as a cover for the handbook is an ingenious choice and it perfectly depicts the perplexities around the debates on the sources of international law.

[9] d'Aspremont, 'Bindingness', 17.

[10] d'Aspremont, Besson, and Knuchel, *The Oxford Handbook of the Sources of International Law*.

[11] d'Aspremont, Besson, and Knuchel, 13–14.

international lawyers, "distantiate themselves from what they have come to call the 'traditional' or 'classical' (list of) sources and identify new ones, together with new doctrines of sources."[12]

Rightly, it would have been ignorant for international lawyers to turn a blind eye to an obvious fact: More and more, countless norms at the global level—even though they are not legally binding in terms of international law—are in fact much more elaborated, precise and impactful than many other legally binding but vague treaties or conventions. For example, Agenda 21 was, in fact, more "hard law" and "binding" than the 1985 Vienna Convention for the Protection of the Ozone Layer given its normative content prescribing more elaborated and precise obligations.[13] This is, of course, from an international relations' perspective rather than being a legal conclusion. Nevertheless, it is a reality that there are countless similar examples where the compliance with global norms are more and more ensured outside the realm of international law.[14]

In that perspective, I demonstrated in this volume that the SDGs are "legally binding," not according to their validity as rules of international law and their membership to the international legal order, but rather as a normative injunction, as binding as proper legal rules of GLSD, distinct from the concept of international law and their significance and normative value therein.[15]

Given their nature as global rules and as they were unanimously adopted in an UNGA resolution, the SDGs are mostly described by international lawyers as a classic example of soft law.[16] In some specific situations, UNGA resolutions might be considered as a customary rule of international law,

[12] d'Aspremont, Besson, and Knuchel, 13–14.

[13] Abbott et al., 'The Concept of Legalization'.

[14] Berman and Pauwelyn, *Informal International Lawmaking*; see also; Pauwelyn, Wessel, and Wouters, *Informal International Lawmaking*.

[15] There is a massive literature about the binding force of the concept of sustainable development within the context of international law. It goes without saying that all the arguments in favour of the bindingness of the concept of sustainable development strengthen the argument of this book about the lawlike quality of the SDGs in terms of GLSD. However, as this book is about the emergence of a new concept of "law" at the global level, I intentionally avoided to refer to this literature in order not to give mixed signals and to put better light on GLSD. In addition, the focus in this book is on the SDGs as being the very first rules of GLSD while, in the context of international law, the subject of examination is essentially the concept of sustainable development.

[16] Pavoni and Piselli, 'The Sustainable Development Goals and International Environmental Law', 35.

but that is not the case for the SDGs because, while adopting the SGDs, there was no intention on the part of States to lay down rules of international law.[17]

Soft law is defined as "a convenient description for a variety of non-legally binding instruments used in contemporary international relations by States and international organizations."[18] There exist abundant scholarly discussions about the significance of soft law within the context of international law.[19] However, both the proponents and critics of soft law largely agree on the fact that soft law instruments are not binding and, therefore, not law per se.[20]

Duncan French argues that, based on the sui generis nature of the SDGs, "international law is not viewed as an acceptable conduit for the advancement of global development" and he proposes to "re-imagine" international law to better explicate the legal nature of the SDGs.[21] He also notes that soft law is not a proper categorisation for the SDGs because they were not adopted with "an intention to regulate in the absence of law" and they are not "on a journey to some form of 'hardness'" in term of international law.[22]

[17] Paragraph 32 of the International Law Association Report on Formation of Customary International Law reads as follows: "Resolutions accepted unanimously or almost unanimously, and which evince a clear intention on the part of their supporters to lay down a rule of international law, are capable, very exceptionally, of creating general customary law by the mere fact of their adoption." For further details, see; *Statement of Principles Applicable to the Formation of General Customary International Law*, ILA London Conference 2000, Final Report of the Committee on Formation of Customary (General) International Law, pages 55–65.

[18] Boyle, 'Soft Law in International Law-Making', 118–19.

[19] Weil, 'Towards Relative Normativity in International Law'; Chinkin, 'The Challenge of Soft Law'; Dupuy, 'Soft Law and the International Law of the Environment'; Higgins, *Problems and Process*, chap. 2; Klabbers, 'The Redundancy of Soft Law'; Hillgenberg, 'A Fresh Look at Soft Law'; Klabbers, 'The Undesirability of Soft Law'; Koskenniemi, 'The Politics of International Law – 20 Years Later'.

[20] Nevertheless, Alan E. Boyle adds the following "If it is true that some soft law instruments are—like treaties—part of the process by which customary law evolves, then it is equally true that in the evolutionary stage they have not yet generated actual law, and we should not pretend otherwise. Identifying when law in the making has become law is of course precisely the point on which States and international lawyers will often disagree, but it is precisely at that point that 'soft law' is in reality no longer soft. Our focus in this chapter is on soft law as one element in the law-making process precisely because it leads to law, not to something less than law." see in Boyle, 'Soft Law in International Law-Making', 119.

[21] French, 'The Global Goals', 151.

[22] French, 175.

In another article co-authored with Louis J. Kotzé, Duncan French is contemplating and re-imagining what is beyond international law based on the significant global norm-making exercises. The authors inquire whether the efforts about the codification of various international environmental law principles under a "Global Pact for the Environment"[23] would constitute the foundations of *Lex Anthropocenae*.[24] They propose a new "*lex*" for filling existing gaps in existing normative system.[25]

Despite the initial enthusiasm, Global Pact for the Environment did not see the sunrise, with the exception of the recognition of "the right to a clean, healthy, and sustainable environment as a human right" by a UNGA Resolution. Unlike the Resolution adopting the SDGs unanimously, this Resolution was adopted with eight UN Member States' abstention.[26] This is yet another example where global actors opted "non-binding" instruments instead of traditional instruments of international law. This is also one of many paths of change in international law.[27]

Marcel Brus notes that "the development of international law can be better understood by placing legal statements on a continuum from weak to strong legal pronunciations instead of using the binary approach that distinguishes between hard and soft law and that qualifies soft law as non-law."[28] In that sense, Brus supports the categorisation of soft law for the SDGs for the sake of not qualifying the SDGs as non-law. Therefore, he is also in search of a better description of the legal nature of the SDGs and he mentions global law as one of the options. He notes: "there is no historic pedigree for the development of global law. Interstate law has developed in the course of centuries. The development of global law has only

[23] Following a French initiative, an UNGA resolution was adopted establishing an "an ad hoc open-ended working group, under the auspices of the General Assembly, to [...] discuss possible options to address possible gaps in international environmental law [...] with a view to making recommendations, which may include the convening of an intergovernmental conference to adopt an international instrument[.]". For further information see; 'Towards a Global Pact for the Environment, UNGA Resolution, UN Doc. A/RES/72/277'; Kotzé and French, 'A Critique of the Global Pact for the Environment'.

[24] Kotzé and French, 'A Critique of the Global Pact for the Environment'.

[25] Kotzé and French, 835.

[26] 'The Human Right to a Clean, Healthy and Sustainable Environment, UNGA Resolution, UN Doc. A/RES/76/300'.

[27] Krisch et al., *The Many Paths of Change in International Law*.

[28] Brus, 'Soft Law in Public International Law'.

recently begun. [...] The SDGs and the Paris Agreement can be regarded as examples of global law rather than interstate law.[29]

There are also other reasons against simple categorisation of the SDGs as another example of soft law. First, soft law is not a type of law. Soft law is a qualification about a potential rule of law, and very frequently, a rule of international law. So, here the term soft is used as an adjective with respect to the quality of these norms because they are not binding. Therefore, soft law is not a type of law, it is like the concept of comparative law. It is not like, Swiss law, Chinese law or international law. However, GLSD is a type of law and is particularly different from the idea of soft law.[30]

Secondly, the reactions around the world after the adoption of the SDGs provide more than enough incentive for internalising the true legal nature of GLSD, well beyond being another example of soft law. For example, before the adoption of the SDGs, back in 2015, the Inter-Parliamentary Union adopted the Hanoi Declaration on the Sustainable Development Goals and declared that they "commit to translating the goals into enforceable domestic laws" and "to hold governments accountable for the goals they have subscribed to."[31]

In this declaration, these parliamentarians from over 130 countries do not give the impression that the SDGs are another example of soft law. They all know that, in terms of international law, the SDGs are not legally binding. Nevertheless, these parliamentarians seem to be quite motivated to go beyond the formalities of international law and even hold their governments accountable for the Global Goals and to make sure that enabling laws are legislated.

In terms of comparison, there exists a massive amount of difference with respect to the parliamentarians' reactions around the globe, respectively, to the Global Compact on Migration (GCM) and to the SDGs. The GCM caused significant political chaos at the domestic level in many countries around the world, especially in Europe.[32] In Switzerland, the

[29] Brus, 262–66. In Brus' words, this volume demonstrates, through the decades-long process leading to the adoption of the SDGs, that, in fact, a historic pedigree exists in the case of GLSD.

[30] For example, in this regard, see the criticism of Richard Collins about the Neil Walker's concept of global law where he explains how Walker qualifies global law as not a type of law but rather as an "Adjectival category" in Collins, 'The Slipperiness of "Global Law"', 725–26.

[31] 'Hanoi Declaration: The Sustainable Development Goals: Turning Words into Action (132nd IPU Assembly)'.

[32] Regarding political chaos in other countries in relation to GCM, it caused the fall of the Belgian government on 18 December 2018. Many other European countries also expressed reluctance about the GCM.

right-wing populist party (largest party in the Swiss parliament), was worried about the legal implications of the GCM and prevented Swiss Government from signing the GCM. Due to similar discussions in many European countries, the GCM was only endorsed in UNGA in 2018, with 152 votes in favour, 5 against and 12 abstentions. Switzerland abstained at the vote. Regarding political chaos in other countries the GCM caused the fall of the Belgian government on 18 December 2018. Brazil voted in favour but later withdrew from it. Many other European countries also made expressed reluctance about the GCM.

Things are significantly different when it comes to the SDGs. For instance, in Kenya, a partnership among Kenyan Parliamentary Human Rights Association, the Kenya Human Rights Commission, the Office of the Attorney General and the Office of the Chief Justice resulted in Goal 16 being integrated "into the Legal Aid Bill, the Access to Information Bill and the Community Land Bill" and "[i]ndicators to track Goal 16 were also integrated into the draft National Human Rights Policy and Action Plan."[33]

Based on the 64 Voluntary National Reviews submitted to the High-Level Political Forum in 2016 and 2017, UN Department for Economic and Social Affairs ("UN DESA") prepared a Compendium of National Institutional Arrangements for implementing the 2030 Agenda for Sustainable Development. The following are some examples of the actions taken at the parliamentary level in different countries to establish new institutional mechanisms for the implementation of the SDGs:

> [I]n Argentina, the 2030 Agenda Parliamentary Observatory was established to promote the adaptation and implementation of the SDGs. The Belgian parliament has established an "SDG Group of Friends" and is planning to integrate relevant SDGs within the work of each parliamentary committee. In Denmark, the parliament established a cross-party network bringing together members from standing committees relevant to the 2030 Agenda. Guatemala's Congress has established working groups pertaining to the SDGs. In Kenya, a Parliamentary SDGs Caucus will be formed. In Nigeria, to enhance the legislative and oversight roles of Parliamentarians on

[33] The Transparency, Accountability & Participation for 2030 Agenda Network, 'Goal 16 Advocacy Toolkit: A Practical Guide for Stakeholders for National-Level Advocacy around Peaceful, Just and Inclusive Societies', 24.

> SDGs implementation process, two select committees on SDGs have been established in the Senate and House of Representatives. The National Legislative Assembly of Thailand has established a Sub-committee on Monitoring the Implementation of Sustainable Development Goals. Zimbabwe created a Parliamentary Thematic Committee on SDGs (emphasis added).[34]

Another handbook prepared as a result of a cooperation among various actors[35] about engaging parliaments on the 2030 Agenda and the SDGs,[36] refers to the following examples, among many others, with respect to better incorporation of the SDGs at the domestic level, through parliaments:

> **Sierra Leone**: The SDGs were linked to the country's 8 Pillars of the Agenda for Prosperity, the 3rd Poverty Reduction Strategy Paper, and aligned to each spending category of the 2016 National Budget which was approved by parliament in November 2015.
> **Serbia**: The National Assembly is working together with GOPAC Serbia and UNDP to establish budget monitoring tools that track its SDG expenditures and impacts.
> **Brazil** [:] [T]he Federal Court of Accounts developed a framework to aggregate performance audit results to monitor and review the implementation of the SDGs at the national level.
> **India** [:] [T]he Office of the Comptroller and Auditor General has scrutinised funding for SDG implementation, and is currently planning an audit on the government's SDG preparedness.
> [**Korea:**] The Korean National Assembly's SDG Forum has been holding open meetings, public hearings and has run two campaigns on the SDGs with the purpose of creating more awareness among civil society actors and citizens at large.[37]

[34] UN Department for Economic and Social Affairs, 'Compendium of National Institutional Arrangements for Implementing the 2030 Agenda for Sustainable Development', 7–8.

[35] The Handbook was produced and published by Together 2030 in partnership with Newcastle University, Philippine Social Enterprise Network, Sightsavers, World Vision and Global Focus. Funding support was provided by Global Focus, Sightsavers and World Vision. Technical support provided by the United Nations Development Programme (UNDP).

[36] Together 2030, 'Engaging Parliaments on the 2030 Agenda and the SDGs: Representation, Accountability and Implementation A Handbook for Civil Society'.

[37] Together 2030, 20, 35, 37.

In addition to parliament and parliamentarians, Governments are also entirely committed to the SDGs. In 2023, the UNGA noted that "Voluntary National Reviews have been strengthened over the past few years with 188 countries participating in this process, representing 97 per cent of the whole United Nations membership."[38]

All the above is to demonstrate that, the SDGs are far beyond being an ordinary UNGA resolution, and, accordingly, it would be very simplistic, traditional and classical to determine their legal nature based on them being a UNGA resolution. It was thus inevitable to wonder that sustainable development might have its own legal field at the global level, and this book illustrates that there might well exist a new concept of law entitled as GLSD.

The year 2023 was the midpoint for the SDGs. "[T]he progress on most of the SDGs is either moving much too slowly or has regressed below the 2015 baseline."[39] This of course puts the SDGs' impact into question. In fact, in 2022, a group of researchers analysed more than 3000 scientific studies on the SDGs (2016 to April 2021) and found that "the 17 SDGs have thus far had only a limited political impact on global, national and local governance since their adoption in 2015."[40] This project "searched for three types of effects: discursive, normative and institutional changes" and defined discursive effects as "changes in global and national debates that make them more aligned with the SDGs." The project found that there is "sound evidence that [...] the SDGs have had some impact from global governance to local politics" but "this impact has so far been largely discursive."[41] Thus, the project's article concludes as follows:

> Yet we are far from the ambition expressed by the [UNGA] of "free[ing] the human race from the tyranny of poverty and want and heal[ing] and secur[ing] our planet". More fundamental change is needed for the SDGs to become "the bold and transformative steps ... to shift the world on to a

[38] 'Strengthening Voluntary National Reviews through Country-Led Evaluation, UNGA Resolution, UN Doc. A/RES/77/283', para. Preamble, 2.

[39] 'Political Declaration of the High-Level Political Forum on Sustainable Development Convened under the Auspices of the General Assembly, UNGA Resolution, UN Doc. A/RES/78/1', para. 8.

[40] Biermann et al., 'Scientific Evidence on the Political Impact of the Sustainable Development Goals', 798.

[41] Biermann et al., 798.

sustainable and resilient path" that the 2030 Agenda of the United Nations has promised.[42]

Although I agree with this conclusion, what I emphasised in this book is that the SDGs are not only about the content of the Global Goals and the promises of 2030 Agenda. They are global rules of sustainable development, they are adopted by global actors and they are recognised as such by the same actors. This recognition is also confirmed by the aforementioned project's conclusion. The project's conclusion that there is sound evidence that the SDGs had discursive impact is the global actors' recognition of the SDGs as global rules of sustainable development. In this sense, what this book illustrates is one of the most tangible achievements of the SDGs.

The promise to free the human race from the tyranny of poverty and to heal the planet is the global actors' promise. The adoption of the SDGs is a key milestone towards achieving this promise, but it is not enough. How far this will be achieved also depends on all of us. International humanitarian law is today much more than it was when Henry Dunant pioneered for the adoption of the first Geneva Convention. Same goes for international criminal law, international human rights law, etc. This is also an endless process. Neither international humanitarian law nor international criminal law is where it should be. Same goes of GLSD. Yet, humanity came so far and it is indeed possible to leave no one behind.

[42] Biermann et al., 798.

Bibliography

Articles

Abbott, Kenneth W. "Engaging the Public and the Private in Global Sustainability Governance." *International Affairs* 88, no. 3 (May 1, 2012): 543–64. https://doi.org/10.1111/j.1468-2346.2012.01088.x.

Abbott, Kenneth W., and Steven Bernstein. "The High-Level Political Forum on Sustainable Development: Orchestration by Default and Design." *Global Policy* 6, no. 3 (2015): 222–33. https://doi.org/10.1111/1758-5899.12199.

Abbott, Kenneth W., Robert O. Keohane, Andrew Moravcsik, Anne-Marie Slaughter, and Duncan Snidal. "The Concept of Legalization." *International Organization* 54, no. 3 (ed 2000): 401–19. https://doi.org/10.1162/002081800551271.

Amariles, David Restrepo. "Legal Indicators, Global Law and Legal Pluralism: An Introduction." *The Journal of Legal Pluralism and Unofficial Law* 47, no. 1 (January 2, 2015): 9–21. https://doi.org/10.1080/07329113.2015.1046739.

———. "Supping with the Devil? Indicators and the Rise of Managerial Rationality in Law." *International Journal of Law in Context* 13, no. 4 (December 2017): 465–84. https://doi.org/10.1017/S1744552317000398.

Aspremont, Jean d'. "Bindingness." SSRN Scholarly Paper. Rochester, NY: Social Science Research Network, November 13, 2015. https://papers.ssrn.com/abstract=2690155.

———. "Bypassing the Authority of International Law: The Virtue of Modern Self-Referentiality." SSRN Scholarly Paper. Rochester, NY: Social Science

H. Göksan, *Global Law of Sustainable Development*, Global Issues, https://doi.org/10.1007/978-3-031-74547-8

Research Network, September 21, 2017a. https://papers.ssrn.com/abstract=3040975.

———. "Herbert Hart in Post-Modern International Legal Scholarship." SSRN Scholarly Paper. Rochester, NY: Social Science Research Network, October 2, 2012. https://papers.ssrn.com/abstract=2155629.

———. "International Lawyers and Legal Forms: Transatlantic Denials." SSRN Scholarly Paper. Rochester, NY: Social Science Research Network, September 14, 2017b. https://papers.ssrn.com/abstract=3036973.

———. "Non-State Actors and the Formation of International Customary Law: Unlearning Some Common Tropes." SSRN Scholarly Paper. Rochester, NY: Social Science Research Network, November 10, 2017c. https://papers.ssrn.com/abstract=3068842.

———. "Softness in International Law: A Self-Serving Quest for New Legal Materials." *European Journal of International Law* 19, no. 5 (November 1, 2008): 1075–93. https://doi.org/10.1093/ejil/chn057.

———. "The Control Over Knowledge by International Courts and Arbitral Tribunals." SSRN Scholarly Paper. Rochester, NY: Social Science Research Network, September 9, 2017d. https://papers.ssrn.com/abstract=3034682.

———. "The Idea of 'Rules' in the Sources of International Law." *British Yearbook of International Law* 84, no. 1 (January 1, 2014): 103–30. https://doi.org/10.1093/bybil/bru025.

———. "The International Court of Justice and the Irony of System-Design." *Journal of International Dispute Settlement* 8, no. 2 (July 1, 2017e): 366–87. https://doi.org/10.1093/jnlids/idw020.

———. "Towards a New Theory of Sources in International Law." *The Oxford Handbook of the Theory of International Law*, June 2, 2016. https://doi.org/10.1093/law/9780198701958.003.0028.

———. "What Was Not Meant to Be: General Principles of Law As a Source of International Law." SSRN Scholarly Paper. Rochester, NY: Social Science Research Network, October 14, 2017f. https://papers.ssrn.com/abstract=3053158.

Barr, Michael S., and Geoffrey P. Miller. "Global Administrative Law: The View from Basel." *European Journal of International Law* 17, no. 1 (February 1, 2006): 15–46. https://doi.org/10.1093/ejil/chi167.

Barral, Virginie. "Sustainable Development in International Law: Nature and Operation of an Evolutive Legal Norm." *European Journal of International Law* 23, no. 2 (May 1, 2012): 377–400. https://doi.org/10.1093/ejil/chs016.

Baxter, Hugh. "Niklas Luhmann's Theory of Autopoietic Legal Systems." *Annual Review of Law and Social Science* 9, no. 1 (2013): 167–84. https://doi.org/10.1146/annurev-lawsocsci-102612-134027.

Been, Wouter de. "Rapprochement in Legal Theory? Michael Giudice's Case for Constructive Conceptual Explanation." *Jurisprudence* 8, no. 3 (September 2, 2017): 685–95. https://doi.org/10.1080/20403313.2017.1380898.

Berman, Paul Schiff. "A Pluralist Approach to International Law." *Yale Journal of International Law* 32 (2007a): 301–30.

———. "From International Law to Law and Globalization," April 18, 2005. https://papers.ssrn.com/abstract=700668.

———. "Global Legal Pluralism." *Southern California Law Review* 80 (2007b 2006): 1155–238.

———. "The New Legal Pluralism." *Annual Review of Law and Social Science* 5, no. 1 (2009): 225–42. https://doi.org/10.1146/annurev.lawsocsci.093008.131539.

Besson, Samantha. "How to Theorise Law in a Transnational Context." *Transnational Legal Theory* 2, no. 4 (2011): 573–79.

———. "The Authority of International Law - Lifting the State Veil." *Sydney Law Review* 31 (2009): 343–80.

Bissio, Roberto. "Civil Society and the MDGs." *Development Policy Journal* 3, no. April 2003 (April 2003): 151–60.

Biswas, Margaret R., and Asit K. Biswas. "Environment and Sustained Development in the Third World: A Review of the Past Decade." *Third World Quarterly* 4, no. 3 (1982): 479–91.

Bodansky, Daniel. "The Legal Character of the Paris Agreement." *Review of European, Comparative & International Environmental Law* 25, no. 2 (2016): 142–50. https://doi.org/10.1111/reel.12154.

Bogdandy, Armin von, and Ingo Venzke. "Beyond Dispute: International Judicial Institutions as Lawmakers Beyond Dispute: International Judicial Institutions as Lawmakers: I. Framing the Issue." *German Law Journal*12 (2011): 979–1004.

Boyle, A. E. "Some Reflections on the Relationship of Treaties and Soft Law." *International & Comparative Law Quarterly* 48, no. 4 (October 1999): 901–13. https://doi.org/10.1017/S0020589300063739.

Campbell, Tim E.J. "The Political Meaning of Stockholm: Third World Participation in the Environment Conference Process." *Stanford Journal of International Studies* 8 (1973): 138–53.

Chasek, Pamela S., and Lynn M. Wagner. "Breaking the Mold: A New Type of Multilateral Sustainable Development Negotiation." *International Environmental Agreements: Politics, Law and Economics* 16, no. 3 (June 1, 2016): 397–413. https://doi.org/10.1007/s10784-016-9320-2.

Chasek, Pamela S., Lynn M. Wagner, Faye Leone, Ana-Maria Lebada, and Nathalie Risse. "Getting to 2030: Negotiating the Post-2015 Sustainable Development Agenda." *Review of European, Comparative & International Environmental Law* 25, no. 1 (2016): 5–14. https://doi.org/10.1111/reel.12149.

Chinkin, C. M. "The Challenge of Soft Law: Development and Change in International Law." *International & Comparative Law Quarterly* 38, no. 4 (October 1989): 850–66. https://doi.org/10.1093/iclqaj/38.4.850.

Cohen, Edward S. "Normative Modeling for Global Economic Governance: The Case of the United Nations Commission on International Trade Law (UNCITRAL)." *Brooklyn Journal of International Law* 36 (2011 2010): 567–604.

Cohen, Harlan Grant. "Finding International Law, Part II: Our Fragmenting Legal Community." *New York University Journal of International Law and Politics* 44 (2012 2011): 1049–108.

Coleman, Jules L. "Beyond Inclusive Legal Positivism." *Ratio Juris* 22, no. 3 (September 1, 2009): 359–94. https://doi.org/10.1111/j.1467-9337.2009.00430.x.

———. "Incorporationism, Conventionality, and the Practical Difference Thesis." *Legal Theory* 4, no. 4 (1998): 381–425.

———. "Negative and Positive Positivism." *Journal of Legal Studies* 11 (1982): 139–64.

Coleman, Jules L., and Ori Simchen. "'Law.'" *Legal Theory* 9, no. 1 (March 2003): 1–41. https://doi.org/10.1017/S1352325203000016.

Collins, Richard. "The Slipperiness of 'Global Law.'" *Oxford Journal of Legal Studies* 37, no. 3 (September 1, 2017): 714–39. https://doi.org/10.1093/ojls/gqx002.

Cotterrell, Roger. "Law's Community: Legal Theory and the Image of Legality." *Journal of Law and Society* 19, no. 4 (1992): 405–22. https://doi.org/10.2307/1410061.

———. "Transnational Communities and the Concept of Law." *Ratio Juris* 21, no. 1 (March 1, 2008): 1–18. https://doi.org/10.1111/j.1467-9337.2007.00377.x.

———. "What Is Transnational Law?" *Law & Social Inquiry* 37, no. 2 (March 1, 2012): 500–524. https://doi.org/10.1111/j.1747-4469.2012.01306.x.

Culver, Keith. "Leaving the Hart-Dworkin Debate." *The University of Toronto Law Journal* 51, no. 4 (2001): 367–98. https://doi.org/10.2307/825911.

———. "Sensing Possibility in International Law – Concepts and Categories for the 21st Century: A Response to Fleur Johns." *AJIL Unbound* 111 (ed 2017): 200–204. https://doi.org/10.1017/aju.2017.53.

D'Amato, Anthony. "Is International Law Really Law." *Northwestern University Law Review* 79 (1985 1984): 1293–1314.

———. "It's a Bird, It's a Plane, It's Jus Cogens Essay." *Connecticut Journal of International Law* 6 (1991 1990): 1–6.

———. "The Concept of Human Rights in International Law." *Columbia Law Review* 82, no. 6 (1982): 1110–59. https://doi.org/10.2307/1122161.

———. “The Neo-Positivist Concept of International Law.” *The American Journal of International Law* 59, no. 2 (1965): 321–24. https://doi.org/10.2307/2196972.

———. “Trashing Customary International Law.” *The American Journal of International Law* 81, no. 1 (1987): 101–05. https://doi.org/10.2307/2202136.

Domingo, Rafael. “Gaius, Vattel, and the New Global Law Paradigm.” *European Journal of International Law* 22, no. 3 (August 1, 2011): 627–47. https://doi.org/10.1093/ejil/chr050.

———. “Global Law and the New Global Human Community.” SSRN Scholarly Paper. Rochester, NY: Social Science Research Network, May 11, 2015. https://papers.ssrn.com/abstract=2943447.

———. “The Crisis of International Law.” *Vanderbilt Journal of Transnational Law* 42 (2009): 1543–94.

———. “The New Global Human Community.” *Chicago Journal of International Law* 12 (2012 2011): 563–88.

Duncanson, Ian W. “The Strange World of English Jurisprudence.” *Northern Ireland Legal Quarterly* 30 (1979): 207–24.

Dupuy, Pierre-Marie. “L’unité de l’ordre Juridique International : Cours Général de Droit International Public (2000) (Volume 297),” December 31, 2002a.

———. “Soft Law and the International Law of the Environment.” *Michigan Journal of International Law* 12 (1991 1990): 420–35.

———. “Vers Une Unité Matérielle de l’ordre Juridique International ?” *Collected Courses of the Hague Academy of International Law*, December 31, 2002b. https://referenceworks.brillonline.com/entries/the-hague-academy-collected-courses/vers-une-unite-materielle-de-lordre-juridique-international-297-ej.9789041118592.009_489.6#1.

Dworkin, Ronald. “A New Philosophy for International Law.” *Philosophy & Public Affairs* 41, no. 1 (January 1, 2013): 2–30. https://doi.org/10.1111/papa.12008.

———. “Hart’s Posthumous Reply Essays.” *Harvard Law Review* 130 (2017 2016): 2096–2130.

———. “Hart’s Postscript and the Character of Political Philosophy.” *Oxford Journal of Legal Studies* 24, no. 1 (March 1, 2004): 1–37. https://doi.org/10.1093/ojls/24.1.1.

———. “The Model of Rules.” *The University of Chicago Law Review* 35, no. 1 (1967): 14–46. https://doi.org/10.2307/1598947.

Ellis, Jaye. “Has International Law Outgrown Trail Smelter?” SSRN Scholarly Paper. Rochester, NY: Social Science Research Network, February 21, 2011. https://papers.ssrn.com/abstract=1766142.

Finger, Matthias, Tom Princen, and Jack Manno. "Nongovernmental Organizations in World Environmental Politics." *International Environmental Affairs* 7, no. 1 (1995): 42–58.

Fischer-Lescano, Andreas, and Gunther Teubner. "Regime-Collisions: The Vain Search for Legal Unity in the Fragmentation of Global Law Diversity or Cacophony: New Sources of Norms in International Law Symposium." *Michigan Journal of International Law* 25 (2004 2003): 999–1046.

Fischer-Lescno, Andreas, and Gunther Teubner. "Reply to Andreas L. Paulus Consensus as Fiction of Global Law Diversity or Cacophony: New Sources of Norms in International Law: Reply." *Michigan Journal of International Law* 25 (2004 2003): 1059–74.

Frydman, Benoit. "A Pragmatic Approach to Global Law." SSRN Scholarly Paper. Rochester, NY: Social Science Research Network, August 19, 2013. https://papers.ssrn.com/abstract=2312504.

———. "Comment penser le droit global ?," February 2012a. http://hdl.handle.net/2013/ULB-DIPOT:oai:dipot.ulb.ac.be:2013/130337.

———. "Coregulation: A Possible Legal Model for Global Governance." SSRN Scholarly Paper. Rochester, NY: Social Science Research Network, January 5, 2012b. https://papers.ssrn.com/abstract=1980176.

Frydman, Benoît, and Isabelle Rorive. "Regulating Internet Content through Intermediaries in Europe and the USA." *Zeitschrift Für Rechtssoziologie* 23, no. 1 (2016): 41–60. https://doi.org/10.1515/zfrs-2002-0104.

Frydman, Benoît, and William Twining. "A Symposium on Global Law, Legal Pluralism and Legal Indicators." *The Journal of Legal Pluralism and Unofficial Law* 47, no. 1 (January 2, 2015): 1–8. https://doi.org/10.1080/07329113.2015.1030210.

Fukuda-Parr, Sakiko. "From the Millennium Development Goals to the Sustainable Development Goals: Shifts in Purpose, Concept, and Politics of Global Goal Setting for Development." *Gender & Development* 24, no. 1 (January 2, 2016): 43–52. https://doi.org/10.1080/13552074.2016.1145895.

Fukuda-Parr, Sakiko, and David Hulme. "International Norm Dynamics and the 'End of Poverty': Understanding the Millennium Development Goals." *Global Governance: A Review of Multilateralism and International Organizations* 17, no. 1 (February 15, 2011): 17–36. https://doi.org/10.5555/ggov.2011.17.1.17.

Fukuda-Parr, Sakiko, and Amy Orr. "The MDG Hunger Target and the Competing Frameworks of Food Security." *Journal of Human Development and Capabilities* 15, no. 2–3 (July 3, 2014): 147–60. https://doi.org/10.1080/19452829.2014.896323.

Fukui, Yasuhito. "The Arms Trade Treaty: Pursuit for the Effective Control of Arms Transfer." *Journal of Conflict and Security Law* 20, no. 2 (July 1, 2015): 301–21. https://doi.org/10.1093/jcsl/krv003.

Giudice, Michael. "Conceptual Analysis, Legal Pluralism, and EU Law." *Transnational Legal Theory* 6, no. 3–4 (October 2, 2015): 586–607. https://doi.org/10.1080/20414005.2015.1120023.

———. "The Regular Practice of Morality in Law." *Ratio Juris* 21, no. 1 (March 1, 2008): 94–106. https://doi.org/10.1111/j.1467-9337.2007.00381.x.

———. "Ways of Understanding Diversity Among Theories of Law." *Law and Philosophy* 24, no. 5 (September 1, 2005): 509–45. https://doi.org/10.1007/s10982-004-4118-8.

Green, Leslie. "General Jurisprudence: A 25th Anniversary Essay." *Oxford Journal of Legal Studies* 25, no. 4 (2005): 565–80.

———. "Legal Positivism," January 3, 2003. https://stanford.library.sydney.edu.au/entries/legal-positivism/.

———. "Positivism and the Inseparability of Law and Morals Symposium: The Hart-Fuller Debate at Fifty." *New York University Law Review* 83 (2008): 1035–58.

Greenawalt, Kent. "The Rule of Recognition and the Constitution." *Michigan Law Review* 85, no. 4 (1987): 621–71. https://doi.org/10.2307/1288727.

Griffiths, John. "What Is Legal Pluralism." *Journal of Legal Pluralism and Unofficial Law* 24 (1986): 1–56.

Hajjaji, Shams Al Din Al. "Review of the New Global Law by Rafael Domingo Review." *Berkeley Journal of International Law* 32 (2014): 268–80.

Halpin, Andrew. "The Methodology of Jurisprudence: Thirty Years Off the Point." *Canadian Journal of Law & Jurisprudence* 19, no. 1 (January 2006): 67–105. https://doi.org/10.1017/S0841820900005609.

Handl, Gunther F., W. Michael Reisman, Bruno Simma, Pierre Marie Dupuy, and Christine Chinkin. "A Hard Look at Soft Law." *Proceedings of the Annual Meeting (American Society of International Law)* 82 (1988): 371–95.

Harlow, Carol. "Global Administrative Law: The Quest for Principles and Values." *European Journal of International Law* 17, no. 1 (February 1, 2006): 187–214. https://doi.org/10.1093/ejil/chi158.

Hart, H. L. A. "Positivism and the Separation of Law and Morals." *Harvard Law Review* 71, no. 4 (1958): 593–629. https://doi.org/10.2307/1338225.

Hierlmeier, Jodie. "UNEP: Retrospect and Prospect - Options for Reforming the Global Environmental Governance Regime." *Georgetown International Environmental Law Review* 14 (2002 2001): 767–806.

Higgins, Rosalyn. "A Babel of Judicial Voices - Ruminations from the Bench." *International and Comparative Law Quarterly* 55 (2006): 791–804.

———. "The ICJ, the ECJ, and the Integrity of International Law." *International and Comparative Law Quarterly* 52 (2003): 1–20.

Hillgenberg, H. "A Fresh Look at Soft Law." *European Journal of International Law* 10, no. 3 (January 1, 1999): 499–515. https://doi.org/10.1093/ejil/10.3.499.

Horner, Rory, and David Hulme. "From International to Global Development: New Geographies of 21st Century Development." *Development and Change*, n.d., n/a-n/a. https://doi.org/10.1111/dech.12379.

Hulme, David. "Reproductive Health and the Millennium Development Goals: Politics, Ethics, Evidence and an 'Unholy Alliance.'" SSRN Scholarly Paper. Rochester, NY: Social Science Research Network, February 1, 2010. https://papers.ssrn.com/abstract=1545907.

———. "The Millennium Development Goals (MDGs): A Short History of the World's Biggest Promise." SSRN Scholarly Paper. Rochester, NY: Social Science Research Network, September 30, 2009. https://papers.ssrn.com/abstract=1544271.

Ivanova, Maria. "UNEP in Global Environmental Governance: Design, Leadership, Location." *Global Environmental Politics* 10, no. 1 (February 1, 2010): 30–59. https://doi.org/10.1162/glep.2010.10.1.30.

Jabareen, Yosef. "A New Conceptual Framework for Sustainable Development." *Environment, Development and Sustainability* 10, no. 2 (April 1, 2008): 179–92. https://doi.org/10.1007/s10668-006-9058-z.

Joyner, Christopher C., and Nancy D. Joyner. "Global Eco-Management and International Organizations: The Stockholm Conference and the Problems of Cooperation." *Natural Resources Journal* 14, no. 4 (1974): 533–55.

Joyner, Chritopher C. "U.N. General Assembly Resolutions and International Law: Rethinking the Contemporary Dynamics of Norm-Creation." *California Western International Law Journal* 11 (1981): 445–78.

Kaasa, Stine Madland. "The UN Commission on Sustainable Development: Which Mechanisms Explain Its Accomplishments?" *Global Environmental Politics* 7, no. 3 (August 1, 2007): 107–29. https://doi.org/10.1162/glep.2007.7.3.107.

Kelsen, Hans. "Professor Stone and the Pure Theory of Law." *Stanford Law Review* 17 (1965 1964): 1128–57.

Kingsbury, Benedict. "International Law as Inter-Public Law." *Nomos* 49 (2009a): 167–204.

———. "The Concept of Compliance as a Function of Competing Conceptions of International Law." *Michigan Journal of International Law* 19 (1998 1997): 345–72.

———. "The Concept of 'Law' in Global Administrative Law." *European Journal of International Law* 20, no. 1 (February 1, 2009b): 23–57. https://doi.org/10.1093/ejil/chp005.

———. "Weighing Global Regulatory Rules and Decisions in National Courts Part I: Definitional Issues in Global Administrative Law." *Acta Juridica* 2009 (2009c): 90–122.

Kingsbury, Benedict, Nico Krisch, and Richard B. Stewart. "The Emergence of Global Administrative Law." *Law and Contemporary Problems* 68, no. 3/4 (2005): 15–61.

Kiss, Alexandre Charles, and Stéphane Doumbé-Billé. "Conférence des Nations Unies sur l'environnement et le développement (Rio de Janeiro-juin 1992)." *Annuaire Français de Droit International* 38, no. 1 (1992): 823–43. https://doi.org/10.3406/afdi.1992.3097.

Klabbers, Jan. "Constitutionalism Lite." *International Organizations Law Review* 1 (2004): 31–58.

———. "Law, Ethics and Global Governance: Accountability in Perspective." *New Zealand Journal of Public and International Law* 11 (2013): 309–22.

———. "The Redundancy of Soft Law." *Nordic Journal of International Law* 65 (1996): 167–82.

———. "The Undesirability of Soft Law." *Nordic Journal of International Law* 67 (1998): 381–92.

Koskenniemi, Martti. "Constitutionalism as Mindset: Reflections on Kantian Themes about International Law and Globalization Critical Modernities: Politics and Law beyond the Liberal Imagination." *Theoretical Inquiries in Law* 8 (2007a): 9–36.

———. "Empire and International Law: The Real Spanish Contribution." *University of Toronto Law Journal*, February 25, 2011. https://doi.org/10.3138/utlj.61.1.001.

———. "The Fate of Public International Law: Between Technique and Politics." *The Modern Law Review* 70, no. 1 (January 1, 2007b): 1–30. https://doi.org/10.1111/j.1468-2230.2006.00624.x.

———. "The Politics of International Law – 20 Years Later." *European Journal of International Law* 20, no. 1 (February 1, 2009): 7–19. https://doi.org/10.1093/ejil/chp006.

Koskenniemi, Martti, and Päivi Leino. "Fragmentation of International Law? Postmodern Anxieties." *Leiden Journal of International Law* 15, no. 3 (January 1, 2002): 553–80.

Kotzé, Louis J., and Duncan French. "A Critique of the Global Pact for the Environment: A Stillborn Initiative or the Foundation for Lex Anthropocenae?" *International Environmental Agreements: Politics, Law and Economics* 18, no. 6 (December 1, 2018): 811–38. https://doi.org/10.1007/s10784-018-9417-x.

Kramer, Matthew H. "Moral Principles and Legal Validity." *Ratio Juris* 22, no. 1 (March 1, 2009): 44–61. https://doi.org/10.1111/j.1467-9337.2008.00411.x.

———. "The Rule of Misrecognition in the Hart of Jurisprudence." *Oxford Journal of Legal Studies* 8 (1988): 401–33.

Kratochwil, Friedrich. "How (Il)Liberal Is the Liberal Theory of Law? Some Critical Remarks on Slaughter's Approach." *Comparative Sociology* 9, no. 1

(January 1, 2010): 120–45. https://doi.org/10.1163/156913210X12535202814478-2.
Krisch, Nico. "International Law in Times of Hegemony: Unequal Power and the Shaping of the International Legal Order." *European Journal of International Law* 16, no. 3 (June 1, 2005): 369–408. https://doi.org/10.1093/ejil/chi123.
———. "Pluralism in International Law and Beyond." SSRN Scholarly Paper. Rochester, NY: Social Science Research Network, June 3, 2015a. https://papers.ssrn.com/abstract=2613930.
———. "The Pluralism of Global Administrative Law." *European Journal of International Law* 17, no. 1 (February 1, 2006): 247–78. https://doi.org/10.1093/ejil/chi163.
———. "The Structure of Postnational Authority." SSRN Scholarly Paper. Rochester, NY: Social Science Research Network, February 13, 2015b. https://papers.ssrn.com/abstract=2564579.
Krisch, Nico, and Benedict Kingsbury. "Introduction: Global Governance and Global Administrative Law in the International Legal Order." *European Journal of International Law* 17, no. 1 (February 1, 2006): 1–13. https://doi.org/10.1093/ejil/chi170.
Kuo, Ming-Sung. "The Concept of 'Law' in Global Administrative Law: A Reply to Benedict Kingsbury." *European Journal of International Law* 20, no. 4 (November 1, 2009): 997–1004. https://doi.org/10.1093/ejil/chp095.
Le Golf, Pierrick. "Global Law: A Legal Phenomenon Emerging from the Process of Globalization." *Indiana Journal of Global Legal Studies* 14, no. 1 (August 13, 2007): 119–45.
Lefkowitz, David. "Customary Law and The Case Fro Incorporationism." *Legal Theory* 11, no. 4 (December 2005): 405–20. https://doi.org/10.1017/S1352325205050214.
———. "(Dis)Solving the Chronological Paradox in Customary International Law: A Hartian Approach." *Canadian Journal of Law and Jurisprudence* 21 (2008): 129–48.
———. "What Makes a Social Order Primitive? In Defense of Hart's Take on International Law." *Legal Theory* 23, no. 4 (December 2017): 258–82. https://doi.org/10.1017/S1352325217000258.
Leiter, Brian. "Beyond the Hart/Dworkin Debate: The Methodology Problem in Jurisprudence Symposium: Has Law Moral Foundations." *American Journal of Jurisprudence* 48 (2003): 17–52.
———. "Realism, Hard Positivism, and Conceptual Analysis." *Legal Theory* 4, no. 4 (December 1998): 533–47. https://doi.org/10.1017/S1352325200001130.
MacCormick, Neil. "Beyond the Sovereign State." *The Modern Law Review* 56, no. 1 (January 1, 1993): 1–18. https://doi.org/10.1111/j.1468-2230.1993.tb02851.x.

———. "The Concept of Law and 'The Concept of Law.'" *Oxford Journal of Legal Studies* 14, no. 1 (1994): 1–23. https://doi.org/10.2307/764760.

Marks, Gary. "An Actor-centred Approach to Multi-level Governance." *Regional & Federal Studies* 6, no. 2 (June 1, 1996): 20–38. https://doi.org/10.1080/13597569608420966.

Marmor, Andrei. "Legal Conventionalism." *Legal Theory* 4, no. 4 (December 1998): 509–31. https://doi.org/10.1017/S1352325200001129.

———. "What Is Law and What Counts as Law? The Separation Thesis in Context." SSRN Scholarly Paper. Rochester, NY: Social Science Research Network, August 1, 2017. https://papers.ssrn.com/abstract=3011432.

Martinez-Fraga, Pedro J. "Book Review, Rafael Domingo, The New Global Law." *McGill Law Journal* 56 (2011 2010): 767–74.

Mee, Laurence D. "The Role of UNEP and UNDP in Multilateral Environmental Agreements." *International Environmental Agreements: Politics, Law and Economics* 5, no. 3 (September 1, 2005): 227–63. https://doi.org/10.1007/s10784-005-3805-8.

Meguro, M. "Distinguishing the Legal Bindingness and Normative Content of Customary International Law." *ESIL Reflections* 6 (December 12, 2017). https://dare.uva.nl/search?identifier=ce416c72-ded9-4373-b3ec-04340635b9da.

Merry, Sally Engle. "Legal Pluralism." *Law & Society Review* 22, no. 5 (1988): 869–96. https://doi.org/10.2307/3053638.

Meyer, Paul. "A Banner Year for Conventional Arms Control? The Arms Trade Treaty and the Small Arms Challenge." *Global Governance: A Review of Multilateralism and International Organizations* 20, no. 2 (April 1, 2014): 203–12. https://doi.org/10.5555/1075-2846-20.2.203.

Miller, Russell, and Rebecca M. Bratspies. "Transboundary Harm in International Law: Lessons from the Trail Smelter Arbitration." SSRN Scholarly Paper. Rochester, NY: Social Science Research Network, 2006. https://papers.ssrn.com/abstract=1990519.

Mulligen, Anne van. "Framing Deformalisation in Public International Law." *Transnational Legal Theory* 6, no. 3–4 (October 2, 2015): 635–60. https://doi.org/10.1080/20414005.2015.1120025.

Pallemaerts, Marc. "International Environmental Law from Stockholm to Rio: Back to the Future?" *Review of European Community & International Environmental Law* 1, no. 3 (September 1, 1992): 254–66. https://doi.org/10.1111/j.1467-9388.1992.tb00044.x.

———. "International Environmental Law in the Age of Sustainable Development: A Critical Assessment of the UNCED Process." *Journal of Law and Commerce* 15 (1996 1995): 623–76.

———. "International Law and Sustainable Development: Any Progress in Johannesburg?" *Review of European Community & International*

Environmental Law 12, no. 1 (2003): 1–11. https://doi.org/10.1111/1467-9388.00339.

Pavoni, Riccardo, and Dario Piselli. "The Sustainable Development Goals and International Environmental Law: Normative Value and Challenges for Implementation." *Veredas Do Direito* 13 (2016): 13–60.

Perry, Stephen R. "Hart on Social Rules and the Foundations of Law: Liberating the Internal Point of View Symposium: The Internal Point of View in Law and Ethics: Jurisprudence and General Legal Theory." *Fordham Law Review* 75 (2007 2006): 1171–1210.

———. "The Varieties of Legal Positivism." *Canadian Journal of Law and Jurisprudence* 9 (1996): 361–82.

Peters, Anne. "Compensatory Constitutionalism: The Function and Potential of Fundamental International Norms and Structures." *Leiden Journal of International Law* 19, no. 3 (October 2006): 579–610. https://doi.org/10.1017/S0922156506003487.

———. "The Merits of Global Constitutionalism." *Indiana Journal of Global Legal Studies* 16, no. 2 (May 24, 2009): 397–411.

Peters, Anne, and Isabella Pagotto. "Soft Law as a New Mode of Governance: A Legal Perspective." SSRN Scholarly Paper. Rochester, NY: Social Science Research Network, February 28, 2006. https://papers.ssrn.com/abstract=1668531.

Piattoni, Simona. "Multi-level Governance: A Historical and Conceptual Analysis." *Journal of European Integration* 31, no. 2 (March 1, 2009): 163–80. https://doi.org/10.1080/07036330802642755.

Raz, Joseph. "The Future of State Sovereignty." SSRN Scholarly Paper. Rochester, NY: Social Science Research Network, November 18, 2017. https://papers.ssrn.com/abstract=3073749.

———. "Two Views of the Nature of the Theory of Law: A Partial Comparison." *Legal Theory* 4, no. 3 (1998): 249–282.

Reisman, W. Michael. "International Lawmaking: A Process of Communication: The Harold D. Lasswell Memorial Lecture." *Proceedings of the Annual Meeting (American Society of International Law)* 75 (1981): 101–20.

———. "International Non Liquet: Recrudescence and Transformation." *International Lawyer* 3 (1969): 770–86.

———. "Soft Law and Law Jobs." *Journal of International Dispute Settlement* 2, no. 1 (February 1, 2011): 25–30. https://doi.org/10.1093/jnlids/idq014.

Reisman, W. Michael, Siegfried Wiessner, and Andrew R. Willard. "The New Haven School: A Brief Introduction Commentary." *Yale Journal of International Law* 32 (2007): 575–82.

Santos, Boaventura de Sousa. "Law: A Map of Misreading. Toward a Postmodern Conception of Law." *Journal of Law and Society* 14, no. 3 (1987): 279–302. https://doi.org/10.2307/1410186.

Shapiro, Martin. “The Globalization of Law.” *Indiana Journal of Global Legal Studies* 1, no. 1 (1993): 37–64.

Shapiro, Scott J. “On Hart’s Way Out.” *Legal Theory* 4, no. 4 (December 1998): 469–507. https://doi.org/10.1017/S1352325200001117.

———. “The Hart-Dworkin Debate: A Short Guide for the Perplexed.” SSRN Scholarly Paper. Rochester, NY: Social Science Research Network, March 5, 2007. https://papers.ssrn.com/abstract=968657.

Slaughter, Anne-Marie, and Jose E. Alvarez. “A Liberal Theory of International Law.” *Proceedings of the Annual Meeting (American Society of International Law)* 94 (2000): 240–53.

Slaughter, Annie-Marie, and Steven R. Ratner. “Appraising the Methods of International Law: A Prospectus for Readers Symposium on Method in International Law.” *American Journal of International Law* 93 (1999): 291–423.

Sohn, Louis B. “Stockholm Declaration on the Human Environment, The.” *Harvard International Law Journal* 14 (1973): 423–515.

Somek, Alexander. “The Concept of ‘Law’ in Global Administrative Law: A Reply to Benedict Kingsbury.” *European Journal of International Law* 20, no. 4 (November 1, 2009): 985–95. https://doi.org/10.1093/ejil/chp091.

“Statistics and Indicators for the Post-2015 Development Agenda, UN System Task Team’s Report,” July 2013. http://www.un.org/en/development/desa/policy/untaskteam_undf/UNTT_MonitoringReport_WEB.pdf.

Strandenaes, Jan-Gustav. “Participatory Democracy - HLPF Laying the Basis for Sustainable Development Governance in the 21st Century,” March 2014. https://sustainabledevelopment.un.org/content/documents/3682The%20High%20Level%20Political%20Forum,%20major%20groups%20and%20modalities.pdf.

Strong, Maurice. “The Hunger Project Millennium Lecture Hunger, Poverty, Population and Environment,” April 1999. http://old.grida.no/geo/GEO/Geo-1-021.htm.

Summers, Robert S. Review of *Review of Of Laws in General*, by Jeremy Bentham and H. L. A. Hart. *The University of Toronto Law Journal* 21, no. 3 (1971): 445–48. https://doi.org/10.2307/824948.

Tamanaha, Brian Z. “A Non-Essentialist Version of Legal Pluralism.” *Journal of Law and Society* 27 (2000): 296–321.

———. “Necessary and Universal Truths about Law?” *Ratio Juris* 30, no. 1 (March 1, 2017): 3–24. https://doi.org/10.1111/raju.12155.

———. “Socio-Legal Positivism and a General Jurisprudence.” *Oxford Journal of Legal Studies* 21, no. 1 (January 1, 2001): 1–32. https://doi.org/10.1093/ojls/21.1.1.

———. “The Contemporary Relevance of Legal Positivism.” *Australian Journal of Legal Philosophy* 32 (2007): 1–38.

———. “Understanding Legal Pluralism: Past to Present, Local to Global.” *Sydney Law Review* 30 (2008): 375–411.

———. “What Is ‘General’ Jurisprudence? A Critique of Universalistic Claims by Philosophical Concepts of Law.” *Transnational Legal Theory* 2, no. 3 (September 15, 2011): 287–308. https://doi.org/10.5235/204140011800664102.

Tasioulas, John. “The Legitimacy of International Law.” In *The Philosophy of International Law*, edited by Samantha Besson and John Tasioulas. OUP Oxford, 2010a.

Teubner, Gunther. “Global Bukowina: Legal Pluralism in the World-Society.” SSRN Scholarly Paper. Rochester, NY: Social Science Research Network, 1996. https://papers.ssrn.com/abstract=896478.

———. “Global Private Regimes: Neo-Spontaneous Law and Dual Constitution of Autonomous Sectors?” SSRN Scholarly Paper. Rochester, NY: Social Science Research Network, April 4, 2006. https://papers.ssrn.com/abstract=894423.

———. “The Two Faces of Janus: Rethinking Legal Pluralism Closed Systems and Open Justice: The Legal Sociology of Niklas Shumann.” *Cardozo Law Review* 13 (1992 1991): 1443–62.

Twining, William. “Diffusion of Law: A Global Perspective Symposium on Legal Transplants.” *Journal of Comparative Law* 1 (2006): 237–60.

———. “Have Concepts, Will Travel: Analytical Jurisprudence in a Global Context.” *International Journal of Law in Context* 1, no. 1 (March 2005a): 5–40. https://doi.org/10.1017/S1744552305001023.

———. “Normative and Legal Pluralism: A Global Perspective Annual Herbert L. Bernstein Lecture in International and Comparative Law.” *Duke Journal of Comparative & International Law* 20 (2010 2009): 473–518.

———. “Social Science and Diffusion of Law.” *Journal of Law and Society* 32 (2005b): 203–40.

Venzke, Ingo. “Between Power and Persuasion: On International Institutions’ Authority in Making Law.” *Transnational Legal Theory* 4, no. 3 (November 30, 2013a): 354–73. https://doi.org/10.5235/20414005.4.3.354.

———. “Contemporary Theories and International Law-Making.” SSRN Scholarly Paper. Rochester, NY: Social Science Research Network, October 18, 2013b. https://papers.ssrn.com/abstract=2342175.

Vromen, Simone. “The Council Committee on NGOs: An Analysis of the Reports of the Council Committee on NGOs between 2005 and 2015.” *Utrecht Law Review* 13 (2017): 82–98.

Waldron, Jeremy. “The Concept and the Rule of Law.” *Georgia Law Review* 43 (2009a 2008): 1–62.

———. “Who Needs Rules of Recognition?” SSRN Scholarly Paper. Rochester, NY: Social Science Research Network, March 12, 2009b. https://papers.ssrn.com/abstract=1358477.

Walker, Neil. "Making a World of Difference? Habermas, Cosmopolitanism and the Constitutionalization of International Law." SSRN Scholarly Paper. Rochester, NY: Social Science Research Network, December 1, 2005. https://papers.ssrn.com/abstract=891036.

———. "Out of Place and Out of Time: Law's Fading Co-Ordinates." SSRN Scholarly Paper. Rochester, NY: Social Science Research Network, March 24, 2009. https://papers.ssrn.com/abstract=1367591.

———. "The Gap between Global Law and Global Justice: A Preliminary Analysis." SSRN Scholarly Paper. Rochester, NY: Social Science Research Network, December 21, 2016. https://papers.ssrn.com/abstract=2888557.

———. "The Jurist in a Global Age." SSRN Scholarly Paper. Rochester, NY: Social Science Research Network, April 13, 2015. https://papers.ssrn.com/abstract=2580114.

Waluchow, W. J. "The Many Faces of Legal Positivism." *University of Toronto Law Journal* 48 (1998): 387–450.

Waluchow, Wil J. "Defeasibility and Legal Positivism." SSRN Scholarly Paper. Rochester, NY: Social Science Research Network, March 5, 2009a. https://papers.ssrn.com/abstract=1346385.

Weil, Prosper. "Towards Relative Normativity in International Law." *American Journal of International Law* 77 (1983): 413–42.

Willetts, Peter. "From Consultative Arrangements to Partnership: The Changing Status of NGOs in Diplomacy at the UN." *Global Governance* 6 (2000): 191–212.

———. "From Stockholm to Rio and Beyond: The Impact of the Environmental Movement on the United Nations Consultative Arrangements for NGOs." *Review of International Studies* 22, no. 1 (1996): 57–80.

Wirth, David A. "The Rio Declaration on Environment and Development: Two Steps Forward and One Back, or Vice Versa." *Georgia Law Review* 29 (1995 1994): 599–654.

Xifaras, Mikhail. "The Global Turn in Legal Theory." *Canadian Journal of Law and Jurisprudence* 29 (2016): 215–44.

Zemanek, Karl. "Vienna Convention on the Law of Treaties between States and International Organizations or between International Organizations," 2009. http://legal.un.org/avl/ha/vcltsio/vcltsio.html.

Zumbansen, Peer. "Transnational Legal Pluralism." *Transnational Legal Theory* 1, no. 2 (July 1, 2010): 141–89. https://doi.org/10.1080/20414005.2010.11424506.

———. "Why Global Law Is Transnational." *Transnational Legal Theory* 4, no. 4 (December 1, 2013): 463–75. https://doi.org/10.5235/20414005.4.4.463.

Zumbansen, Peer C. "Defining the Space of Transnational Law: Legal Theory, Global Governance & Legal Pluralism." SSRN Scholarly Paper. Rochester, NY: Social Science Research Network, September 26, 2011. https://papers.ssrn.com/abstract=1934044.

Books

Aspremont, Jean d'. *Formalism and the Sources of International Law: A Theory of the Ascertainment of Legal Rules.* Oxford Monographs in International Law. Oxford: Oxford University Press, 2011.

Aspremont, Jean d', Samantha Besson, and Sévrine Knuchel, eds. *The Oxford Handbook of the Sources of International Law.* Oxford Handbooks. Oxford, New York: Oxford University Press, 2017g.

Austin, John, and Wilfrid E. Rumble. *The Province of Jurisprudence Determined.* Cambridge Texts in the History of Political Thought. Cambridge: Cambridge Univ. Press, 1995.

Bentham, Jeremy. *Of Laws in General.* The Collected Works of Jeremy Bentham 2, Principles of legislation. London: The Athlone Press, 1970.

Berman, Ayelet, and Joost Pauwelyn. *Informal International Lawmaking: Case Studies.* Torkel Opsahl Academic EPublisher, 2012.

Berman, Paul Schiff. *Global Legal Pluralism: A Jurisprudence of Law Beyond Borders.* Cambridge University Press, 2012.

Besson, Samantha, and John Tasioulas, eds. *The Philosophy of International Law.* New York, NY: Oxford University Press, 2010.

Betsill, Michele Merrill, and Elisabeth Corell. *NGO Diplomacy: The Influence of Nongovernmental Organizations in International Environmental Negotiations.* MIT Press, 2008.

Birnie, Patricia W., Alan E. Boyle, and Catherine Redgwell. *International Law and the Environment.* Oxford University Press, 2009.

Boyle, Alan, and Christine Chinkin. *The Making of International Law.* OUP Oxford, 2007.

Carson, Rachel. *Silent Spring.* Houghton Mifflin Harcourt, 2002.

Chatterjee, Pratap, Matthias Finger, and Matthias Finger. *The Earth Brokers : Power, Politics and World Development.* Routledge, 2014. https://doi.org/10.4324/9781315832180.

Coleman, Jules L. *The Practice of Principle: In Defence of a Pragmatist Approach to Legal Theory.* Oxford University Press, 2003.

Cotterrell, Roger, and Maksymilian Del Mar. *Authority in Transnational Legal Theory: Theorising Across Disciplines.* Edward Elgar Publishing, 2016.

Culver, Keith, and Michael Giudice. *Legality's Borders: An Essay in General Jurisprudence.* Oxford University Press, 2010.

Dodds, Felix, Ambassador David Donoghue, and Jimena Leiva Roesch. *Negotiating the Sustainable Development Goals: A Transformational Agenda for an Insecure World.* Taylor & Francis, 2016.

Dodds, Felix, Michael Strauss, and Maurice F. Strong. *Only One Earth: The Long Road Via Rio to Sustainable Development.* Routledge, 2012.

Domingo, Rafael. *The New Global Law*. ASIL Studies in International Legal Theory. Cambridge: Cambridge University Press, 2010.
Dworkin, Ronald. *A Matter of Principle*. Clarendon Press, 1985.
———. *Law's Empire*. Harvard University Press, 1986.
———. *Taking Rights Seriously*. Harvard University Press, 1978.
Epps, Dwain C. *The Churches in International Affairs: Reports 1999–2002*. Commission of the Churches on International Affairs of the World Council of Churches, 2005.
Franck, Thomas M. *The Power of Legitimacy among Nations*. Oxford University Press, 1990.
Giudice, Michael. *Understanding the Nature of Law: A Case for Constructive Conceptual Explanation*. Edward Elgar Publishing, 2015.
Hart, H. L. A. *Essays in Jurisprudence and Philosophy*. OUP Oxford, 1983.
———. *The Concept of Law*. 3rd ed. Clarendon Law Series. Oxford: Oxford University Press, 2012.
Heijer, Maarten den, and Harmen van der Wilt. *Netherlands Yearbook of International Law 2015: Jus Cogens: Quo Vadis?* Springer, 2016.
Higgins, Rosalyn. *Problems and Process: International Law and How We Use It*. Clarendon Press, 1995.
Hoof, Godefridus J. H. *Rethinking the Sources of International Law*. Brill Archive, 1983.
Kelsen, Hans. *Principles of International Law*. New York: Rinehart, 1952.
———. *Pure Theory of Law*. University of California Press, 1967.
Kelsen, Hans, and Michael Hartney. *General Theory of Norms*. Oxford: Clarendon Press, 1991.
Kelsen, Hans, and Anders Wedberg. *General Theory of Law and State*. 20th Century Legal Philosophy Series, vol. 1. Cambridge Mass: Harvard University Press, 1945.
Kiss, Alexandre, and Dinah Shelton. *Guide to International Environmental Law*. BRILL, 2007.
Klabbers, Jan. *An Introduction to International Organizations Law*. Cambridge University Press, 2015.
Klabbers, Jan, Anne Peters, and Geir Ulfstein. *The Constitutionalization of International Law*. OUP Oxford, 2009.
Klabbers, Jan, and Touko Piiparinen. *Normative Pluralism and International Law: Exploring Global Governance*. Cambridge University Press, 2013.
Koskenniemi, Martti. *The Politics of International Law*. Bloomsbury Publishing, 2011.
Kramer, Matthew H. *The Legacy of H.L.A. Hart: Legal, Political, and Moral Philosophy*. Oxford University Press, 2008a.
———. *Where Law and Morality Meet*. Oxford University Press, 2008b.

Krisch, Nico. *Beyond Constitutionalism: The Pluralist Structure of Postnational Law*. OUP Oxford, 2010.
MacCormick, John. *The Global Environmental Movement: Reclaiming Paradise*. London: Belhaven Press, 1989.
Marmor, Andrei. *Positive Law and Objective Values*. Clarendon Press, 2001.
Musa, Shavana, and Eefje de Volder. *Reflections on Global Law*. Martinus Nijhoff Publishers, 2013.
Pauwelyn, Joost, Ramses Wessel, and Jan Wouters. *Informal International Lawmaking*. OUP Oxford, 2012.
Peterson, M. J. *The UN General Assembly*. Psychology Press, 2006.
Raz, Joseph. *Between Authority and Interpretation: On the Theory of Law and Practical Reason*. OUP Oxford, 2009a.
———. *The Authority of Law: Essays on Law and Morality*. 2nd edition. Oxford ; New York: Oxford University Press, 2009b.
———. *The Concept of a Legal System: An Introduction to the Theory of Legal System*. Oxford University Press, 1980.
Reid, David. *Sustainable Development: An Introductory Guide*. Routledge, 2013.
Santos, Boaventura de Sousa, and César A. Rodríguez-Garavito. *Law and Globalization from Below: Towards a Cosmopolitan Legality*. Cambridge University Press, 2005.
Schultz, Thomas. *Transnational Legality: Stateless Law and International Arbitration*. OUP Oxford, 2013.
Shapiro, Scott J. *Legality*. Harvard University Press, 2011.
Slaughter, Anne-Marie. *A New World Order*. Princeton University Press, 2009.
Tamanaha, Brian Z. *A General Jurisprudence of Law and Society*. Oxford University Press, 2001.
———. *On the Rule of Law: History, Politics, Theory*. Cambridge University Press, 2004.
Teubner, Gunther. *Global Law without a State*. Ashgate Publishing Company, 1997.
Tolba, Mostafa Kamal, and Programme des Nations Unies pour l'environnement, eds. *The World Environment 1972–1992: Two Decades of Challenge*. Repr. London ; Glasgow [etc.]: Chapman & Hall, 1993.
Twining, William. *General Jurisprudence: Understanding Law from a Global Perspective*. Law in Context. Cambridge: Cambridge University Press, 2009.
———. *Globalisation and Legal Scholarship*. Tilburg Law Lectures Series. Montesquieu Seminars, vol. 4. Nijmegen: Wolf Legal Publ, 2011.
———. *Globalisation and Legal Theory*. Cambridge University Press, 2000.
Viñuales, Jorge E., ed. *The Rio Declaration on Environment and Development: A Commentary*. Oxford University Press, 2015.
Walker, Neil. *Intimations of Global Law*. Cambridge University Press, 2014.
Waluchow, Wil, and Stefan Sciaraffa, eds. *The Legacy of Ronald Dworkin*. Oxford University Press, 2016.

Waluchow, Wilfrid J. *Inclusive Legal Positivism*. Clarendon Press, 1994.
Werksman, Jacob. *Greening International Institutions*. Routledge, 2014.
Willetts, Peter, ed. *"The Conscience of the World": The Influence of Non-Governmental Organisations in the UN System*. Washington, D.C: The Brookings Institution, 1996.
Ziccardi Capaldo, Giuliana. *The Pillars of Global Law*. Aldershot, Hants, England ; Burlington, VT: Ashgate, 2008.

Book Chapters

Aspremont, Jean d'. "Jus Cogens as a Social Construct Without Pedigree." In *Netherlands Yearbook of International Law 2015*, 85–114. Netherlands Yearbook of International Law. T.M.C. Asser Press, The Hague, 2016a. https://doi.org/10.1007/978-94-6265-114-2_4.
———. "Subjects and Actors in International Lawmaking: The Paradigmatic Divides in the Cognition of International Norm Generating Processes." In *Research Handbooks in International Law*, edited by Brölmann, C. and Radi, Y. Edward Elgar, 2016b. http://dare.uva.nl/personal/pure/en/publications/subjects-and-actors-in-international-lawmaking-the-paradigmatic-divides-in-the-cognition-of-international-norm-generating-processes(95ef06fe-c49c-4751-90c5-43d6bb52cc5a).html.
Bache, Ian. "Multi-Level Governance in the European Union." In *The Oxford Handbook of Governance*, edited by David Levi-Faur, 2012. https://www.oxfordhandbooks.com/view/10.1093/oxfordhb/9780199560530.001.0001/oxfordhb-9780199560530-e-44.
Bache, Ian, Ian Bartle, and Matthew Flinders. "Multi-Level Governance." In *Handbook on Theories of Governance*, edited by Christopher Ansell and Jacob Torfing, 2016. https://www.elgaronline.com/view/edcoll/9781782548492/9781782548492.00052.xml.
Besson, Samantha. "Theorizing the Sources of International Law." In *The Philosophy of International Law*, edited by Samantha Besson and John Tasioulas, 163–85, 2010.
———. "Whose Constitution(s)? International Law, Constitutionalism and Democracy." In *Ruling the World? Constitutionalism, International Law and Global Governance*, edited by Jeffrey L. Dunoff and Joel P. Trachtman, 381–407. Cambridge University Press, 2009. http://doc.rero.ch/record/28902.
Bix, Brian. "Natural Law: The Modern Tradition." In *The Oxford Handbook of Jurisprudence and Philosophy of Law*, edited by Jules Coleman and Scott J. Shapiro. Oxford University Press, 2002.

Bodansky, Daniel, ed. "International Law, the International Court of Justice, and Nuclear Weapons." In *Non Liquet and the Incompleteness of International Law*, 153–70. Cambridge, UK: Cambridge University Press, 1999.

———, ed. "Max Planck Encyclopedia of Public International Law." In *Non Liquet*, Vol. 6. International Organizations or Institutions, History of Martens Clause. Oxford: Oxford University Press, 2012.

Boyle, Alan. "Soft Law in International Law-Making." In *International Law*, edited by Malcolm D. Evans, Fourth Edition., 118–36. Oxford University Press, 2014.

Brus, Marcel M. T. A. "Soft Law in Public International Law: A Pragmatic or a Principled Choice? Comparing the Sustainable Development Goals and the Paris Agreement." In *Legal Validity and Soft Law*, edited by Pauline Westerman, Jaap Hage, Stephan Kirste, and Anne Ruth Mackor, 243–66. Law and Philosophy Library. Cham: Springer International Publishing, 2018. https://doi.org/10.1007/978-3-319-77522-7_13.

Coleman, Jules L., and Brian Leiter. "Legal Positivism." In *A Companion to Philosophy of Law and Legal Theory*, edited by Dennis Pattersonessor, 228–48. Wiley-Blackwell, 2010. https://doi.org/10.1002/9781444320114.ch14.

Cotterrell, Roger. "A Concept of Law for Global Legal Pluralism?" In *Concepts of Law: Comparative, Jurisprudential, and Social Science Perspectives*, 193–208. Routledge, 2016.

French, Duncan. "The Global Goals: Formalism Foregone, Contested Legality and 'Re-Imaginings' of International Law." In *Ethiopian Yearbook of International Law 2016*, edited by Zeray Yihdego, Melaku Geboye Desta, and Fikremarkos Merso, 151–78. Ethiopian Yearbook of International Law. Cham: Springer International Publishing, 2017. https://doi.org/10.1007/978-3-319-55898-1_7.

Giudice, Michael. "Imprerialism and Importance on Dworkin's Jurisprudence." In *The Legacy of Ronald Dworkin*, edited by Wil Waluchow and Stefan Sciaraffa, 225–43. Oxford University Press, 2016.

Jörgens, Helge. "Governance by Diffusion: Implementing Global Norms through Cross-National Imitation and Learning," 246–83, 2004.

Lefkowitz, David. "The Sources of International Law: Some Philosophical Reflections." In *The Philosophy of International Law*, 187–203, 2010.

Levrat, Nicolas. "Legal Studies and Global Governance." In *Globalisation, Multilateralism, Europe: Towards a Better Global Governance?*, edited by Mario Telò, 159–72, 2013. https://archive-ouverte.unige.ch/unige:45391.

Marmor, Andrei. "Exclusive Legal Positivism." In *The Oxford Handbook of Jurisprudence and Philosophy of Law*, 2004.

———. "The Ideal of the Rule of Law." In *A Companion to Philosophy of Law and Legal Theory*, edited by Dennis Pattersonessor, 666–74. Wiley-Blackwell, 2010. https://doi.org/10.1002/9781444320114.ch48.

Merry, Sally Engle. "International Law and Sociolegal Scholarship: Toward a Spatial Global Legal Pluralism." In *Special Issue Law and Society Reconsidered*, 41:149–68. Studies in Law, Politics and Society 41. Emerald Group Publishing Limited, 2007. http://www.emeraldinsight.com/doi/full/10.1016/S1059-4337%2807%2900006-3.

Nollkaemper, A., Klabbers, J., Piiparinen, T., and IRL Prog 2009–2016 (ACIL, FdR). "Inside or out: Two Types of International Legal Pluralism." In *ASIL Studies in International Legal Theory*. Cambridge University Press, 2013. http://dare.uva.nl/personal/pure/en/publications/inside-or-out-two-types-of-international-legal-pluralism(f8b99f07-6eac-4e1a-8f97-6f5aa18ce753).html.

Raz, Joseph. "Can There Be a Theory of Law?" In *The Blackwell Guide to the Philosophy of Law and Legal Theory*, edited by Martin P. Golding and William A. Edmundson. Blackwell, 2005.

Tasioulas, John. "The Legitimacy of International Law." In *The Philosophy of International Law*, edited by Samantha Besson and John Tasioulas. OUP Oxford, 2010b.

Waldron, Jeremy. "Hart and the Principles of Legality." In *The Legacy of H.L.A. Hart: Legal, Political, and Moral Philosophy*, edited by Matthew H. Kramer. Oxford University Press, 2008.

Waluchow, Wil J. "Four Concepts of Validity: Reflections on Inclusive and Exclusive Positivism." In *The Rule of Recognition and the U.S. Constitution*, 123–44. Oxford University Press, 2009b.

UNGA Resolutions

"2005 World Summit Outcome, UNGA Resolution, UNGA Resolution, UN Doc. A/RES/60/1," September 16, 2005. http://www.un.org/en/ga/search/view_doc.asp?symbol=A/RES/60/1.

"Declaration and State of Progress and Initiatives for the Future Implementation of the Programme of Action for the Sustainable Development of Small Island Developing States, UNGA Resolution, UN Doc. A/RES/S-22/2," September 28, 1999. http://www.un.org/en/ga/search/view_doc.asp?symbol=A/RES/S-22/2.

"Declaration on Cities and Other Human Settlements in the New Millennium, UNGA Resolution, UN Doc. A/RES/S-25/2," June 9, 2001. http://www.un.org/en/ga/search/view_doc.asp?symbol=A/RES/S-25/2.

"Development and Environment, UNGA Resolution 2849 (XXVI)," December 20, 1971. http://www.un.org/en/ga/search/view_doc.asp?symbol=A/RES/2849(XXVI).

"Dissemination of the Principles of the Rio Declaration on Environment and Development, UNGA Resolution, UN Doc. A/RES/48/190," December

21, 1993. http://www.un.org/en/ga/search/view_doc.asp?symbol=A/RES/48/190.
"Enhancing Complementarities among International Instruments Related to Environment and Sustainable Development, UNGA Resolution, UN Doc. A/RES/54/217," December 22, 1999. http://www.un.org/en/ga/search/view_doc.asp?symbol=A/RES/54/217.
"Environmental Perspective to the Year 2000 and Beyond, UNGA Resolution, UN Doc. A/RES/42/186," December 11, 1987. http://www.un.org/en/ga/search/view_doc.asp?symbol=A/RES/42/186.
"Follow-up to the Outcome of the 2005 World Summit, Including the Millennium Development Goals and the Other Internationally Agreed Development Goals, UNGA Resolution, UN Doc. A/RES/60/265," June 30, 2006. http://www.un.org/en/ga/search/view_doc.asp?symbol=A/RES/60/265.
——— of the Millennium Summit and Integrated and Coordinated Implementation of and Follow-up to the Outcomes of the Major United Nations Conferences and Summits in the Economic and Social Fields, UNGA Resolution, UN Doc. A/RES/58/291," May 6, 2004. http://www.un.org/en/ga/search/view_doc.asp?symbol=A/RES/58/291.
——— of the Millennium Summit, UNGA Resolution, UN Doc. A/RES/55/162," December 14, 2000. http://www.un.org/en/ga/search/view_doc.asp?symbol=A/RES/55/162&Lang=E.
——— of the Millennium Summit, UNGA Resolution, UN Doc. A/RES/56/95," December 14, 2001. http://www.un.org/en/ga/search/view_doc.asp?symbol=A/RES/56/95.
"Follow-up to the Outcome of the Millennium Summit, UNGA Resolution, UN Doc. A/RES/57/144," December 16, 2002. http://www.un.org/en/ga/search/view_doc.asp?symbol=A/RES/57/144.
"Format and Organizational Aspects of the High-Level Political Forum on Sustainable Development, UNGA Resolution, UN Doc. A/RES/67/290," July 9, 2013. http://www.un.org/en/ga/search/view_doc.asp?symbol=A/RES/67/290.
"Further Actions and Initiatives to Implement the Beijing Declaration and Platform for Action, UNGA Resolution, UN Doc. A/RES/S-23/3," June 10, 2000. http://www.un.org/en/ga/search/view_doc.asp?symbol=A/RES/S-23/3.
"Further Initiatives for Social Development, UNGA Resolution, UN Doc. A/RES/S-24/2," July 1, 2000. http://www.un.org/en/ga/search/view_doc.asp?symbol=A/RES/S-24/2.
"Implementation of Agenda 21, the Programme for the Further Implementation of Agenda 21 and the Outcomes of the World Summit on Sustainable Development and of the United Nations Conference on Sustainable Development, UNGA Resolution, UN Doc. A/RES/67/203," December 21, 2012. http://www.un.org/en/ga/search/view_doc.asp?symbol=A/RES/67/203.

——— 21, the Programme for the Further Implementation of Agenda 21 and the Outcomes of the World Summit on Sustainable Development, UNGA Resolution, UN Doc. A/RES/63/212," December 19, 2008. http://www.un.org/en/ga/search/view_doc.asp?symbol=A/RES/63/212.

"Implementation of Agenda 21, the Programme for the Further Implementation of Agenda 21 and the Outcomes of the World Summit on Sustainable Development, UNGA Resolution, UN Doc. A/RES/64/236," December 24, 2009. http://www.un.org/en/ga/search/view_doc.asp?symbol=A/RES/64/236.

"Implementation of and Follow-up to the Outcome of the United Nations Conference on Environment and Development and the Nineteenth Special Session of the General Assembly, UNGA Resolution, UN Doc. A/RES/53/188," December 15, 1998. http://www.un.org/en/ga/search/view_doc.asp?symbol=A/RES/53/188.

——— to the Outcome of the United Nations Conference on Environment and Development and the Nineteenth Special Session of the General Assembly, UNGA Resolution, UN Doc. A/RES/54/218," December 22, 1999. http://www.un.org/en/ga/search/view_doc.asp?symbol=A/RES/54/218.

"Institutional Arrangements to Follow up the United Nations Conference on Environment and Development, UNGA Resolution, UN Doc. A/RES/47/191," December 22, 1992. http://www.un.org/documents/ga/res/47/ares47-191.htm.

"Integrated and Coordinated Implementation of and Follow-up to the Outcomes of the Major United Nations Conferences and Summits in the Economic and Social Fields, UNGA Resolution, UN Doc. A/RES/56/211," December 21, 2001. http://www.un.org/en/ga/search/view_doc.asp?symbol=A/RES/56/211.

"Integrated and Coordinated Implementation of and Follow-up to the Outcomes of the Major United Nations Conferences and Summits in the Economic and Social Fields, UNGA Resolution, UN Doc. A/RES/57/270," December 20, 2002. http://www.un.org/en/ga/search/view_doc.asp?symbol=A/RES/57/270.

"Integrated and Coordinated Implementation of and Follow-up to the Outcomes of the Major United Nations Conferences and Summits in the Economic and Social Fields, UNGA Resolution, UN Doc. A/RES/57/270 B," June 23, 2003. http://www.un.org/en/ga/search/view_doc.asp?symbol=A/RES/57/270B.

"International Co-Operation in the Field of the Environment, UNGA Resolution, UN Doc. A/RES/35/74," December 5, 1980. http://www.un.org/en/ga/search/view_doc.asp?symbol=A/RES/35/74.

——— of the Environment, UNGA Resolution, UN Doc. A/RES/36/192," December 17, 1981. http://www.un.org/en/ga/search/view_doc.asp?symbol=A/RES/36/192.

"International Institutional Arrangements Related to Environment and Development, UNGA Resolution, UN Doc. A/RES/53/186," December 15, 1998. http://www.un.org/en/ga/search/view_doc.asp?symbol=A/RES/53/186.

"Keeping the Promise: United to Achieve the Millennium Development Goals, UNGA Resolution, UN Doc. A/RES/65/1," September 22, 2010. http://www.un.org/en/ga/search/view_doc.asp?symbol=A/RES/65/1.

"Key Actions for the Further Implementation of the Programme of Action of the International Conference on Population and Development, UNGA Resolution, UN Doc. A/RES/S-21/2," July 2, 1999. http://www.un.org/en/ga/search/view_doc.asp?symbol=A/RES/S-21/2.

"Observer Status for the International Committee of the Red Cross, in Consideration of the Special Role and Mandates Conferred upon It by the Geneva Conventions of 12 August 1949, UNGA Resolution, UN Doc. A/RES/45/6," October 16, 1990. http://www.un.org/documents/ga/res/45/a45r006.htm.

"Organization of the Millennium Summit of the United Nations, UNGA Resolution, UN Doc. A/RES/54/281," August 11, 2000. https://digitallibrary.un.org/record/420505/files/A_RES_54_281-EN.pdf.

"Organization of the United Nations Summit for the Adoption of the Post-2015 Development Agenda, UNGA Resolution, UN Doc. A/RES/69/244," December 29, 2014. http://www.un.org/en/ga/search/view_doc.asp?symbol=A/RES/69/244.

"Outcome Document of the Special Event to Follow up Efforts Made towards Achieving the Millennium Development Goals, UNGA Resolution, UN Doc. A/RES/68/6," October 9, 2013. http://www.un.org/en/ga/search/view_doc.asp?symbol=A/RES/68/6.

"Participation of the European Union in the Work of the United Nations, UNGA Resolution, UNGA Resolution, UN Doc. A/RES/65/276," May 3, 2011. https://documents-dds-ny.un.org/doc/UNDOC/GEN/N10/529/10/PDF/N1052910.pdf?OpenElement.

"Problems of the Human Environment, UNGA Resolution 2398 (XXIII)," December 3, 1968. http://www.un.org/en/ga/search/view_doc.asp?symbol=A/RES/2398(XXIII).

"Process of Preparation of the Environmental Perspective to the Year 2000 and Beyond, UNGA Resolution, UN Doc. A/RES/38/161," December 19, 1983. http://www.un.org/en/ga/search/view_doc.asp?symbol=A/RES/38/161.

"Programme for the Further Implementation of Agenda 21, UNGA Resolution, UN Doc. A/RES/S-19/2," June 28, 1997. http://www.un.org/documents/ga/res/spec/aress19-2.htm.
"Registration and Publication of Treaties and International Agreements: Regulations to Give Effect to Article 102 of the Charter of The United Nations, UNGA Resolution 97 (I)," December 14, 1946. https://treaties.un.org/xml/db/msdb/pageregulation_en.html.
"Report of the Commission on Sustainable Development on Its Second Session, UNGA Resolution, UN Doc. A/RES/49/111," December 19, 1994a. http://www.un.org/en/ga/search/view_doc.asp?symbol=A/RES/49/111.
"Report of the Open Working Group of the General Assembly on Sustainable Development Goals, UNGA Resolution, UN Doc. A/68/970," August 12, 2014a. https://digitallibrary.un.org/record/778970/files/A_68_970-EN.pdf.
——— Group on Sustainable Development Goals Established Pursuant to General Assembly Resolution 66/288, UNGA Resolution, UN Doc. A/RES/68/309," September 10, 2014b. http://www.un.org/en/ga/search/view_doc.asp?symbol=A/RES/68/309.
"Report of the United Nations Conference on Environment and Development, UNGA Resolution, UN Doc. A/RES/47/190," December 22, 1992a. http://www.un.org/en/ga/search/view_doc.asp?symbol=A/RES/47/190.
"Report of the World Commission on Environment and Development, UNGA Resolution, UN Doc. A/RES/42/187," December 11, 1987. http://www.un.org/en/ga/search/view_doc.asp?symbol=A/RES/42/187.
"Session of a Special Character of the Governing Council of the United Nations Environment Programme, UNGA Resolution, UN Doc. A/RES/36/189," December 17, 1981. http://www.un.org/en/ga/search/view_doc.asp?symbol=A/RES/36/189.
——— of the Governing Council of the United Nations Environment Programme, UNGA Resolution, UN Doc. A/RES/37/219," December 20, 1982. http://www.un.org/en/ga/search/view_doc.asp?symbol=A/RES/37/219.
"Special Session for the Purpose of an Overall Review and Appraisal of the Implementation of Agenda 21, UNGA Resolution, UN Doc. A/RES/50/113," December 20, 1995. http://www.un.org/en/ga/search/view_doc.asp?symbol=A/RES/50/113.
——— of an Overall Review and Appraisal of the Implementation of Agenda 21, UNGA Resolution, UN Doc. A/RES/51/181," December 16, 1996. http://www.un.org/en/ga/search/view_doc.asp?symbol=A/RES/51/181.
"Status of the European Economic Community in the General Assembly, UNGA Resolution 3208 (XXIX)," October 11, 1974. https://documents-dds-ny.un.org/doc/RESOLUTION/GEN/NR0/738/10/IMG/NR073810.pdf?OpenElement.

"Strengthening of the Economic and Social Council, UNGA Resolution, UN Doc. A/RES/61/16," November 20, 2006. http://www.un.org/en/ga/search/view_doc.asp?symbol=A/RES/61/16.
"Ten-Year Review of Progress Achieved in the Implementation of the Outcome of the United Nations Conference on Environment and Development, UNGA Resolution, UN Doc. A/RES/55/199," December 20, 2000. http://www.un.org/en/ga/search/view_doc.asp?symbol=A/RES/55/199&Lang=E.
"The Future We Want, UNGA Resolution, UN Doc. A/RES/66/288," July 27, 2012. http://www.un.org/en/ga/search/view_doc.asp?symbol=A/RES/66/288.
"The Millennium Assembly of the United Nations, UNGA Resolution, UN Doc. A/RES/53/202," September 17, 1998. http://www.un.org/en/ga/search/view_doc.asp?symbol=A/RES/53/202&Lang=E.
"Towards a Global Pact for the Environment, UNGA Resolution, UN Doc. A/RES/72/277," May 10, 2018. https://digitallibrary.un.org/record/1617171/files/A_RES_72_277-EN.pdf.
"Transforming Our World: The 2030 Agenda for Sustainable Development, UNGA Resolution, UN Doc. A/RES/70/1," September 25, 2015. http://www.un.org/en/ga/search/view_doc.asp?symbol=A/RES/70/1.
"United Nation Conference on the Human Environment, UNGA Resolution 2581 (XXIV)," December 15, 1969. http://www.un.org/en/ga/search/view_doc.asp?symbol=A/RES/2581(XXIV).
——— on the Human Environment, UNGA Resolution 2657 (XXV)," December 7, 1970. http://www.un.org/en/ga/search/view_doc.asp?symbol=A/RES/2657(XXV).
——— on the Human Environment, UNGA Resolution 2850 (XXVI)," December 20, 1971. http://www.un.org/en/ga/search/view_doc.asp?symbol=A/RES/2850(XXVI).
"United Nations Conference on Environment and Development, UNGA Resolution, UN Doc. A/RES/43/196," December 20, 1988. http://www.un.org/en/ga/search/view_doc.asp?symbol=A/RES/43/196.
——— and Development, UNGA Resolution, UN Doc. A/RES/44/228," December 22, 1989. http://www.un.org/en/ga/search/view_doc.asp?symbol=A/RES/44/228.
——— and Development, UNGA Resolution, UN Doc. A/RES/45/211," December 21, 1990. http://www.un.org/en/ga/search/view_doc.asp?symbol=A/RES/45/211.
——— and Development, UNGA Resolution, UN Doc. A/RES/46/168," December 19, 1991. http://www.un.org/en/ga/search/view_doc.asp?symbol=A/RES/46/168.

"United Nations Millennium Declaration, UNGA Resolution, UN Doc. A/RES/55/2," September 8, 2000. http://www.un.org/en/ga/search/view_doc.asp?symbol=A/RES/55/2&Lang=E.

"World Summit on Sustainable Development, UNGA Resolution, UN Doc. A/RES/56/226," December 24, 2001. http://www.un.org/en/ga/search/view_doc.asp?symbol=A/RES/56/226.

"World Summit on Sustainable Development, UNGA Resolution, UN Doc. A/RES/57/253," December 20, 2002. http://www.un.org/en/ga/search/view_doc.asp?symbol=A/RES/57/253.

UN ECOSOC Resolutions

"Consultative Relationship between the United Nations and Non-Governmental Organizations, ECOSOC Resolution, UN. Doc. E/RES/1996/31.," July 25, 1996. http://www.un.org/documents/ecosoc/res/1996/eres1996-31.htm.

"Establishment of the Commission on Sustainable Development, ECOSOC Resolution, UN. Doc. E/RES/1993/207.," February 12, 1993. http://www.un-documents.net/1993-207.htm.

"Full Participation of the European Community in the Commission on Sustainable Development, ECOSOC Decision 1995/201.," February 8, 1995. http://www.un.org/documents/ecosoc/dec/1995/edec1995-201.htm.

"General Review of the Arrangements for Consultation with Non-Governmental Organizations, ECOSOC Decision 1995/304.," July 26, 1995. http://www.un.org/documents/ecosoc/dec/1995/edec1995-304.htm.

"Integrated and Coordinated Implementation of and Follow-up to the Outcomes of the Major United Nations Conferences and Summits, UN. Doc. E/RES/2001/21.," July 26, 2001. https://www.un.org/ecosoc/sites/www.un.org.ecosoc/files/documents/2001/resolution-2001-21.pdf.

"Procedural Arrangements for the Commission on Sustainable Development, ECOSOC Decision 1993/215.," February 12, 1993. http://www.un-documents.net/1993-215.htm.

"Review of the Arrangements for Consultation with Non-Governmental Organizations, ECOSOC Decision 1993/214.," February 12, 1993a. http://www.un-documents.net/1993-214.htm.

——— for Consultation with Non-Governmental Organizations, ECOSOC Resolution, UN. Doc. E/RES/1993/80.," July 30, 1993b. http://www.un-documents.net/1993-80.htm.

"Rules of Procedure of the Functional Commissions of the Economic and Social Council, ECOSOC Resolution, UN. Doc. E/5975/Rev.1.," 1983. https://digitallibrary.un.org/record/50230?ln=en.

Reports of the UN Secretary-General

"Problems of the Human Environment: Report of the Secretary-General, E/4667," May 26, 1969. https://digitallibrary.un.org/record/729455?ln=en.
"Report of the Secretary-General, A Life of Dignity for All: Accelerating Progress towards the Millennium Development Goals and Advancing the United Nations Development Agenda beyond 2015, UN Doc. A/68/202," July 26, 2013a. https://digitallibrary.un.org/record/754891/files/A_68_202-EN.pdf.
———, Environment and Sustainable Development: Special Session for the Purpose of an Overall Review and Appraisal of Agenda 21, UN Doc. A/51/420," October 1, 1996. http://www.un.org/documents/ga/docs/51/plenary/a51-420.htm.
———, Implementation of Agenda 21, the Programme for the Further Implementation of Agenda 21 and the Outcomes of the World Summit on Sustainable Development, UN Doc. A/64/275," August 10, 2009. https://digitallibrary.un.org/record/672676/files/A_64_275-EN.pdf.
———, Integrated and Coordinated Implementation of and Follow-up to the Outcomes of the Major United Nations Conferences and Summits, Including the Millennium Summit UN Doc. A/57/75-E/2002/57," May 7, 2002. https://documents-dds-ny.un.org/doc/UNDOC/GEN/N02/373/86/PDF/N0237386.pdf?OpenElement.
———, Lessons Learned from the Commission on Sustainable Development, UN Doc. A/67/757," February 26, 2013b. https://digitallibrary.un.org/record/746313/files/A_67_757-EN.pdf.
"Report of the Secretary-General on the Work of the Organization, UN Doc. A/61/1," August 16, 2006. https://digitallibrary.un.org/record/582048/files/A_61_1-EN.pdf.
"Report of the Secretary-General, Preparatory Process for the United Nations Conference on Environment and Development, UN Doc. A/CONF.151/PC/2," February 23, 1990. https://digitallibrary.un.org/record/86729?ln=en.
"Report of the Secretary-General, Proposals on the Format, Scope and Organizational Aspects of the 1997 Special Session of the General Assembly on the Overall Review and Appraisal of Agenda 21, UN Doc. A/50/453," September 20, 1995. http://www.un.org/documents/ga/docs/50/plenary/a50-453.htm.
"Report of the Secretary-General, Question of the Convening of a United Nations Conference on Environment and Development, A/44/256 E/1989/66," May 2, 1989. https://digitallibrary.un.org/record/60950/files/A_44_256_E_1989_66-EN.pdf.

"Report of the Secretary-General, Road Map towards the Implementation of the United Nations Millennium Declaration, UN Doc. A/56/326," September 6, 2001. https://undocs.org/A/56/326.

"Report of the Secretary-General, Rules of Procedure of the Commission on Sustainable Development, E/1993/12," January 29, 1993. http://www.un.org/documents/ecosoc/docs/1993/e1993-12.htm.

"Report of the Secretary-General, We the Peoples: The Role of the United Nations in the Twenty-First Century, UN Doc. A/54/2000," March 27, 2000. https://digitallibrary.un.org/record/410974/files/A_54_2000-EN.pdf§.

"Synthesis Report of the Secretary-General on the Post-2015 Sustainable Development Agenda, The Road to Dignity by 2030: Ending Poverty, Transforming All Lives and Protecting the Planet, UN Doc. A/69/700," December 4, 2014. https://digitallibrary.un.org/record/754891/files/A_68_202-EN.pdf.

Other UN Documents

"A Millennium Assembly, the United Nations System (Special Commission) and a Millennium Forum: Note by the Secretary-General, UN Doc. A/52/850," March 31, 1998. https://digitallibrary.un.org/record/252281/files/A_52_850-EN.pdf.

"A New Global Partnership: Eradicate Poverty and Transform Economies Through Sustainable Development, The Report of the High-Level Panel of Eminent Persons on the Post-2015 Development Agenda," May 2013. https://www.un.org/sg/sites/www.un.org.sg/files/files/HLP_P2015_Report.pdf.

"A Renewed Global Partnership for Development, UN System Task Team's Report," March 2013. http://www.un.org/en/development/desa/policy/untaskteam_undf/glob_dev_rep_2013.pdf.

"Agenda 21, Report of the United Nations Conference on Environment and Development, A/CONF.151/26/Rev.1 (Vol.1) Annex II," June 14, 1992. http://www.un-documents.net/agenda21.htm.

"Corporate Sustainability and the United Nations Post-2015 Development Agenda, UN Global Compact's Report to the UN Secretary-General," June 2013. https://www.unglobalcompact.org/docs/news_events/9.1_news_archives/2013_06_18/UNGC_Post2015_Report.pdf.

"List of NGO Observers, United Nations Conference on the Human Environment, UN Doc. A/CONF.48/INF.6," June 5, 1972.

"List of Participants, United Nations Conference on the Human Environment, UN Doc. A/CONF.48/INF.5/Rev.1," June 5, 1972.

"Methods of Work, Open Working Group on Sustainable Development Goals," 2013. https://sustainabledevelopment.un.org/content/documents/1692OWG_methods_work_adopted_1403.pdf.

"Millennium Forum, Note by the Secretariat, UN Doc. A/54/959," August 8, 2000. https://digitallibrary.un.org/record/421341/files/A_54_959-EN.pdf.

"Note by the President of the General Assembly, Environment and Sustainable Development: Special Session for the Purpose of an Overall Review and Appraisal of Agenda 21, UN Doc. A/51/864," April 7, 1997. https://digitallibrary.un.org/record/232856/files/A_51_864-EN.pdf.

——— of the General Assembly, Summary of the First Meeting of the High-Level Political Forum on Sustainable Development, UN Doc. A/68/588," November 13, 2013. https://digitallibrary.un.org/record/761077/files/A_68_588-EN.pdf.

"Note by the Secretariat, Draft Provisional Rules of Procedure of the United Nations Conference on Sustainable Development, UN Doc. A/CONF.216/PC/4," April 26, 2010. https://digitallibrary.un.org/record/681810/files/A_CONF.216_PC_4-EN.pdf.

"Note by the Secretary-General, List of Non-Governmental Organizations in Consultative Status with the Economic and Social Council as of 1 September 2015, UN. Doc. E/2015/INF/5.," August 22, 2016. https://undocs.org/E/2015/INF/5.

"Provisional Rules of Procedure of the Conference, United Nations Conference on the Arms Trade Treaty, A/CONF.217/L.1.," March 7, 2012. http://www.un.org/ga/search/view_doc.asp?symbol=A/CONF.217/L.1&Lang=E.

"Realizing the Future We Want for All, UN System Task Team's Report to the UN Secretary-General," June 2012. http://www.un.org/en/development/desa/policy/untaskteam_undf/untt_report.pdf.

"Reference Document on the Participation of Civil Society in United Nations Conferences and Special Sessions of the General Assembly during the 1990s," August 1, 2001. http://www.un.org/ga/president/55/speech/civilsociety1.htm.

"Report of the Commission on Sustainable Development on Its Fourth Session, UN Doc. E/1996/28.," May 3, 1996. https://digitallibrary.un.org/record/216959/files/E_1996_28-EN.pdf.

——— on Sustainable Development on Its Second Session, UN Doc. E/1994/33.," May 27, 1994b. https://digitallibrary.un.org/record/163245/files/E_1994_33_E_CN.17_1994_20-EN.pdf.

——— on Sustainable Development on Its Third Session, UN Doc. E/1995/32.," April 28, 1995. https://digitallibrary.un.org/record/209124/files/E_1995_32-EN.pdf.

"Report of the Executive Director of UNEP, International Environmental Governance, UNEP/IGM/1/2.," April 4, 2001. http://www.un.org/ga/president/61/follow-up/environment/Report-010404.pdf.

"Report of the First Meeting of the High-Level Political Forum on Sustainable Development Convened under the Auspices of the Economic and Social Council, UN Doc. E/HLPF/2014/2.," October 15, 2014. https://digitallibrary.un.org/record/783717/files/E_HLPF_2014_2-EN.pdf.

"Report of the Fourth World Conference on Women, UN Doc. A/CONF.177/20," October 17, 1995. https://digitallibrary.un.org/record/208677/files/A_CONF-177_20-EN.pdf.

"Report of the Global Conference on the Sustainable Development of Small Island Developing States, UN Doc. A/CONF.167/9," May 6, 1994. https://digitallibrary.un.org/record/198168/files/A_CONF.167_9-EN.pdf.

"Report of the International Conference on Population and Development, UN Doc. A/CONF.171/13," October 18, 1994. https://digitallibrary.un.org/record/172777/files/A_CONF.171_13-EN.pdf.

"Report of the Preparatory Committee for the United Nations Conference on Environment and Development on Its First Session, A/45/46," August 31, 1990. https://digitallibrary.un.org/record/114260/files/A_45_46-EN.pdf.

"Report of the Preparatory Committee for the United Nations Conference on Environment and Development on Its Organizational Session, A/44/48," March 16, 1990. https://digitallibrary.un.org/record/87763/files/A_44_48-EN.pdf.

"Report of the Preparatory Committee for the United Nations Conference on Environment and Development on Its Second Session, A/46/48(Vol.I)," April 5, 1991. https://digitallibrary.un.org/record/128321/files/A_46_48%28Vol.I%29-EN.pdf.

"Report of the Preparatory Committee for the United Nations Conference on Environment and Development on Its Third Session, A/46/48(Vol.II)," September 4, 1991. https://digitallibrary.un.org/record/143314/files/A_46_48%28Vol.II%29-EN.pdf.

"Report of the Preparatory Committee for the United Nations Conference on the Human Environment on Its First Session, UN Doc. A/CONF.48/PC/6," April 6, 1970. https://digitallibrary.un.org/record/730064/files/A_CONF.48_PC_6-EN.pdf.

——— for the United Nations Conference on the Human Environment on Its Forth Session, UN Doc. A/CONF.48/PC/17," March 15, 1972. https://digitallibrary.un.org/record/730272/files/A_CONF.48_PC_17-EN.pdf.

——— for the United Nations Conference on the Human Environment on Its Second Session, UN Doc. A/CONF.48/PC/9," February 26, 1971. https://digitallibrary.un.org/record/730067/files/A_CONF.48_PC_9-EN.pdf.

"Report of the Preparatory Committee for the United Nations Conference on the Human Environment on Its Third Session, UN Doc. A/CONF.48/PC/13," September 30, 1971. https://digitallibrary.un.org/record/730069/files/A_CONF.48_PC_13-EN.pdf.

"Report of the Second Meeting of the High-Level Political Forum on Sustainable Development Convened under the Auspices of the Economic and Social Council, UN Doc. E/HLPF/2014/4.," August 18, 2015. http://www.un.org/ga/search/view_doc.asp?symbol=E/HLPF/2015/4&Lang=E.

"Report of the United Nations Conference on Environment and Development, A/CONF.151/26/Rev.1 (Vol.1)," June 14, 1992b. https://digitallibrary.un.org/record/160453/files/A_CONF.151_26_Rev.1%28Vol.I%29-EN.pdf.

——— Conference on Human Environment, A/CONF.48/14/Rev.1," June 5, 1972. https://digitallibrary.un.org/record/523249/files/A_CONF.48_14_Rev.1-EN.pdf.

"Report of the United Nations Conference on Human Settlements, UN Doc. A/CONF.165/14," August 7, 1996. https://digitallibrary.un.org/record/222703/files/A_CONF.165_14-EN.pdf.

"Report of the United Nations Conference on Sustainable Development, UN Doc. A/CONF.216/16," August 13, 2012. https://digitallibrary.un.org/record/737074/files/A_CONF.216_16-EN.pdf.

"Report of the World Commission on Environment and Development, UN Doc. A/42/427," August 4, 1987. https://digitallibrary.un.org/record/139811/files/A_42_427-EN.pdf.

"Report of the World Summit for Social Development, UN Doc. A/CONF.166/9," April 19, 1995. https://digitallibrary.un.org/record/208677/files/A_CONF-177_20-EN.pdf.

——— on Sustainable Development, UN Doc. A/CONF.199/20," September 4, 2002. https://digitallibrary.un.org/record/478154/files/A_CONF-199_20-EN.pdf.

"Rio Declaration on Environment and Development, Report of the United Nations Conference on Environment and Development, A/CONF.151/26/Rev.1 (Vol.1) Annex I," June 14, 1992. http://www.un.org/documents/ga/conf151/aconf15126-1annex1.htm.

"Transcript of Press Conference Given by Secretary-General Kofi Annan and Other Officials to Launch Joint Report 'A Better World for All', UN Doc. SG/SM/7466." United Nations Press Release, June 26, 2000. https://www.un.org/press/en/2000/20000626.sgsm7466.doc.html.

UN Department for Economic and Social Affairs, Division for Public Administration and Development Management. "Compendium of National Institutional Arrangements for Implementing the 2030 Agenda for Sustainable Development." UN DESA, 2018. http://workspace.unpan.org/sites/Internet/Documents/UNPAN97468.pdf.

"United Nations Environment Programme: Report of the Governing Council on the Work of Its Eleventh Session, UN Doc. A/38/25," May 24, 1983. https://digitallibrary.un.org/record/62941/files/A_38_25-EN.pdf.

"United Nations Environment Programme: Report of the Governing Council on the Work of Its Nineteenth Session, UN Doc. A/52/25," April 4, 1997. https://digitallibrary.un.org/record/243368/files/A_52_25-EN.pdf.

"United Nations Environment Programme: Report of the Governing Council (Session of a Special Character and 10th Session, UN Doc. A/37/25," May 18, 1982. https://digitallibrary.un.org/record/45429/files/A_37_25-EN.pdf.

Other Documents

Aeschi, Thomas. "Parliamentary Initiative 14.433: Recommandations et Décisions de l'OCDE et de Ses Organismes Spécialisés. Obligation d'informer et de Consulter La Commission Législative Compétente," June 20, 2014. https://www.parlament.ch/fr/ratsbetrieb/suche-curia-vista/geschaeft?AffairId=20140433.

———. "Parliamentary Motion 18.3838: La Suisse Ne Doit Pas Signer Le Pacte de l'ONU Sur Les Migrations," September 26, 2018. https://www.parlament.ch/fr/ratsbetrieb/suche-curia-vista/geschaeft?AffairId=20183838.

"Better World for All: Progress Towards the International Development Goals." International Monetary Fund, June 26, 2000. https://www.imf.org/external/pubs/ft/jointpub/world/2000/eng/bwae.pdf.

Bolton, John. United States Mission to the United Nations. "Letter from Amb. Bolton on Millennium Development Goals." United States Mission to the United Nations, August 26, 2005. https://www.globalpolicy.org/images/pdfs/0826bolton.pdf.

"Founex Report on Development and Environment, 1971," 1971. https://www.stakeholderforum.org/fileadmin/files/Earth%20Summit%202012new/Publications%20and%20Reports/founex%20report%201972.pdf.

Germann, Hannes. "Parliamentary Motion 18.3935: La Suisse Ne Doit Pas Signer Le Pacte de l'ONU Sur Les Migrations," September 27, 2018. https://www.parlament.ch/fr/ratsbetrieb/suche-curia-vista/geschaeft?AffairId=20183935.

Glenn, Jerome C., Elizabeth Florescu, and Theodore J. Gordon. "Analysis of United Nations Millennium Summit Speeches," April 2001. https://apps.dtic.mil/docs/citations/ADA593926.

"Hanoi Declaration: The Sustainable Development Goals: Turning Words into Action (132nd IPU Assembly)," April 1, 2015. http://archive.ipu.org/conf-e/132/Rpt-gendebate.htm.

"Joint Report to the High-Level Panel on the Post-2015 Development Agenda, The UN Global Compact and the World Business Council for Sustainable

Development," March 2013. https://www.unglobalcompact.org/docs/issues_doc/development/Joint_Report_HLP.pdf.

"Parliamentary Motion 18.4103: Pacte de l'ONU Sur Les Migrations. Soumettre à l'Assemblée Fédérale La Décision d'approbation," November 8, 2018. https://www.parlament.ch/fr/ratsbetrieb/suche-curia-vista/geschaeft?AffairId=20184103.

"Postulat 18.4104: Consultation et Participation Du Parlement Dans Le Domaine Du Droit Souple ('soft Law')," November 12, 2018. https://www.parlament.ch/fr/ratsbetrieb/suche-curia-vista/geschaeft?AffairId=20184104.

Romano, Marco. "Parliamentary Initiative 14.474: Sauvegarder Les Compétences Du Parlement En Matière de Politique Étrangère et de Législation," December 12, 2014a. https://www.parlament.ch/fr/ratsbetrieb/suche-curia-vista/geschaeft?AffairId=20140474.

———. "Parliamentary Question 14.1075: Qui a Approuvé Les Recommandations Du GAFI de 2012?," September 23, 2014b. https://www.parlament.ch/fr/ratsbetrieb/suche-curia-vista/geschaeft?AffairId=20141075.

"Shaping the 21st Century: The Contribution of Development Co-Operation." OECD, May 6, 1996. https://www.oecd.org/dac/2508761.pdf.

The Transparency, Accountability & Participation for 2030 Agenda Network. "Goal 16 Advocacy Toolkit: A Practical Guide for Stakeholders for National-Level Advocacy around Peaceful, Just and Inclusive Societies," 2016. https://tapnetwork2030.org/wp-content/uploads/2016/04/TAP_Toolkit_FINAL_web.pdf.

Together 2030. "Engaging Parliaments on the 2030 Agenda and the SDGs: Representation, Accountability and Implementation A Handbook for Civil Society," July 2018. https://www.together2030.org/wp-content/uploads/2018/07/Engaging-parliaments-on-the-2030-Agenda-and-the-SDGs.pdf.

Blog Articles

Akande, Dapo. "What Is the Meaning of 'Consensus' in International Decision Making?" *EJIL: Talk!* (blog), April 8, 2013. https://www.ejiltalk.org/negotiations-on-arms-trade-treaty-fail-to-adopt-treaty-by-consensus-what-is-the-meaning-of-consensus-in-international-decision-making/.

"Who Was Rachel Carson?" *SafeChemicalPolicy.Org* (blog), March 2, 2007. http://www.safechemicalpolicy.org/who-was-rachel-carson/.

Newspaper Articles

Borger, Julian. "Bolton Throws UN Summit into Chaos." *The Guardian*, August 26, 2005, sec. World news. https://www.theguardian.com/world/2005/aug/26/usa.julianborger.

Griswold, Eliza. "How 'Silent Spring' Ignited the Environmental Movement." *The New York Times*, September 21, 2012, sec. Magazine. https://www.nytimes.com/2012/09/23/magazine/how-silent-spring-ignited-the-environmental-movement.html.

Websites

"Geneva 2000: WCC General Secretary Writes to UN SecretaryGeneral Kofi Annan, WCC Press Release, PR-00-18, of 20 June 2000." United Nations Press Release, June 28, 2000. http://www.wcc-coe.org/wcc/news/press/00/22pu.html.

"Secretary-General Appoints High-Level Panel on Post-2015 Development Agenda." United Nations Press Release, July 31, 2012. https://www.un.org/sg/sites/www.un.org.sg/files/documents/management/PRpost2015.pdf.

"Secretary-General Assembles High-Level Panel on Post-2015 Development Agenda, Appointing 26 Members of Government, Civil Society, Private Sector, UN Doc. SG/A/1364-DEV/2949." United Nations Press Release, July 31, 2012. https://www.un.org/press/en/2012/sga1364.doc.htm.

Index[1]

[1] Note: Page numbers followed by 'n' refer to notes.

H. Göksan, *Global Law of Sustainable Development*, Global Issues,
https://doi.org/10.1007/978-3-031-74547-8

SPRINGER NATURE

GPSR Compliance

The European Union's (EU) General Product Safety Regulation (GPSR) is a set of rules that requires consumer products to be safe and our obligations to ensure this.

If you have any concerns about our products, you can contact us on ProductSafety@springernature.com

In case Publisher is established outside the EU, the EU authorized representative is:

Springer Nature Customer Service Center GmbH
Europaplatz 3
69115 Heidelberg, Germany

The manufacturer's authorised representative in the EU is Springer Nature Customer Service Centre GmbH, Europaplatz 3, 69115 Heidelberg, Germany. If you have any concerns regarding our products, please contact ProductSafety@springernature.com

Printed and bound by CPI Group (UK) Ltd, Croydon, CR0 4YY
30/09/2026
02225583-0003